The Challenges of Highland Development in Vietnam

edited by
A. Terry Rambo, Robert R. Reed,
Le Trong Cuc, and Michael R. DiGregorio

October 1995

East-West Center
Program on Environment
Honolulu, Hawaii

Center for Natural Resources
and Environmental Studies,
Hanoi University

Center for Southeast Asia Studies,
University of California
at Berkeley

A. Terry Rambo
Director, Program on Environment
East-West Center
1777 East-West Road
Honolulu, HI 96848 USA

Robert R. Reed
Chair, Center for Southeast Asia Studies
University of California, Berkeley
2223 Fulton Street, Room 617
Berkeley, CA 94720 USA

Le Trong Cuc
Deputy Director
Center for Natural Resources
and Environmental Studies
Hanoi University
Hanoi, Vietnam

Michael R. DiGregorio
Graduate School of Architecture and Urban Planning
University of California, LA
405 Hilgard Avenue
Los Angeles, CA 90025 USA

LIBRARY OF CONGRESS CATALOGING-IN-PUBLICATION DATA

The challenges of Highland development in Vietnam / edited by A. Terry Rambo . . . [et al.].
p. cm.
Includes bibliographical references.
ISBN 0-86638-176-7
1. Natural resources—Vietnam—Central Highlands—Management—Congresses. 2. Central Highlands (Vietnam)—Economic conditions—Congresses. 3. Central Highlands (Vietnam)—Economic policy—Congresses. I. Rambo, A. Terry.
HC444.Z7C463 1995
338.9597—dc20 95-41204

Cover photo: Thai village in Mai Chau district, Hoa Binh province (photo taken in January 1992).

Cover photo credit: A. Terry Rambo

To secure copies, write to the:

Publication Sales Office
East-West Center
1777 East-West Road
Honolulu, HI 96848 USA
Phone: 808-944-7145
Fax: 808-944-7376
E-mail: ewcbooks@ewc.bitnet

Contents

Maps, Figures, and Tables

Maps

Figures

Tables

Preface

This volume is the proceedings of a conference held at the East-West Center in Honolulu, Hawaii, in July 1994. It makes available to a wider audience revised versions of most of the papers presented at that meeting, which was jointly sponsored by the Indochina Initiative of the East-West Center, the Center for Southeast Asia Studies of the University of California at Berkeley, and the Center for Natural Resources and Environmental Studies of Hanoi University.

The goals of the conference were to review existing knowledge about Vietnam's highland regions and to explore specific issues relating to the development of the human and natural resources of the uplands. A number of papers provide comparative analyses of highland development issues in neighboring countries. Taking part in the discussions were some thirty scholars and development policy specialists from Vietnam, China, Hong Kong, and the United States (see Appendix).

All of the conference papers contribute to sharpening our definition of the challenges of developing Vietnam's highlands in two ways. On the one hand, they provide us with a great deal of information about the highlands as a human landscape, a specific place in space and time characterized by a unique array of geographic, ethnological, demographic, and economic characteristics. We can learn much about these different characteristics and the ways that they have interacted to generate the specific developmental trajectory traced by the highlands. For those with a positivist bent, these papers offer convenient access to what we currently understand to be the "facts" of the matter. On the other hand, the papers offer many insights into the diverse and often contradictory ways in which the highlands are conceptualized as a development arena. They allow us to see, however imperfectly, the mental models that guide perception of reality and determine which aspects of empirical experience are granted recognition as constituting "facts." Thus, in studying these papers we simultaneously can learn both about the highlands as an empirical landscape and about the different ways in which different observers construct their visions of that landscape. Both kinds of information are important; both are equally real. Indeed, the major dilemmas of formulating and implementing development policies for the highlands reflect the complex interplay between them.

Finally, we would note that although we have lightly edited all papers for style we have made no attempt to impose any kind of common viewpoint on the diverse arguments presented. Individual authors are solely responsible for the ideas and information contained in their papers.

Acknowledgments—Major financial support for this conference was provided by the East-West Center and the Center for Southeast Asia Studies of the University of California at Berkeley, using funds provided by the Pacific Rim Program of the University of California and the Henry B. Luce Foundation. Additional funding was provided by a grant to the East-West Center Program on Environment (ENV) from the John D. and Catherine T. MacArthur Foundation.

The difficult work of organizing the conference was ably done by Vy Ton, ENV Project Specialist, with the assistance of Keith Fahrney and Michael Rucker. The complex logistic arrangements for participants were handled by ENV Program Officer June Kuramoto.

Translation of presentations was done by Trinh Xuan Vu and Le Minh Hang who dealt with complex and often unfamiliar terminology with great skill. The maps, except for Chapter 4, were prepared by Michael DiGregorio. Daniel Bauer, Mary Hayano, Lisa Nhomi, and Monica Geng contributed to the production of this volume. Final editing was done by ENV Senior Editor Helen Takeuchi. To all of them, we owe a debt of gratitude.

A. Terry Rambo
Robert R. Reed
Le Trong Cuc
Michael R. DiGregorio

Defining Highland Development Challenges in Vietnam: Some Themes and Issues Emerging from the Conference

A. Terry Rambo
Program on Environment, East-West Center, Honolulu

This conference was an exciting one because of the great diversity of ideas and viewpoints that were represented. Emerging from the papers and the lively discussions that accompanied their presentation are several major themes and key issues. In this introductory essay, I attempt to identify some of the major themes and examine their implications for our understanding of the challenges of development of Vietnam's highlands. It should be understood that the perspective offered on these issues is my personal one; this introductory essay does not pretend to represent an objective synthesis of the viewpoint of all the participants. Indeed, no such synthesis is possible because no such consensus existed. This reflects the fact that participants held different and often contradictory views and opinions regarding many of these points. The existence of these contradictions is healthy to the extent that it succeeds in drawing attention to these themes as central questions that must be addressed in future dialogues about development strategies for the highlands. In this essay, three major themes will be explored: the natural resource endowment of the highlands, the human dimensions of highland development, and the nature of the highlands as an arena for future development.

THE NATURAL RESOURCE ENDOWMENT OF THE HIGHLANDS

The conventional view in Hanoi of the development potential of the highlands is not unlike the somewhat schizophrenic view of America's Western frontier held in Washington in the late 1800s. The American West was simultaneously perceived as the Great American Desert, a vast expanse of barren land capable of supporting only a handful of nomadic Indians, and as a virgin fertile plain needing only the application of modern technology by white settlers to be transformed into the home of prosperous farming, ranching, and mining communities. In much the same way, Vietnam's highlands are perceived as being on the one hand, remote, isolated, and poor—lands capable only of supporting scattered populations of culturally backward nomadic shifting cultivators—and on the other hand as an almost limitless frontier endowed with immense unexploited resources that only await Kinh settlement and application of modern technology for their development. Just as was true in the case of the American West, there is some truth to both of these contradictory perceptions of the highlands: The natural resource potential is real but the constraints on its development are also real.[1] Thus, it is important to achieve a realistic assessment of the natural resource endowment of the highlands and to understand the multiple constraints operating to restrict the success of efforts to sustainably develop these resources.

As pointed out by Chu Huu Quy in his overview paper, the highlands cover three-quarters of the surface area of Vietnam and are home to one-third of the national population. Although the highlands are often thought of as lightly populated, it might be noted that the 25 million inhabitants of Vietnam's highlands considerably outnumber the total national populations of several neighboring countries.

Vietnam's highlands are extremely diverse from a geographical standpoint. No uniform system of classification of the different regions, zones, and subzones in the highlands exists, however. Chu Huu Quy describes five subnational regions; Hoang Xuan Ty employs a different classification consisting of seven subnational regions, while Nguyen Tran Cau delineates eight subnational regions.

Existing terminology for classifying different land forms and types of land use are often misleading or internally contradictory. For example, Le Trong Cuc reports that only 10.7 percent of the land classified as "forest land" in the Da River watershed is actually covered with trees; the rest is "nonforested forest land." At the same time, land being used for shifting cultivation is not included in the category "agricultural land." Chu Huu Quy reports that "barren hills" cover 35 percent of the natural land, but Thomas Sikor notes that this category is as much a political as an ecological one. Land is classified as "barren" when its current use does not coincide with the use for which it has been designated by government land-use planners. Sikor presents his own useful system for classifying barren lands. There is clearly a need for better systems for delineating and classifying upland regions to provide an improved basis for development planning.

There is no question but that many of Vietnam's most valuable natural resources, including minerals, hydropower potential, forests, and agricultural land suitable for growing of industrial crops, are located in the highlands. There is still much room for debate about the absolute magnitude of these resources, their real economic value, and the difficulties confronting efforts to exploit them. The following sections review the development potential of several key natural resources.

Mineral Resources

Although not yet fully explored geologically, the highlands are known to contain substantial reserves of valuable minerals including gold, gemstones, and tungsten, wolfram, and other rare earths. Many mines are located in remote inaccessible sites so that development is difficult and expensive. The environmental consequences of mining are often serious and irreversible. For example, gold mining employing primitive methods of extracting the mineral from the ore using mercury and arsenic is already polluting rivers with highly toxic chemicals, threatening the health of downstream riverine ecosystems and human populations.

Energy Resources

That the highlands are endowed with a very large hydropower potential is well known; it is the desirability of developing this potential that is in dispute. At present, northern Vietnam has surplus electricity, although this surplus is expected to shortly disappear with the completion of the transmission line from the Hoa Binh dam to Ho Chi Minh city and the growth of local demand by the expanding northern economy. To meet this anticipated increase in demand, national economic planners advocate construction of several new hydropower facilities including the giant Ta Bu dam in Son La province. Cognizant of the many social and environmental problems resulting from the construction of the Hoa Binh dam, some scientists have questioned the advisability of the Ta Bu project.

A central concern is the need to relocate more than 100,000 people, mostly members of the Black Thai ethnic minority, from the area to be flooded by the reservoir. The ineptly handled resettlement of the much smaller number of people displaced by the Hoa Binh dam provides a case study in the high social and environmental costs associated with such hydropower projects. In the case of the Hoa Binh dam more than 30,000 people, mainly members of the Muong minority, lost their highly productive irrigated rice fields in the valley bottoms. Because inadequate compensation was provided to allow resettlement elsewhere, most families simply moved their houses up onto the steep hillslopes above the reservoir where they now scratch out a bare subsistence from swidden cultivation. As Le Trong Cuc observes, erosion from their swiddens contributes to the extremely heavy sediment load that is silting the reservoir at rates far faster than projected when it was designed, reducing its life from several hundred years to several tens of years.

Of course, not all hydropower projects have such high social and environmental costs. Some potential sites in the Central Highlands are in sparsely settled zones where displacement of local people will be much less of a problem. Such projects may well meet the criteria proposed by Leslie Lipper for evaluation of the economic and environmental costs and benefits of watershed projects. But even in those cases where imputed benefits are large and social and environmental costs are modest, however, the economics of dam construction appear problematic. Up-front capital costs are immense, the lag between beginning of construction and the actual delivery of power often a decade or more, and the distance between point of generation and end-users often uneconomically long. Thus, as Charles Johnson shows in his analysis of the comparative costs of developing new generating capability, natural gas (a resource that Vietnam has in great abundance) offers a much cheaper alternative to hydropower. Construction and operation of generators fueled by natural gas is also associated with fewer social and environmental externalities, although use of this fossil fuel source, unlike hydropower, does release greenhouse gases to the atmosphere.

Forest Resources and Biological Diversity

Most of Vietnam's remaining primary forests are located in the highlands, especially Gia Lai and Kontum provinces in the Tay Nguyen. These forests, which are already being cut at a rate far exceeding their natural regenerative capacity, will be exhausted by the turn of the century unless stronger protective measures are taken. In addition to commercial logging, much of it illegal, and clearance of land for agricultural resettlement projects, shifting cultivation is a major cause of deforestation. According to Le Duy Hung, 100,000 hectares of forest are destroyed each year by the three million members of ethnic minorities practicing shifting cultivation. Nguyen Van Thang, however, reports a 200,000 hectare annual loss to shifting cultivation, but attributes some three-quarters of the total damage to immigrants from the lowlands.

Whatever the relative importance of its various causes, deforestation is a major threat to preservation of biological diversity. The vast majority of Vietnam's known plant and animal species, many of them rare endemics, are found only in the upland forests. Several large wild mammals such as the rhinoceros, wild cattle, and tiger can only survive in large tracts of undisturbed primary forest. Other species, notably deer and wild pigs, can thrive in secondary forests as long as human predation is not excessive. Virtually no indigenous wild animal species are able to survive in the monocultural Eucalyptus plantations planted under the auspices of the Ministry of Forestry and the World Food Program.

Although human activities threaten survival of many highland species, people are the victims of other species, particularly microorganisms such as malaria plasmodia. Swidden agriculture, by opening gaps in the forest cover, creates ideal breeding conditions for the species of Anopheles mosquito that is the most dangerous vector for malaria in Vietnam. Numerous other disease organisms, including a wide variety of arboviruses, make large parts of the highlands an unhealthy environment for human settlement. Consequently, mortality rates among indigenous people were historically extremely high, which may account for the relatively low population density displayed by the highlands until recent times. One of the proudest accomplishments of the socialist government was the extension of health-care facilities into even the remotest mountain settlements. The structure and functioning of this system of primary health care in the Central Highlands province of Lam Dong is described by Dominic Montagu.

Forest destruction also threatens to undermine the success of tourism, which is one of Vietnam's fastest growing industries and a major source of foreign exchange. Hill stations such as Dalat, whose attractions are so well described by Robert Reed, draw tourists because of their pleasant climates and beautiful scenery. Dalat is famous for its pine forests, which are now endangered by cutting to make golf courses and expand residential areas. Its beautiful lakes, streams, and waterfalls are polluted with siltation by soil eroded from the now barren slopes. In more remote parts of the highlands, the possibilities for ecotourism and cultural tourism are considerable but only if both natural and cultural diversity are maintained.

Loss of forests is important not only because of its negative impacts on the national economy but even more because it deprives poor rural people of an important part of their subsistence base. In a manner similar to that described in Carol Ireson's case study of rural communities in Laos, households in highland Vietnam make use of forests as supermarkets, gold mines, and welfare support. Traditionally, the mountain minorities have relied on the forest to supply many vital resources including timber and bamboo for house construction, wild animals for meat, jungle vegetables and wild roots that substituted for rice at times of crop failure, and medicinal plants. It is the loss of access to these survival resources that helps to explain why, as Bui Cach Tuyen reports, 54 percent of ethnic minority families surveyed in Lam Dong province in the Central Highlands are classified as living in poverty. The commercial trade in forest products is also a major source of cash income for many highland groups, leading Hoang Xuan Ty to suggest that the best way to ensure protection of the forests is to expand the reach of the market economy so that highlanders can trade forest products for rice, thus reducing their dependence on swidden agriculture.

Agricultural Resources

The fact that many parts of the highlands contain vast expanses of land with only a sparse population is responsible for the perception of their great potential for agricultural development. There are, however, serious unanswered questions about the long-term carrying capacity of upland agricultural systems that make this development potential problematic. With the exception of a restricted area of basaltic soils in the Central Highlands, most upland soils are of inferior quality with poor structure, very low nutrient levels, and high vulnerability to erosion. Traditional systems of rotational swidden agriculture as practiced by many ethnic minorities were well adapted to these conditions but can only function satisfactorily when population densities are very low so that fields can be allowed to remain fallow for long periods after a few years of cropping. Shortening the fallow period in the effort to intensify production results in rapid land degradation. As Hoang Xuan Ty describes in his paper, research is needed to find ways to make swiddening more sustainable, especially by developing methods for accelerating forest regeneration during the fallow period.

As Le Duy Hung describes in his paper, the government has for many years encouraged swidden-farming highland people to adopt more permanent forms of agriculture as part of the "Fixed Cultivation and Sedentarization Program" (*dinh canh dinh cu*). Almost two million shifting cultivators have officially been "sedentarized," but according to Hung only 30 percent of them actually lead a stable life. An additional one million people have not yet been reached by this program.

Unfortunately, few of the alternatives to swiddening are ecologically sustainable and economically viable. The steep topography and limited supplies of surface water restrict the development of irrigated wet rice fields to only a small fraction of the total area of the highlands. Attempts to cultivate dryland annual crops on a continuing basis have often resulted in severe land degradation and subsequent abandonment of fields. Planting of industrial tree crops such as tea and coffee appears to offer one sustainable alternative, although, as Eric Crystal points out in his paper describing the history of smallholder coffee cultivation in Indonesia, there are many constraints on the successful performance of such a system of farming. Successful cultivation of industrial crops depends on good transportation systems providing ready access to markets to sell produce and purchase staple foods, provision of technical inputs and advice, and stable prices. All these factors are frequently absent in the highlands where, according to Le Duy Hung, only one-half of the villages are reached by a motorable road. Even when successful, tree crop-based systems are capable of supporting only one or two hundred people per square kilometer, a density far lower than that of the wet rice agricultural systems of the deltas.

Agroforestry systems, in which growing of trees is integrated with production of annual crops, offer another promising approach to sustainable development of highland areas. The papers by Nguyen Khanh Quac et al. and Bui Cach Tuyen describe some of the experimental efforts to develop such systems being carried on by Bac Thai University for the Northern Highlands and the University of Agriculture and Forestry for the Central Highlands.

Overall, the current density of rural population in the highlands is probably close to the maximum that can be sustainably supported using existing agricultural technology. In some areas, notably the Da River watershed in northwestern mountains described by Le Trong Cuc, population has already exceeded carrying capacity as manifested by environmental degradation and declining standards of living. Thus, the central problem in many highland areas is no longer that of how to best develop virgin natural resources but instead is one of how to restore ecological productivity. According to Chu Huu Quy, the cost of restoring the 13.4 million hectares of land classified as "barren hills" using existing technology would exceed thirteen billion dollars, an impossibly large sum given the scarcity of capital for rural development in Vietnam's highlands. (According to Bui Cach Tuyen, over a two-year period the State Agricultural Bank made only US$135,000 in loans available to the 735,000 people of Lam Dong province.) Unless cheaper and more efficient methods for restoring the productivity of severely degraded upland ecosystems are broadly adopted, the conditions of life in many mountain zones can only continue to worsen. Reversing this downward slide in the quantity and quality of natural resources is thus a major challenge of highland development.

HUMAN DIMENSIONS OF HIGHLAND DEVELOPMENT

The extraordinary complexity of the human dimensions of highland development is discussed in my own paper in this volume. Cultural diversity is very high with more than fifty ethnic minority groups ranging in population from a few hundred (the Ruc) to more than one million (the Tay) residing in the highlands. Although minorities comprise only 12 percent of the total national population, they constitute a much larger percentage of the population in many highland provinces. This share has been rapidly declining, however, particularly in the Tay Nguyen, as a consequence of massive resettlement of Kinh in this region subsequent to national reunification in 1975. Thus, the highlands today constitute a gigantic experiment in ethnic mixing and acculturation.

As in all countries with multi-ethnic populations, including the United States, the question of ethnic relations is a politically sensitive one in Vietnam. Officially, no problems in ethnic relations are admitted because the constitution guarantees members of minorities equal rights of citizenship, including the right to preservation of their cultural traditions. Historically, the Party and the government have displayed great interest in the welfare of the mountain minorities. A not inconsiderable number of individuals from highland minorities have achieved prominence in the Party, the government, the military, and cultural affairs. That the late President Ho Chi Minh had his official residence in Hanoi constructed in the style of a Tay mountain house on piles (*nha san*) evidences the seriousness of the commitment of the Vietnam's revolutionary leadership to valorizing minority cultures and transcending majority cultural chauvinism. Certainly, the record of socialist Vietnam in this regard compares quite favorably to that of many of its neighbors in Southeast Asia or, for that matter, to the United States and the Latin American nations.

Despite Vietnam's generally positive record with regard to treatment of minorities, the issue of ethnic relations in the highlands is not as unproblematic as it is officially portrayed. Granting of the constitutional right to minorities to preserve their cultures should not be mistaken for a genuine acceptance of cultural relativism. Official tolerance of minority cultural traits is restricted to those elements (e.g., traditional dress, folk songs, and dances) that are viewed as socially benign. Traits viewed as backward (e.g., religious beliefs and rituals labeled as "superstitions," multi-family longhouses) or reactionary (e.g., feudalistic forms of social organization) have been at times subject to quite ruthless suppression. Thus, the relationship between the Vietnamese state and its ethnic minorities remains a paternalistic one in which the ultimate authority to make decisions about appropriate directions for cultural change remains in the hands of the central government, not in those of the minorities themselves. The Vietnamese national ethnic community may constitute, as one Kinh ethnologist has written, a garden in which a hundred flowers of different colors and perfume bloom, but the overall plan for the garden is exclusively determined by the head gardener (i.e., the state). Not surprisingly, therefore, Kinh values most strongly shape national development policies for the highlands. This reality is reflected most strongly with regard to questions of minority land rights, educational and language policies, and the role of indigenous knowledge in highland development.

Minority Land Rights

Reference has already been made to the Kinh perception of the highlands as essentially vacant lands, thinly inhabited by nomadic tribes wandering at random across the landscape practicing shifting cultivation. This perception is reified in the official title of the sedentarization program of *dinh canh dinh cu* (fixed fields, fixed residence), which is designed to replace the supposed traditional way of life of *du canh du cu* (migratory fields, migratory residence). As Vietnamese ethnologists have clearly documented, however, only a small percentage of highland people are even quasi-nomadic in the sense of more or less frequently moving their villages, and even these groups often reside in the same locality for decades.[2] Many highland minority groups have lived in the same homelands for generations, even centuries, by practicing a form of shifting cultivation called rotational swiddening. In this type of swidden agriculture, a new field is cleared from the forest, cultivated for one or two years, and then fallowed for ten to twenty years to allow the forest to regenerate before it is again cleared and farmed for a couple of years in an essentially endless cycle. For each cultivated hectare, there must be a reserve of ten to twenty hectares in forest fallow. These fallow areas are not vacant or unused land but instead are an integral part of the total system of rotational swidden agriculture and are recognized as such in the traditional systems of land tenure of many of the highland ethnic minorities.

In the eyes of Kinh development planners, however, only the small area of fields currently under cultivation are seen as being developed land to which the indigenous users may have rights of tenure; the much larger area under fallow is seen as vacant wasteland that may be freely alienated for other uses, including resettlement of migrants from the lowlands. The loss of any part of the fallow areas upsets the delicate balance between population and land, however, forcing the swidden farmers to lengthen the period of cultivation of each plot and shorten the period for which it is fallowed. This accelerated cultivation cycle does not allow sufficient time for the forest to regenerate. Soil fertility declines because nutrient levels are no longer restored by the trees. Eventually, the overworked plots are invaded by weed species, including Imperata grass. Crop yields decline rapidly while the amount of time needed for weeding increases. The current crisis in highland subsistence agriculture is not the result of an inherent flaw in swidden agriculture but has instead been precipitated by land-use changes introduced by exogenous agencies that have failed to recognize the rational basis of indigenous highland systems of land tenure. As noted by Nguyen Van Thang, this land became "ownerless" only after it was taken over by the state and the cooperatives were established. Unless changes in land tenure are quickly made, this problem can only become more serious as highland populations continue to increase and the quality of land further declines.

Unfortunately, there are no easy solutions for the land tenure problems of the highlands. It is much too late to simply return to the status quo ante by recognizing "indigenous rights" and restoring alienated lands to tribal control. In many cases the traditional social institutions that controlled land allocation, such as those described for the Hmong and Dzao by Nguyen Van Thang, have already disappeared or atrophied beyond repair. It should also be recognized that not all ethnic minorities in the highlands are truly indigenous. Significant numbers of Hmong, for example, only migrated into northern Vietnam from China and Laos in the late nineteenth and early twentieth centuries so that their settlement of the uplands is virtually coterminous with that of the Kinh. As Hoang Xuan Ty reports, many recent immigrants to the Tay Nguyen are members of ethnic minorities coming from the overpopulated and environmentally degraded northern mountains. In any case there are now several million Kinh residents of the highlands, many now second- or third-generation inhabitants, who have put down roots and acquired their own de facto rights to the land they cultivate. To date, little is known of the extent and ecological impacts of settler agriculture in the highlands. And the populations of many highland indigenous minorities have also increased greatly, particularly in the northwestern mountains, so that they can no longer be accommodated under traditional systems of land tenure. The challenge now is to create new systems of tenure appropriate to the changed conditions of the highlands.

Implementation of Decree 327, which mandates a uniform national system of private holdings based on long-term leases, as described by Thomas Sikor, does not necessarily offer the optimum approach to sustainable management of highland areas, particularly forested zones. There is evidence already from the midlands of Vinh Phu province that such privatization is producing very serious socioeconomic differentiation, as some privileged households succeed in amassing large-scale holdings while poorer households are left out entirely. Community-based systems of resource management, such as are described for the Central Highlands by Bui Cach Tuyen, offer one promising alternative to total privatization with its accompanying loss of equitability.

Education and Language Policy

As the papers by Tran Lanh and Nguyen Viet Tung reveal, formal education levels in the highlands are on average considerably lower than in the lowlands. There is considerable variation among different ethnic groups, with Muong and Thai displaying relatively high levels of school attendance among children of both sexes and relatively high levels of adult literacy. The Hmong, Dzao, and several groups in the Central Highlands have much lower rates of school attendance, especially of girls, and very low levels of adult literacy. Thus, only 15 percent of Hmong men and fewer than 5 percent of Hmong women are literate, compared to the national average of 88 percent.

Expanding the access to education for highland populations is a major challenge, given the limited resources available. Tran Lanh describes some of the approaches that are being tested, including establishment of boarding schools to offer higher grades of education to children from isolated villages that lack the means to offer post-primary schooling. The paper by Nguyen Khanh Quac et al. describes the efforts of Agricultural University No. 3 at Bac Thai to expand minority enrollment at the tertiary level.

The place of minority languages in the educational system was the focus of considerable discussion among conference participants, with overtones somewhat reminiscent of the continuing debate in the United States about "multiculturalism" in the school curriculum. At present, schools in the mountains teach according to the standard national curriculum employing the national language. In the past, however, serious attempts were made to use minority languages in primary schools and adult education programs. Thus, following the defeat of the French in 1954, considerable effort was devoted to development of alphabets for several minority languages, notably Tay, Thai, and Hmong. Although these scripts were widely employed in the schools of the Thai-Meo Autonomous Zone, use of the national language became dominant following the abolition of this special zone in 1975. Teaching in minority languages at the primary level is again under consideration and is already being done as a matter of local option in some districts in the northwestern mountains. Shortage of qualified minority teachers and lack of suitable textbooks are major constraints on expansion of this approach, however. Also in many highland areas, several different ethnic groups live interspersed in a single community, and children from two or more groups share a common classroom. Given Vietnam's historical experience with colonial encouragement of minority aspirations for autonomy as a divide-and-rule tactic, there are also legitimate concerns about the possible contribution that encouragement of use of minority languages might make to emergence of a stronger sense of ethnonationalism among highlanders. Nevertheless, this concern must be balanced against the benefits of native language literacy as a tool in cultural preservation and dissemination of indigenous knowledge.

The Place of Indigenous Knowledge in Highland Development

The role to be played by indigenous knowledge in the process of highland development is perhaps the issue on which there was the least agreement among conference participants. To put it bluntly, the central point at issue is whether indigenous ethnic groups have backward cultures that should be changed as rapidly as possible to conform to the advanced (Kinh) model or whether they have different, but not inferior, cultures that are already well adapted to local conditions and therefore offer the optimum basis for their future development. The view of minority cultures as backward was manifested in presentations by many of the Vietnamese participants. (It should be noted that the papers by Le Trong Cuc, Hoang Xuan Ty, and Nguyen Van Thang represent clear exceptions in this regard.)

The tendency to devalue indigenous knowledge may reflect in part the fact that ethnocentrism is at least as prevalent among Kinh as it is among members of majority cultures everywhere in the world. But, probably much more important is the fact that this natural tendency of members of the majority group to devalue minority cultures is reinforced, in the Vietnamese case, by the Marxist model of unilineal cultural evolution, which assigns most of the minority groups of the highlands to a primitive or backward status in contrast to the putatively civilized society of the lowlands. Thus, Marxist evolutionary theory offers scientific sanction to the tendency to place the blame for all failings of development in the highlands on alleged shortcomings in the cultures of the ethnic minorities. In this context, Le Duy Hung's statement that "such vices as superstitions and false beliefs detrimental to production and social life are quite rife" is unremarkable, shocking as it may be to the sensibilities of professional social scientists.

Opposing the conventional Kinh view is an alternative perspective, derived both from Darwinian evolutionary theory and contemporary studies of cultural ecology, that conceives of traditional cultures as being highly adapted to their natural environment as the result of many centuries of natural selection. From this perspective, which is most fully articulated in the paper in this volume by Nguyen Van Thang, the cultures of the highland minorities represent examples of successful and sustainable adaptation to this environment. Thus, in his view, the breakdown in traditional social organization and customs caused by state interference, rather than any supposed backwardness of the minorities themselves, is responsible for most environmental degradation. Serious deforestation, for example, occurred only after the Hmong and Dzao kinship groups lost their rights to control land use to the cooperatives.

As will be evident to readers of my own contribution to the conference, I believe that indigenous knowledge can be of very great value in the development process. At the same time, however, I am concerned that we avoid over-romanticization of traditional minority cultures. Hmong clearance of primary forests to plant opium poppies has been recognized since the colonial period as causing serious environmental degradation, including being responsible for a not inconsiderable part of the area of anthropogenic grasslands in northern Indochina. Although practicing an environmentally more benign form of rotational swiddening, the Katu of Quang Nam until recently believed that human sacrifices were essential to maintain the fertility of their fields and engaged in bloody intervillage raiding to ensure the supply of victims. Even the admirable "composite swidden system" practiced by the Tay of the Da River watershed may have evolved as a consequence of expropriation of paddy fields by the feudal nobility forcing the commoners to expand their fields into the hill slopes.

In any case, while the philosophical differences between the two positions on the value of indigenous knowledge can probably never be fully resolved, at the level of praxis neither extreme position is supportable. There is ample evidence that efforts to develop the highlands employing models based on lowland experience have generally resulted in failure, much as comparable attempts in China's upland areas described by R. D. Hill have also been unsuccessful. At the same time it should be equally evident that radical social and environmental changes in the highlands have greatly reduced the viability of traditional modes of adaptation of the indigenous ethnic minorities. Survival strategies that were highly successful when population density was fewer than ten persons per square kilometer face collapse when densities are increased by a factor of ten- or twenty-fold. For example, swidden agriculture, a traditional system of production that has been described as a successful adaptation in earlier sections of this essay, is no longer sustainable in most parts of the highlands. As the papers by Le Trong Cuc and Hoang Xuan Ty indicate, alternative subsistence strategies must be found if the basic survival needs of the growing highland population are to be met in the future. The search for such strategies will proceed faster and more efficiently if it takes full advantage of the vast existing storehouse of empirically derived knowledge of the specific environmental conditions of the highlands that is encoded in the form of indigenous systems of practice and knowledge. Thus, finding effective ways to incorporate the ethnic minorities as active partners in the development planning process to take maximum advantage of their indigenous knowledge is a major challenge of highland development.

THE HIGHLANDS AS AN ARENA FOR DEVELOPMENT

The papers in this volume all challenge in one way or another the conventional perception of the highlands as constituting a marginal area or a remote and unimportant frontier zone that can be safely ignored as development effort is concentrated in the cities and agricultural plains of the lowlands. Instead, the collective picture that emerges is of the highlands as a critical arena for development where success or failure has immense implications for the well-being not only of the 25 million people living in the highlands but for the nation as a whole. Indeed, the recognition of the great extent of interdependency between Vietnam's highlands and its lowlands is perhaps the most important point on which general agreement was reached at this meeting. This interdependency has received scant recognition in past thinking about the highlands.

Historically, the Vietnamese state has paid attention to the highlands only in terms of ensuring military security and exploiting natural resources needed by the lowland economy. Development of the highlands to improve the lives of the ethnic minorities was hardly a matter of concern.

Before the French occupation, the Vietnamese state was concerned with the highlands primarily for strategic reasons. The mountain passes offered a route for foreign invasions and the forests provided a refuge for rebels and bandits. At various times, military camps and walls were built to separate particularly unruly upland areas from the lowlands. Economic exchange was sporadic and limited in volume, although there was a flow of highly valued forest products from the highlands to the lowlands (sometimes in the guise of tribute to the imperial court) while salt and iron went back upstream. Settlement of Kinh (lowland Vietnamese) into the highlands was actively discouraged by the court, although fear of malaria and tribal attacks may have been more effective than imperial policies in limiting pioneer settlement.

French colonial involvement in the highlands was initially also motivated by strategic concerns. Anti-colonial guerrillas remained active in the northwestern mountains until well after the turn of the century, forcing the French to maintain substantial military forces there. Indeed, large areas remained under military administration rather than being incorporated into the ordinary provincial administrative system until after World War I. The economic potential of the highlands soon attracted the French, however, and exploration for minerals began early in the colonial era. Agricultural development was also attempted with plantations for industrial crops being established in several locales. In the Central Highlands, as Eric Crystal points out, coffee proved a successful crop both on French-owned plantations and for independent smallholders, both Kinh and members of ethnic minorities. The potential of the highlands for tourism and health was also quickly recognized and ambitious plans drawn up for establishment of several hill stations, a major experiment in regional development planning that is recounted in detail by Robert Reed. Dalat soon became the largest and economically most successful of these European highland settlements. Attempts to resettle Kinh into the Northern Highlands to relieve population pressure in the Red River Delta were much less successful, in part because these projects were poorly funded, but mainly because of the very high mortality from malaria suffered by the migrants.

During the Resistance War, economic development virtually ceased as the highlands became a battleground. Many ethnic minorities strongly supported the revolutionary forces. Ho Chi Minh's first headquarters was in a Tay community in Viet Bac, and many of the first recruits for the new People's Army of Vietnam were drawn from this minority group. The vast areas of forested mountains provided safe havens for the Viet Minh forces from which they could infiltrate units into the French-controlled lowlands. With their limited personnel and restricted mobility, the French could never establish long-term control over most of the highlands, although they maintained several footholds in areas where they retained some support from the local elites. In order to win support from the highlanders, the French employed a divide-and-rule strategy, establishing Muong and Thai autonomous zones in the northwestern mountains, and separating the Central Highlands from Vietnam under the guise of the *Pays Montagnard du Sud* (PMS), which was administered as a "crown domain" directly under Emperor Bao Dai.

The defeat of the French at Dien Bien Phu in 1954 again shifted attention to the economic potential of the highlands. In both north and south, large-scale schemes to resettle Kinh from the lowlands into the highlands were undertaken. The provinces of the northern midlands such as Vinh Phu absorbed hundreds of thousands of migrants from the overcrowded Red River Delta. Within a few years the area was almost wholly deforested as settlers converted valleys into paddy fields and cleared the hill slopes to grow cassava and corn. The ecological consequences of resettlement were disastrous as forest clearance exposed the fragile soils to erosion, creating vast areas of barren hills that are only now being gradually revegetated at great expense. In the Central Highlands, the Diem regime also resettled tens of thousands of lowlanders, many of them refugees from the north, in its "land development centers" where they cleared the forest to plant rubber, coffee, and tea plantations. Again, the ecological consequences were often negative although, because of the much smaller scale of the program, not generally as severe as in the northern midlands. In many areas, establishment of the land development centers also resulted in considerable friction between the settlers and the indigenous ethnic minorities whose traditional land rights were ignored, sometimes even explicitly denied, by those planning the resettlement projects. By the early 1960s the increased level of conflict in the Central Highlands caused a cessation of the land development program. Instead, the focus became wholly on security with the Saigon government regrouping, often forcibly, the majority of highlanders into "strategic hamlets." Recruitment of tribal minorities into partisan units, such as the Civilian Irregular Defense Groups organized by the American Special Forces, fostered aspirations for local autonomy, contributing to the evolution of the United Front for the Liberation of the Oppressed Races (usually known by its French acronym as FULRO) separatist movement. Military activity was intense, and the traditional ways of living of the indigenous peoples of Tay Nguyen were severely disrupted.

Following unification of the country in 1975, ambitious new projects were undertaken to resettle lowlanders into the highlands, including the northwestern mountains, the Central Highlands, and the southern midlands. Accurate statistics are unavailable but somewhere between two and four million people were involved in this massive effort to implant thousands of new economic zones, state farms, and state forestry enterprises in the highlands. Map I.1, which is based on official census figures, illustrates the extent of this movement of people as expressed in changing population densities. As in the past, the emphasis of these projects was on meeting the needs of the lowlands by alleviating population pressure through resettlement schemes, extraction of timber and other natural resources, production of industrial crops, and generation of electricity.

Of course, indigenous highland populations enjoyed some benefits from these development efforts. Especially important was the extension of the educational and public health systems into even the most remote areas, as described in papers in this volume by Dominic Montagu and Tran Lanh. But they also bore a disproportionate share of the costs. Living conditions were often harsh, relations between indigenous and migrant populations sometimes strained, natural resources overexploited, and the environment subject to severe degradation. The low priority that Vietnamese development planners attached to providing benefits to the people of the highlands is clearly illustrated by the fact that for many years after the completion of the Hoa Binh dam all power transmission lines led into the lowlands while no electricity was provided to the people of the upland districts that suffered most of the social and environmental costs of this project.

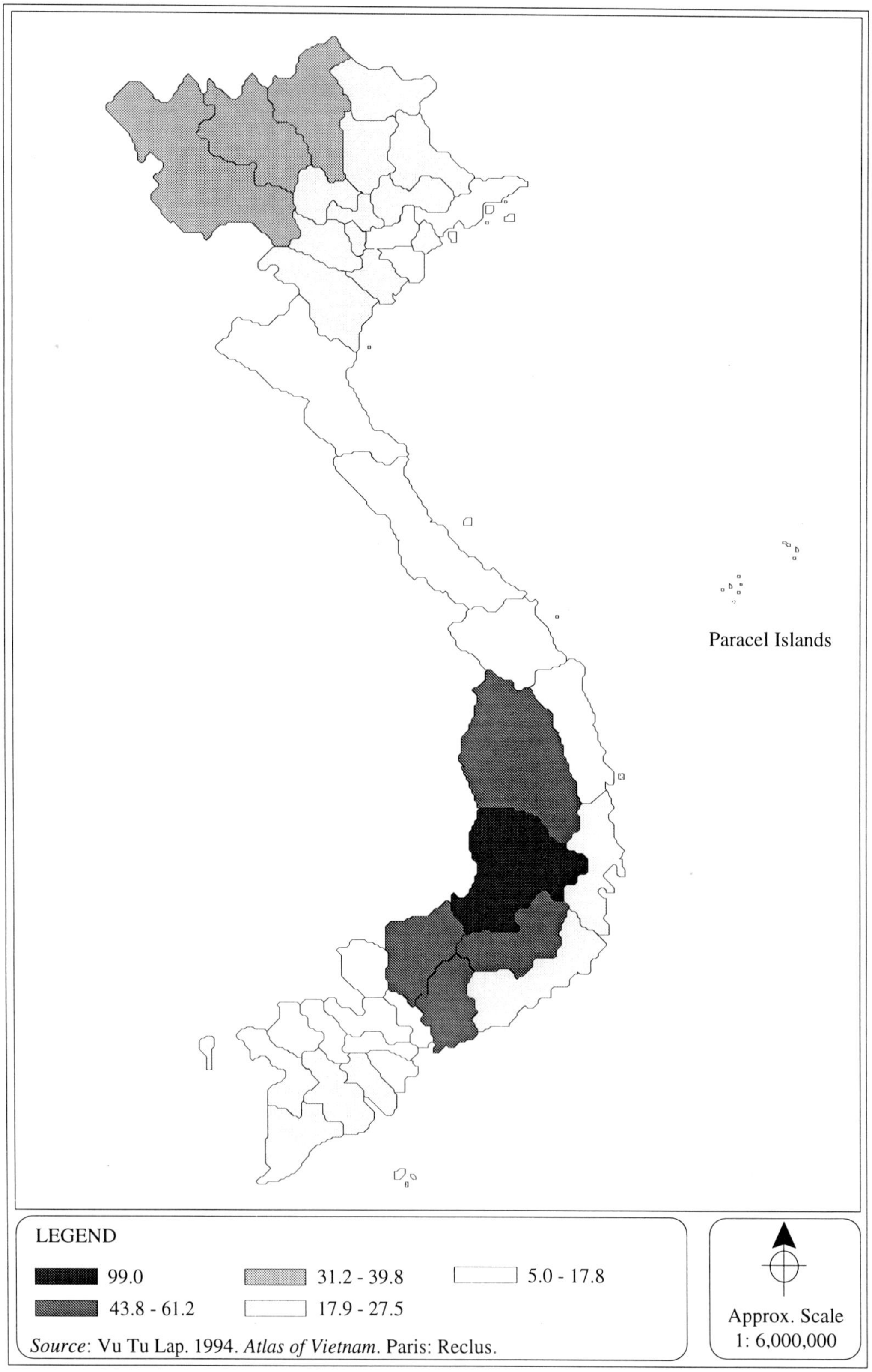

Map I.1 Percent change in gross population density, 1979-89

The "development" of highland areas in ways that primarily served the interests of the lowland-based political and economic systems, and only secondarily met the needs of the highland people themselves, is not, of course, a phenomenon unique to Vietnam. The Appalachian Mountain region in the United States offers a textbook example of the exploitation of highland natural resources (in this case timber, coal, and hydropower) for the benefit of lowland society, leaving the upland people the impoverished inhabitants of a permanently degraded environment. R. D. Hill recounts similar experiences of upland development in the People's Republic of China. More or less identical stories can be told about development of ethnic minority areas in Indonesia, the Philippines, and Malaysia. If Vietnamese national development is to be done on a truly sustainable basis, however, new strategies will have to be envisioned for meeting the needs of the country's most disadvantaged people living in its ecologically most fragile area—the highlands.

Development of the highlands is deserving of attention for the sake of the highland populations in their own right. After all, one-third of the national population lives in this region. No part of the population made greater sacrifices to ensure the success of the revolution but none has gained less from victory. It would be unwise to ignore the potential dangers to national unity if a sense of jealousy and discontent should spread among highlanders, particularly members of ethnic minorities, as a consequence of the failure of national development schemes to provide them with benefits comparable to those enjoyed by compatriots in the prospering lowlands and commensurate with the suffering that they have endured. Chu Huu Quy is quite correct in calling our attention to the problem of increased inequality, both inequalities between the highlands and the lowlands and inequalities among different groups within the highlands, as a major threat to the long-term sustainability of Vietnamese development.

Development of the highlands is also a matter of great importance to the people of the lowlands. These people depend on the highlands for many critical resources, especially electrical power and water. As Le Trong Cuc points out, the downstream environmental impacts of human activities in the highlands are also worthy of attention. Thus, national development policies need to take into full account the significant interdependencies that already exist between the peoples of the highlands and the peoples of the lowlands to which Chu Huu Quy refers. There are a number of encouraging indicators that this imperative has been recognized by the national leadership. Establishment of the Ministerial-level Committee on Ethnic Minorities and Mountain Area Development is one such indicator of the concern felt at the highest political levels. Allocation of massive budgetary resources to the Fixed Cultivation and Sedentarization Program, as described in the paper by Le Duy Hung, is another indicator of the desire to extend the benefits of development to highland people.

The enthusiastic participation of senior officials and scholars in this conference, and their willingness to discuss even the most sensitive questions, is a further indicator of the urgency with which the search for new strategies for highland development is now being pursued within Vietnam. The greatest challenge of highland development is not to overcome physical or economic obstacles but to discover and promote innovative ways of thinking about this unique region and the role it should play in Vietnam's national development.

CONCLUSIONS

In this introductory essay, I have touched on a number of critical issues relating to development of Vietnam's highlands. Although some of these issues are matters of considerable sensitivity, it is impossible to seriously discuss development policies for the highlands without invoking them. It is to be hoped, however, that readers will recognize that no malice lies behind this discussion. Instead, it is pursued in the belief that the best way to minimize the inevitable social problems and conflicts arising out of the development process is by honestly and openly acknowledging the difficulties that must be overcome.

It is clear that the challenges of highland development in Vietnam are enormous in number and vast in scale. Moreover, these challenges are multiplying at a rapid rate as a consequence of population growth, expanding levels of economic activity, and introduction of new technologies and forms of organization. Coping with these changes and, if possible, formulating policies that permit getting ahead of the curve of change are matters of highest priority for Vietnam's national development planning. It is hoped that the papers in this volume will contribute to this process by helping to more clearly define the nature of the challenges of highland development and suggesting some possible strategies for achieving the twin goals of sustainable and equitable development of this vital part of the Vietnamese nation.

Acknowledgments—This essay was written while I was a Visiting Scientist at the National Institute of Environmental Studies (NIES) of the Japan Environment Agency. I am grateful to the Japan Environment Agency and the Environmental Research Center for having made my stay at NIES possible. Neil L. Jamieson and Michael DiGregorio made many helpful comments and suggestions for revision on an earlier draft of this essay. My understanding of the history of efforts to develop the Vietnamese highlands owes much to the scholarly work of Gerald C. Hickey. My own research in the midlands and mountains of northern Vietnam has been made possible by the generous financial support of the John D. and Catherine T. MacArthur Foundation and the Rockefeller Brothers Fund. Le Trong Cuc has freely shared his deep knowledge of human relations with the upland environment in Vietnam and has been a valued colleague in several field studies that we have carried out since 1988.

NOTES

1. In the case of the American West, shortage of water has proven to be the key limiting factor for sustainable agricultural development; in the case of Vietnam's highlands, the quality of the land itself may be the greatest constraint on development.

2. The several different types of swidden agriculture practiced by highland minority peoples, including the stable form referred to in this paper as "rotational swiddening," are well described in *Vien Dan Toc Hoc* [Institute of Ethnology], *Cac dan toc it nguoi o Viet Nam: Các tinh phia bac* [Ethnic

minorities of Vietnam: Northern provinces], *Nha Xuat Ban Khoa Hoc Xa Hoi* [Social Sciences Publishing House], Hanoi, 1978, 43 ff. Unfortunately, these distinctions are generally ignored by Vietnamese development planners who refer to all swiddeners as nomadic (*du canh du cu*).

PART ONE

The Highlands As an Area for Development

CHAPTER 1

Overview of Highland Development in Vietnam: General Characteristics, Socioeconomic Situation, and Development Challenges

Chu Huu Quy
Vietnam's Integrated Rural Development Program, Hanoi

GENERAL CHARACTERISTICS

The uplands of Vietnam, which consist of fourteen highland provinces and twenty-three provinces with some hill and mountain districts or communes, cover three-fourths of the national territory. They extend as a continuous band from the northeast to northwest and all along the Truong Son chain to the eastern part of southern Vietnam for a total distance of more than 4,000 kilometers (Map 1.1). Passes in the highlands of the north and the west serve as communication channels between Vietnam, China, Laos, and Cambodia (State Planning Committee 1993).

Limitations in the availability of land for cultivation of food crops, combined with a growing population, have led to deforestation throughout the highlands. Although better controlled at present than in the past, deforestation still causes serious environmental problems that affect not only local populations but also people living in other regions through the general degradation of watersheds (Ministry of Agriculture and Food Industries 1993). One means of reversing these patterns may involve the replacement of low value and only moderately productive food crops with high value and more prolific tropical tree and vegetable crops.

In 1945 forest covered about 45 percent of Vietnam's total natural territory. In the fifty years since then, the area under forest has been reduced to approximately 26 percent of the natural territory, or 8,630,965 hectares. In some formerly forested highland provinces, however, only 5 to 7 percent of the area remains forested. Similarly, barren land, a category that includes seashores, true desert, and degraded forest land, currently occupies 13,420,391 hectares, or 34.5 percent of natural territory (ibid.). However, it should be noted that barren land in Vietnamese upland areas is generally not as seriously degraded as some African regions where formerly forest and grassland areas have been degraded to true deserts. Rather, much of the highlands are still amenable to interventions directed to the regeneration of the tropical forest and the cultivation of new forest or diversified agricultural crops.[1]

Approximately 24 million people, one-third of the total population of Vietnam, live in the highlands (State Planning Committee 1993). Nevertheless, because hill and mountain territories cover a much larger geographic area than the lowlands, average population densities are much lower than either the national average or averages for the lowlands. For example, the average population density of the highlands is nearly 100 people/km^2 as

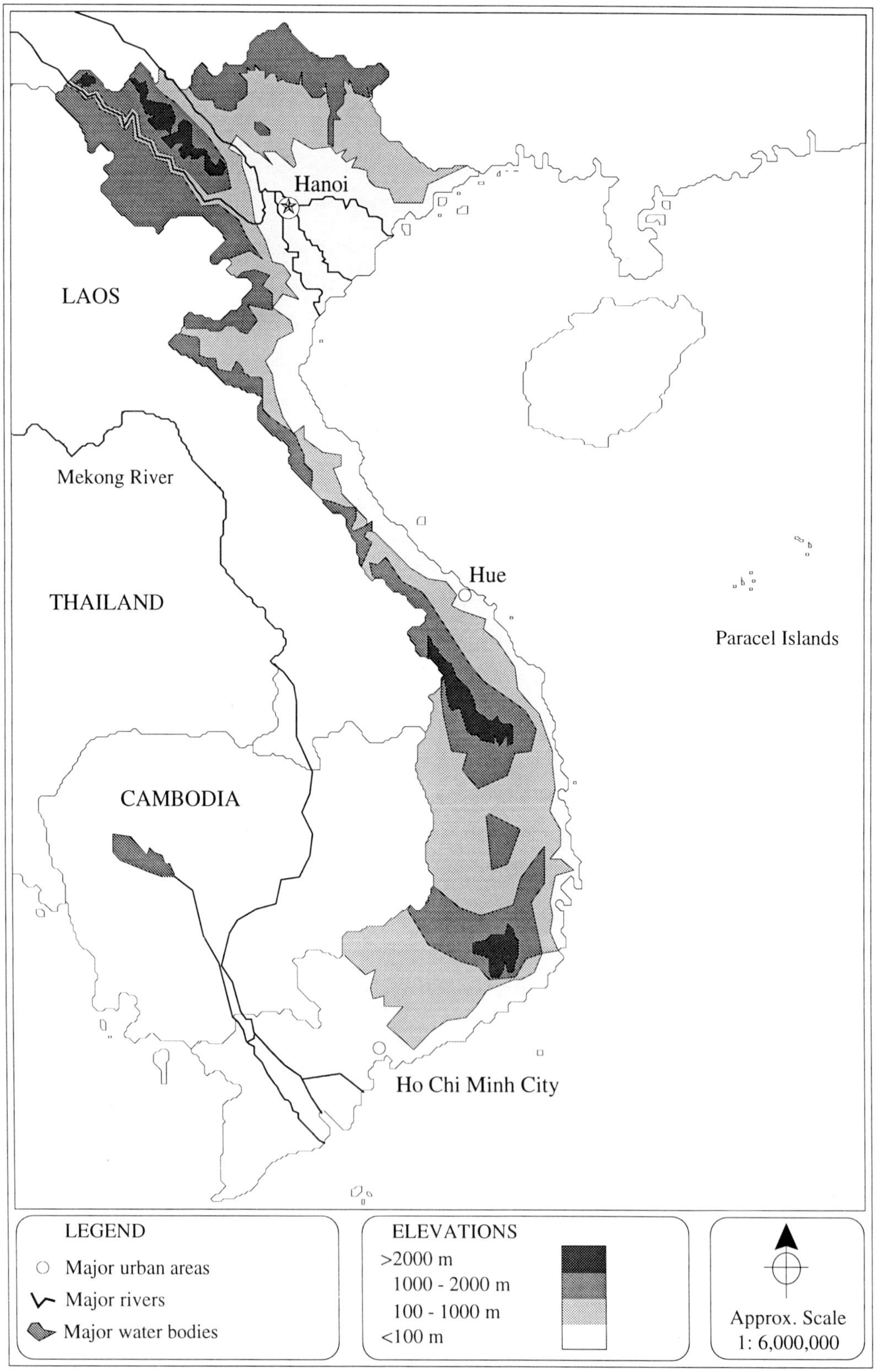

Map1.1 Topography of Vietnam

compared with a national average of more than 200 persons/km^2. Furthermore, since the population of uplanders is distributed very unevenly, in some remote, high mountainous areas, population density reaches only 5 to 7 people/km^2. For comparison, several provinces in the lower Red River Delta support population densities greater than 1,200 persons/km^2.

The highlands are the home of the majority of Vietnam's minority populations, among which Tay, Nung, Thai, Muong, Hmong, Dzao, Ede, Bana, and Jarai are the most numerous. Both the educational attainment levels and levels of material-cultural life of the upland population are generally very low. These factors have received special and systematic attention by the Vietnamese Communist Party and the state throughout the course of national socioeconomic construction and development.[2]

The Vietnamese highlands have potential advantages in the development of branches of the economy such as forestry, perennial industrial crops, fruits, medicinal plants, and animal husbandry. In addition, the mountainous realms contain the majority of Vietnam's nonpetroleum mineral deposits. These resources and resource potentials have been developed by a variety of socioeconomic units, both private and under state management, including cooperative and private enterprises, agricultural and silvicultural households, and centrally managed and local state enterprises.

The highlands are also the source of many of Vietnam's major rivers[3] with an annual flow of more than 450 billion cubic meters. Although varying seasonally, the hydraulic capacity of the mountain regions is sufficient to meet the increased demands of industry, the daily water needs of the people, and large-scale hydroelectric power. Every year, in addition to water, highland rivers supply billions of cubic meters of alluvium to augment the fertility of cultivated soils in the plains (State Planning Committee 1993).

HIGHLAND ZONES

Vietnam's rich and diversified highland areas have been divided into a variety of natural ecological-climatic zones by a number of authors.[4] In this chapter, the hill and mountain territories have been divided into five zones (Map 1.2).

The *Northeastern Highlands* extend from the coast along the common border with China to the Red River. They are the ancestral home of Tay, Nung, and Dzao peoples, among other less numerous minority groups. The population density here, at 150 to 300 persons/km^2, is significantly higher than other upland zones. The educational level of people in the Northeastern Highlands also exceeds that of most other minority areas, while their material-cultural standards have also improved significantly in recent years. Similarly, the transportation network in the northeast is better developed than other mountainous areas. The main economic activities here are food-crop farming, forestry, industrial and fruit-crop cultivation, and animal husbandry. Commerce is well developed along the border with China and through seaports.

The *Northwestern Highlands* cover an area extending from the western side of the Red River along the border with China to the beginning of the common border with Laos. The

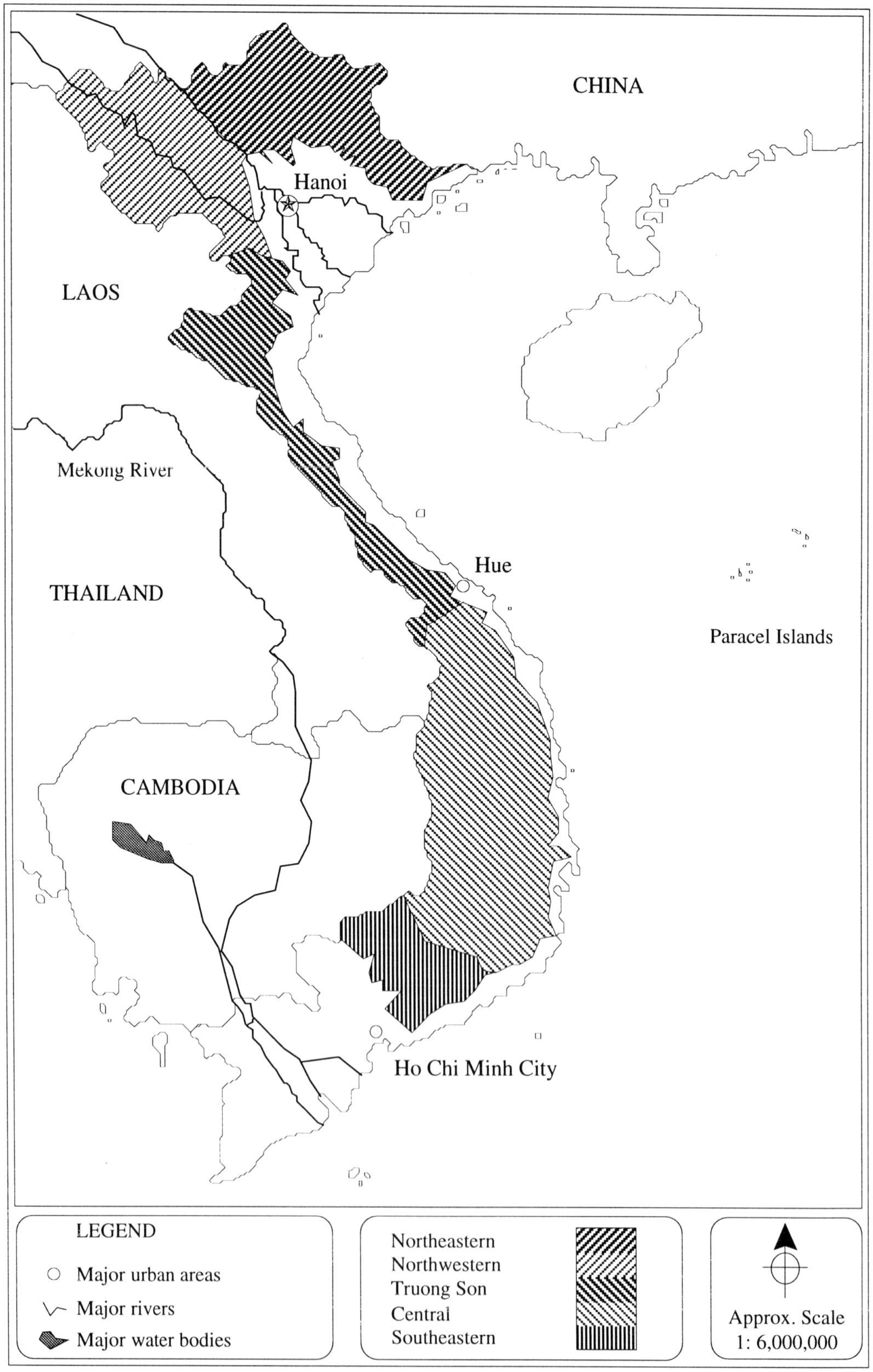

Map 1.2 Five highland zones

Northwestern Highlands, penetrating more than 500 kilometers into the center of the North, are larger in land area than the Northeastern Highlands. The knowledge level and material-cultural standards of the people, however, are generally lower. The Northwestern Highlands are the home of Thai, Muong, and Hmong peoples. Their main economic activities are silviculture, terraced rice culture in hills, wet rice culture in the valleys, animal husbandry, industrial and fruit-crop cultivation, and cultivation of medicinal plants.

The *Truong Son Highlands* extend as a long band of high, steep land from Hoa Binh and Thanh Hoa provinces south to the Central Highlands. Its minimum width is 20 to 30 kilometers and maximum more than 100 kilometers. Its landscape is dissected by numerous rivers. The Truong Son Highlands are affected both by strong typhoons moving in from the east over the South China Sea and hot dry winds moving down from the mountainous areas of Laos to the west. The educational levels and material-cultural standards of its population are uneven, often lower than that of other zones. Although many distinct minority peoples live in the Truong Son Highlands, their population by group often totals only in the hundreds. Although the economic activities of these people are similar to other upland zones, they are often more primitive due to isolation and severe natural conditions.

The *Central Highlands* encompass four provinces with a less diverse landscape than other hill and mountain regions. It has a common border in the west with Laos and Cambodia. The climate is dry and hot, with a clear rainy season and dry season. Its forest reserves remain rather vast. Forest coverage is about 40 percent. The zone possesses a wide area of basalt red soil, which is at present used to cultivate high-value industrial plants such as coffee, rubber trees, tea, cashew, and other fruit crops. The main minority people in the Central Highlands are Ede, Bana, and Jarai. Their knowledge level and material-cultural standards vary, but in general are better than that of the Northwestern and Truong Son zones. Its economic potential is rated high. The transportation network is also better than the two other zones.

The *Southeastern Highlands*, a hill area, border the Central Highlands and the Mekong River Delta and share a boundary in the west with Cambodia. This is the most advantaged zone. The landscape is rather smooth; the soil is suitable for high-value industrial and fruit crops. The transport system is favorable, near Ho Chi Minh city and open to easy economic and cultural communications with other regions within the country as well as abroad. The Southeastern Highlands have a number of more developed industrial and services units specialized in agriculture, forestry products processing, construction material, porcelain, fine art, and light industries. The population density is about 250 people/km^2. Local population was very thin in the past, but since the 1950s people from other zones in the country have settled here. This has resulted in a higher, more diverse population than other mountain areas. Minority peoples are thus only a small percentage of the total population. Average income per capita of its population is higher than all other highland and plain zones throughout the country.

SOCIOECONOMIC SITUATION

Regional Inequalities

At present, comparative socioeconomic statistics point out significant inequalities between high-mountain, deep and remote areas and those in the plains, city suburbs, around industrial centers or towns. This phenomenon is quite well known and has been recorded in other underdeveloped countries as they have begun their "total renovation." Such regional inequalities should not be glossed over lightly but rather vigorously and systematically addressed given the potential they have to cause social instability during the development process (Chu 1993b).

According to a General Statistical Office (1994) survey of farmer incomes for 1993, the average income of a farm household in the most prosperous of Vietnam's seven administrative regions is more than double the average for the poorest. While this survey accurately depicts large-scale regional disparities, data provided by research organizations, line ministries, and local authorities suggest that the true depth of these regional disparities in income and, as a consequence, cultural and social welfare, can only be understood when disaggregated to the district and village level (Chu and Ha 1991).

State Policy and the Alleviation of Regional Inequalities

Agriculture, Livestock, and Forestry Food production, nutrition, and the avoidance of famine have been the primary concern of all Vietnamese from the time of our ancestors up to now. In recent years, these issues have been broadly addressed on a national level. Food production for Vietnam's population of 72 million is now sufficient and has, in fact, supported a limited reserve and export capacity (GSO 1992). The possibility of sustaining food self-sufficiency, as well as increasing the level held in reserve or exported, is quite real, barring disasters.

Due to the attainment of a national food production goal of 25 million tons in 1993, two years before the national plan target date, and to sound food circulation policies, food prices[5] have stabilized over the past several years. As a result, though food crises may still arise in isolated highland areas, the threat of grave famines, as have occurred in the past, has been removed.

Food production within the mountain territories has increased by nearly 500,000 tons in the last four years, despite a stabilization, and in some places a decrease, in the area devoted to food crop cultivation. This has been due to improved cultivation methods, to the impact of technical renovation, and more important, to government interventions in food production through the improvement of irrigation systems, new crop varieties, tax policies, credit, and marketing support. Increases in food production have occurred alongside incentives to improve agricultural technology, to reduce the need for each household to produce sufficient food for its own consumption, to grant more agricultural land to crops with higher commodity value, and to sell high-value products outside and buy additional food at a comparative price advantage. In the past few years, therefore, the number of households with insufficient food has decreased rapidly to between 10 and 15 percent, despite high population growth rates, averaging between 2.5 and 3.4 percent, which have resulted in rates of food production per capita lower than the national average, under 250 kg/person/yr compared to 350 kg/person/yr (Ministry of Agriculture and Food Industries 1993).

As mentioned, industrial crops, fruit plants, and animal husbandry generally have comparative advantages in the highlands. The development trends in the production of these high-valued agricultural products in recent years have been quite encouraging (see Table 1.1).

Table 1.1 Increases in the cultivation of selected agricultural products

Product (1,000 ha)	1989	1993	Increase (%)
Coffee	123	146	+11.9
Rubber	215	243	+11.3
Tea	58	70	+12.1
Cashew	80	116	+14.5

Source: Ministry of Agriculture and Food Industries (1993).

The production of other industrial crops such as tobacco, mulberry, cotton, and sugarcane, fruit crops such as apricot, plum, orange, tangerine, banana, litchi, longan, mango, and pear, and tuber plants such as cassava, as well as medicinal plants, have all rapidly expanded in appropriate areas. For the moment, accurate statistical data on the production of these crops are unavailable. Nevertheless, widespread acceptance of the government policy to expand "house gardens, hill gardens, and forest gardens," supported by land policies that have given farmers rights to land for integrated agroforestry production, indicates increasing diversification of agricultural production to these marketable crops.[6]

In addition to these agricultural products, production of livestock such as cattle, milk cows, goats, deer, horses, pigs, poultry, and silkworms has increased greatly. Currently, innovations in milk cow and silkworm production are spreading from research centers in Son La (for the North) and Lam Dong province (for the South). Water buffalo and oxen, previously raised for local use as draft animals, have increasingly shifted toward production for sale to other regions. Meanwhile, the use of horses as draft animals, a use which has declined over recent years, is being re-established and developed. In addition, the raising of goats and deer for their exchange value has been developed in a large way in several localities. Finally, pig and poultry production in highland areas has shown the same growth as in lowland regions. In general, animal husbandry in the uplands is being shifted into a new stage: breed improvement, application of technical advances, and reduction in free-ranging husbandry (ibid.).

Forest conservation and lumber production are high priority strategic issues for the country and, more particularly, for all highland zones. As far back as the early 1960s, the government began transferring forest and barren lands to local authorities, state-managed forestry enterprises, and farmer households. The outcome of these early attempts at forest management has been very modest. Only after issuance of Politburo Resolution No. 22 and Government Decision No. 72 five years ago, and especially since government Decision No. 327 two years ago, have transfer policies, now described as a forest contract system, begun to show positive outcomes. This has been due to a number of reasons:

- Increases in government investment.
- With the improvement of life in highland areas, about 5 percent of farming households have been able to accumulate enough capital to undertake forestry alongside their agricultural work. The majority of these farming households have received 2 to 3 hectares for use in agroforestry production, although a number of households were allotted 10 to 20 hectares. Some particularly well-established households received between 100 and 300 hectares. In the future, these households will become major upland businesses, specializing not only in forestry, but also other industries and services activities under state guidance and support.
- The governments of some countries and international agencies have allocated aid for forestry development, exploitation of the highland's diverse potential, environmental protection, and improvement of living standards in hill and mountain areas.
- Both government and local macro-economic policies have encouraged forestry development.
- The government's strict prohibition of deforestation, together with a policy of zoning cultivation to regenerate the forest, has shown increasing effect.
- Better awareness among the population of the high economic value of forestry combined with agriculture has encouraged farming households to conserve and develop forest land in conjunction with agricultural production.

In total, more than 5 million hectares of forest land has been transferred to the farmers for self-management and agroforestry development (Table 1.2). Expansion of concentrated forest plantation land has seen a twofold increase in recent years, rising from a 110,000-hectare per year average (1976–90) to a current average of 200,000 hectares (GSO 1968–92).

Industry, Services, and Commerce Industrial, service, and commercial activities in the uplands have increased rapidly over the last decade. More specifically, such industries as agriculture and forest products processing, mineral mining and construction material production, light industry, handicrafts, and indigenous arts have been expanding in both number and type of firms and total output, especially in recent years. This has been most rapid in the Southeastern Highlands where infrastructure and agro-industrial bases have been historically more developed.

Table 1.2 Rate of transfer of forest land

Period	Amount of forest land transferred
1968–82	2.5 million hectares transferred to 4,000 cooperatives and farmer households
1983–89	1.9 million hectares
1990–92	0.8 million hectares

Industrial, commercial, and tourism centers are being formed gradually in different places, even in the most disadvantaged zones such as the Northwestern and Central Highlands. Of special attention is the phenomenon of increasingly developed markets, even in remote high mountain areas. For example, according to data provided by the Ministry of Commerce, in 1993 there were 592 district, border, and commune markets in the ten northern upland provinces, a nearly threefold increase over 1980. In Son La, Lai Chau, Tuyen Quang, and Yen Bai provinces, the increase has been six- to sevenfold. The number of small traders in eight of these upland provinces has also rapidly increased from 16,271 households in 1989 to 27,263 households in 1992 for a substantial 68 percent increase. In addition, provincially managed state-trading companies and organizations maintain shops in each of these districts and in a number of the communes (Ministry of Commerce 1993). Local authorities engage in these trading activities in an effort to carry out state policy directed to providing remote areas with locally unavailable commercial goods such as foodstuffs, kerosene, medicines, tissue, paper, and salt. Every year, reserves of these goods are shipped to the highlands before the wet season, when transport is very difficult. In Lai Chau, the most remote highland province, there were seven to ten state-run trading points in every district, or 61 in total, by 1992.

In spite of these achievements in commerce, industry and services remain underdeveloped in most highland areas. Sustained effort over the long term will be required to adequately develop these sectors for the benefit of far-flung highland peoples (ibid.).

Education, Health Care, and Social Welfare At present, the adult literacy rate for the whole country is over 80 percent, while for highland zones the same figure is on average about 60 percent. In some remote upland areas, this figure is even lower, reaching roughly 30 percent. The situation is further complicated because illiteracy eradication for minority people requires learning both their own language and the national language.

Over the last three years, the government has paid special attention to education of indigenous peoples living in mountain areas. Between 1991 and 1993, the government investment fund for highland education has increased 3.73 times (Ministry of Finance 1993). Pilot programs for minority children have been inaugurated in almost every district, as well as in many communes and villages. Nevertheless, due to the low income and difficult daily life of upland peoples, insufficient construction of schools, and lack of teachers and teaching materials, highland illiteracy programs have been unable to achieve their goals.

In contrast to literacy programs, recent government efforts to improve health services in the highlands, assisted by foreign countries and international agencies, have shown very positive results. For example, government investment in health care for people living in hill and mountain realms saw a fourteenfold increase between 1991 and 1993.[7] As a result, between 1990 and 1993 the number of highland districts with health centers rose from only 18.5 percent to 88.1 percent (Ministry of Health 1993). In addition, some upland provinces and districts have formed mobile health-care teams for emergency assistance.

Similar increases have occurred in the communes. Currently, 80 percent of highland communes have health centers. Each of these health centers is staffed by at least two health-care personnel. Unfortunately, due to difficulties in recruiting and training health-care personnel for work in upland areas, the majority have received only specialized secondary education. The training of additional health-care personnel for work in the highlands is a subject of special concern of Ministry of Health and other government line agencies.

Numerous outmoded superstitions and social illnesses—such as drug addiction and gambling—are prevalent throughout the highlands. They remain especially acute in certain areas where opportunities for contact with and assimilation of new, healthy cultural practices are limited (ibid).

Socioeconomic Infrastructure The principal transportation systems in upland zones were seriously damaged during the war. Their restoration and improvement will require large investments far beyond the capacity of either the state or private capital. Significant efforts, however, have already been made. By combining investment capital for prioritized projects over the last two years, the two Northern Highland rail lines were restored and main roads through high hill towns and district centers were repaired. Additionally some important national roads that pass through the North, South, and Central Highlands were repaired. According to the Ministry of Transportation, a bus trip from Hanoi to Lai Chau, which in the past took three days, now only takes one-and-a-half to two days; a trip from Hanoi to Ha Giang, which in the past took two days, now takes only one day. Some important roads that serve border crossings were also restored (Ministry of Transport and Communications 1993).

Progress has been made in repairing, upgrading, and constructing provincial, district, and communal roads in highland areas. In three years, according to the Ministry of Transportation, nearly 15,000 kilometers of new roads were constructed in the ten Northern Highland and four Central Highland provinces, and thousands of bridges were built or repaired. Overall, there are now 181 meters of roadway per square kilometer of hill and mountain regions. The corresponding figure for Thailand is 200 meters, for Malaysia it is 250 meters, and for the Philippines it is 450 meters (Ministry of Transportation 1993). Compared to these countries, however, the quality of rural roads in Vietnam is much lower.

Despite this progress, difficult terrain has made it impossible to extend all-weather transport routes to many highland communities. Currently, 146 district centers and 2,347 communes within eleven Northern Highland and four Central Highland provinces are served by all-weather roads. For the most part, the remaining 563 communes (20 percent) that have not been reached are in quite remote or high mountain areas. In these regions, horses and human power remain the chief means of transport. Predictably this has significantly limited the possibility of opening such areas to the commodity economy (ibid.).

At present, the average per capita electricity consumption in the highland zones is only 10 to 15 percent of the national average. The reason for this disparity is due principally to a lack of electrical services in upland territories. To meet growing demands, some localities near the northern border and some inner areas have provided electricity for themselves through the use of diesel generators (State Planning Committee 1993).

Hydropower is a second source of local electrical-generating capacity. Large-, medium-, and small-scale hydropower stations, designed to meet the needs of highland communities, have received technical and financial support from both the government and local authorities. In recent years, hydropower projects have taken the form of public-private joint ventures promoted under a policy calling for the government and the people to work together. These hydropower projects not only provide electricity, but also provide irrigation water to local agriculture and forestry, processing water to industry and clean water to households. The multiple benefits of such projects have attracted the attention of international agencies, many of which have provided significant project and program assistance.

Post services, radio, and television have also received an increasingly large investment, mainly in the last three years.

In summary, while infrastructure construction in the highlands has received increased investment in the last three to four years, the amount invested has not been sufficient to the tasks at hand (Chu and Ha 1991).

DEVELOPMENT TARGETS AND CHALLENGES

The general target to the year 2000 is to accelerate the rate of socioeconomic development of the highlands as a whole and pay more attention to the material and cultural life of minority people in particular.

Agriculture and Forestry

Agriculture should develop in accordance with the natural conditions of the highland areas and life traditions of minority people. The government has thus targeted promotion of high-value industrial crops in particular regions, fruit crops in others, and intensive gardening by farmer households throughout the region (Table 1.3). The purpose of these projects is to increase production of agricultural commodities for their exchange value and the development of processing industries which, by increasing rural incomes, can serve as a basis for wide-scale improvement in living standards.

This emphasis on commodity production is not meant to exclude food production. Nevertheless, highland standards of living cannot improve on self-provisioning alone. Any development program should encourage mutual exchanges based on comparative advan-

Table 1.3 Crop production targets

Crop	1993	2000
Food production per capita	200–250 kg	250–300 kg
Rubber tree area	243,000 ha	380,000 ha
Coffee tree area	146,000 ha	200,000 ha
Tea plant area	70,000 ha	150,000 ha
Cashew tree area	116,000 ha	240,000 ha
Fruit plants	Data not available	
Livestock and poultry value		1.5–2-fold increase

Source: Ministry of Agriculture and Food Industries (1993).

tages that broaden both economic and cultural contact. It is thus essential to give state and local priority to irrigation work, crop improvement, introduction of new crops, and application of technical innovations for the intensification of crop and livestock productivity. At the same time, attention should be focused on regulation of food circulation[8] and prices as highland households are increasingly drawn into the sale of forestry and diversified agroproducts as their income source.

Forest conservation and development, a high priority in highland planning, should become an essential component in the settlement of nomadic minority people. This view is contained within government policy, particularly Decision No. 202 on the contract system for forest preservation, cultivation for forest regeneration and afforestation issued May 2, 1994 (Anon. May 2, 1994). Under the provisions of this decision, government organizations such as forest protection and specialized forest management teams, agricultural and forestry enterprises, educational and professional schools, and other government organizations can receive rights to forests and forest land. These organizations can then contract farmer households, private individuals, government organizations, army units, schools, and other social entities to carry out forest preservation, reforestation, and afforestation. Land transfers will be based on land suitability, feasibility of the project, and capacity of the contractor to provide accurate accounting. Despite these formidable entrance barriers, priority will be given to nomadic minority people and the local population. Funding sources for specific projects include state and foreign grants and credit, and the self-procured capital of contractors. Contractors are obliged to realize all items of signed contracts and have the right to earn profits in accordance with contract stipulations regarding duration, products to be harvested, method of integrating forest production and agriculture, transfer of rights to other households, and the use of forest resources for self-provisioning.

The intent of these policies is to preserve and enrich nearly 9 million hectares of remaining forest by 1995, to increase this area by 1.5 to 2 times by the year 2000, and to create stable protection forests and high-value forest plantations. Currently, 100,000 to 150,000 hectares of forest are destroyed annually. Given the reliance of local people on forest areas for food production, a secondary purpose of state forestry policy is to conduct, along with forest preservation, afforestation and reforestation, production of agricultural crops that promote soil conservation and meet local needs. The ultimate intent of these policies, however, is to raise the current forest coverage from 26 percent to between 30 and 32 percent by the year 1995, and to between 40 and 45 percent by 2000. This calls for a 5-million hectare annual increase in forests, forest plantations, and stabilized forest land area over the next fifteen years (Ministry of Forestry 1993).

Industry, Commerce, and Services

Recent government policies encourage the formation of investment capital through the reorganization of state enterprises, creation of private enterprises, solicitation of foreign aid, formation of joint venture companies with foreign partners, government funding for equipment upgrading, and the opening of new state enterprises. Current state-managed industrial and service units in upland areas need to be reorganized in accordance with these policies. Processing industries for agriculture and forest products should be the first priority. Appropriate attention should also be given to mining and construction materials industries. In conjunction with these two priorities, machinery production and repair industries are very important to meet the demands of highland development, while light industry is required to meet the demands for consumer goods fit to the demands of households in the uplands. Finally, arts and craft export products with minority motifs should be developed as a source of additional income to highland households (Chu 1994).

State trade organizations, through provincial trading companies, operate shops in district centers, stable or mobile shops in communes, and trade points in communes or groups of communes with participation of private traders. State policy should encourage the expansion of these trading companies to fill gaps left through spontaneous development, especially those that exploit highland people. At the same time, state policies should encourage private traders to provide essential goods to upland communities at reasonable prices and to encourage farming households that specialize in small trade to open new markets in the countryside.

Trade and commerce in remote areas are subjects of special concern of different authorities from the central to local level. Recently, the National Assembly adopted a proposal to increase investment in highland trading in 1994 by twofold compared to 1993. The government has decided to provide four items free of charge to the most remote highland communities: iodized salt, medicines, paper, and kerosene. The government will also provide price support and transportation costs for seven kinds of goods which, in addition to the four items listed above, include tissue, insecticides, and chemical fertilizers (Anon. May 23, 1994).

Commercial policy should also include the highland's rich tourism potential. Up to now, tourism has been developed primarily in the seashore areas near cities and industrial centers. Highland tourism has not yet been fully exploited. In the coming period, there are numerous possibilities to develop tourism in hill and mountain areas that would attract both domestic and foreign tourists. As these potentials are exploited, income from tourism should occupy an increasing part of the total income of local authorities and highland households.

Infrastructure

Infrastructure construction in highland zones has become an urgent priority in state policy. The target for the year 2000 is to upgrade all national roads in highland zones and to expand and gradually pave the principal roads from Hanoi and Ho Chi Minh city to all provincial towns. At the provincial level, the target is to upgrade provincial road systems and bridges to provide for the movement of heavy trucks in both dry and rainy seasons. To facilitate trade, roads from airports, railway stations, river and sea ports, and border entrances will be upgraded as well. To further develop tourism and commercial potential, district roads to communal centers and cultural or tourist attractions will be upgraded for all-weather travel.

State policy should encourage joint public-private and domestic-international investment to improve the highland transportation system. It is necessary to pay special attention to river-transport systems. To provide basic investment capital for highland transport development, the Ministry of Transportation has presented a huge budget for consideration by the government.

State irrigation policy should facilitate the exploitation of the highland's agro-industrial potential, combining development and upgrading of large, medium, and small hydropower projects with irrigation work. In addition, state policy should pay special attention to medium and small hydropower stations for high mountain areas (Ministry of Transport and Communications 1993).

Education, Health, and Social Welfare

Illiteracy, including first-language illiteracy, is targeted for eradication in highland areas by the year 2000. Government funding should be given to increase the knowledge of highland people through construction of schools, provision of equipment and teaching materials, and the training of teachers. In addition, to develop a wider cultural experience, the government should place instructional and cultural media such as books and video tapes in highland libraries.

In regards to health, the target is to provide early diagnosis of diseases and to prevent their spread. In particular, state policy will seek to control goiter, malaria, and leprosy, three diseases common in the highlands. In conjunction with a general policy to reduce highland population growth rates to 2 percent or less per year, state policy should also seek to improve health care for mothers and children and to decrease the death rate of new-born children. To facilitate these health-care targets will require raising the number of health-care personnel in each commune from its present figure of two trained workers to three or four by the year 2000, to build new polyclinics, organize mobile health-care teams and upgrade current health-care centers, and to provide a reserve supply of medicines in case of emergency (Ministry of Health 1993). Finally, in conjunction with state policies on trade and transportation, the age-old threat of local famine will be addressed, as well as persistent social problems such as drug addiction and social responsibilities such as care of the elderly and children.

DEVELOPMENT CHALLENGES

Highland minority people have a long, deep tradition of communal solidarity and mutual assistance. Through different historical periods, especially during the revolution and war for national independence and unity, they have made major contributions and suffered great losses. The lives of many upland peoples still face numerous limitations. Given the historic sacrifices endured by highland minority people, these limitations are a special concern of the Communist Party and the state. Thus, every effort will be made to assist highland minority people to develop endogenous resources for their own benefit and the benefit of the country as a whole.

Although major progress has already been made, great challenges lie ahead. These challenges, cataloged throughout this chapter, can be summarized as (1) very poor material and technical infrastructure; (2) seriously damaged environment; (3) poorly developed economy; (4) low level of knowledge; (5) high population increase; (6) unemployment; and (7) poor education and training for local professional staff and administrators.

Besides these challenges, there are new opportunities and advantages. Among these is more concentrated efforts of the government, evidenced over the last three years, to provide a new and effective momentum for highland development. While government inputs continue to increase, the aid and assistance of foreign governments and international agencies have also become more important. Nevertheless, it will always be the endogenous sources of upland people themselves that will be the most decisive for highland development (Chu and Tran 1993).

NOTES

1. According to one source, between US$1,000 and US$1,500 are needed to create a complete agroforestry environment on 1 hectare of degraded land using local labor and state support. Such investments have had high returns on investment, as well as ecological benefits. For some other countries, a similar investment should be two to four times higher or even more (Chu 1966).

2. See, for example, Resolution No. 10 of the Politbureau of Communist Party of Vietnam, April 5, 1988; Political Report of the Central Committee of Communist Party of Vietnam at the Seventh National Party Congress, June 1991, pp. 18, 19, 51, 61, 66; *Strategy of Stabilization and Socioeconomic Development Toward the Year 2000*, Seventh National Party Congress, June 1991, pp. 51, 21; and Document of the Fifth Plenum of Party Central Committee, June 1993, pp. 74, 75.

3. The Mekong River has its source in China and flows through Burma, Thailand, Laos, and Cambodia before entering the South China Sea in Vietnam.

4. There exists no unified method of highland zoning. Rather, the division of highland areas into specific zones has depended on the specific purpose of the authors of papers. One can list at least four different zoning methods: the first is that of the author, the second belongs to the Forestry Planning Institute under the Ministry of Forestry, the third is that of Dr. Nguyen Tran Cau, and the fourth is that of Dr. Nguyen Van Ty. The related data in these three papers are complementary to one another.

5. The price of paddy, at 1,000 to 1,200 *dong* per kilogram, varies by $.02 per kilogram throughout the country ("Price and Market Information," 1993–94).

6. Long-term usufruct rights are given to farmers in areas with abundant land while shorter-term rights are given to farmers in land-scarce areas.

7. Roughly 36 percent of this fund was spent on malaria eradication, 43 percent on goiter control programs, 18 percent for demography and family planning, and 3 percent on vaccinations against six common diseases.

8. Highland households are increasingly relying on lowland rice as their basic staple as they convert their own low-productivity rice lands to more productive, higher income crops.

BIBLIOGRAPHY

Anon. May 2, 1994. Decision no. 202 of the Prime Minister. *Nhan Dan.*

Anon. May 23, 1994. Investment for mountainous areas. *Nhan Dan.*

Anon. June 2, 1994. To pay more attention to mountainous areas. *Nhan Dan.*

Bui Dinh Thanh, ed. 1993. *Social policy: Some theoretical and practical issues.* Hanoi: Scientific Research Program No. KX.04.

Center on Population and Labour Resources and the Center for the Development of Rural Human Resources in Asia. July 1993. *Famine and poverty in Vietnam: Some research results of the Labour, Invalids and Social Affairs Branch.* Hanoi: Authors.

Central Committee of the Communist Party of Vietnam. April 5, 1988. Resolution No. 10 of the Politbureau of the Communist Party of Vietnam.

Central Committee of the Communist Party of Vietnam. June 1991. Political Report of the Central Committee of Communist Party of Vietnam at the Seventh National Party Congress. Hanoi: Authors.

Central Committee of the Communist Party of Vietnam. November 27, 1989. Some Essential Directions and Policies on Socio-Economic Development of Mountainous Areas. Resolution No. 22 NQ/TW of the Politbureau.

Chu Huu Quy. 1966. Dissertation for doctorate on economics. Leningrad.

Chu Huu Quy. 1993a. Vietnam's rural development: The past, present and future. Paper presented at a scientific seminar of Agriculture University No. 1, Hanoi.

Chu Huu Quy. April 1993b. *Results of the research theme No. KX.08.01 of the scientific research program on Vietnam rural development.* Hanoi: NISTFASS.

Chu Huu Quy. October 25, 1993c. *Strategic directions and socio-economic rural development, national industrialization promotion forecasting for the coming period.* Hanoi: NISTFASS.

Chu Huu Quy. April 18, 1994. On industrialization and modernization of the country. *Nhan Dan.*

Chu Huu Quy, ed. 1994. *Vietnam's integrated rural development program, 1992–93.* Hanoi: NISTFASS.

Chu Huu Quy and Ha Nhan Thang, eds. 1991. *The socio-economics of the Vietnamese countryside at present.* Vols. 1 and 2. Hanoi: Ideology and Culture Publishing House.

Chu Huu Quy and Tran Thanh Binh, eds. 1993. *The state-level scientific research program on Vietnam's integrated socio-economic rural development: An overview of the program's activities in 1992.* Hanoi: Social Sciences Publishing House.

Committee on Nationalities and Mountainous Areas. September 1993. Draft report on highland socio-economic development. Hanoi: Authors.

Council of Ministers. March 13, 1990. Some Practical Directions and Policies on Socio-Economic Development of Mountainous Areas. Decree No. 72 of the Council of Ministers.

General Statistical Office. 1968–94. *Statistical annual.* Hanoi: Statistical Publishing House.

General Statistical Office. 1985–94. *Statistical data on Vietnam's agriculture, forestry and fisheries.* Hanoi: Statistical Publishing House.

Institute of Social Sciences. 1990. *World agriculture, countryside and peasants.* Hanoi: Authors.

Johnson, N., and B. Cabarde. 1993. *Surviving the cut: Natural forest management in the humid tropics.* Washington, D.C.: World Resources Institute.

Le Trong Cuc, Kathleen Gillogly, and A. Terry Rambo. 1992. *Agroecosystems of the midlands of northern Vietnam.* Occasional Paper No. 12. Honolulu: East-West Center.

Ministry of Agriculture and Food Industries. September 1993. Draft report on highland socio-economic development. Hanoi: Authors.

Ministry of Commerce. September 1993. Draft report on highland socio-economic development. Hanoi: Authors.

Ministry of Finance. September 1993. Draft report on highland socio-economic development. Hanoi: Authors.

Ministry of Forestry. September 1993. Draft report on highland socio-economic development. Hanoi: Authors.

Ministry of Health. September 1993. Draft report on highland socio-economic development. Hanoi: Authors.

Ministry of Transport and Communication. September 1993. Draft report on highland socio-economic development. Hanoi: Authors.

Nguyen Sinh Cuc. 1991. *Real situation of Vietnamese agriculture, countryside and peasants 1976–90.* Hanoi: Statistical Publishing House.

Nguyen Van Tiem. 1993. *Rich and poor in the countryside at present.* Hanoi: Agriculture Publishing House.

Nguyen Van Truong. 1985. *Designing integrated agroforestry models.* Hanoi: Agriculture Publishing House.

Olivier, George. 1992. *Human ecology.* Hanoi: World Publishing House.

Phan Dai Doan. 1992. *Vietnamese village: Some socio-economic issues.* Hanoi: Social Sciences Publishing House.

Seventh National Party Congress. June 1991. *Strategy of stabilization and socio-economic development towards the year 2000.* Hanoi: Authors.

State Planning Committee. September 1993. Draft report on highland socio-economic development. Hanoi: Authors.

Tuong Lai, ed. 1992. *Some population problems under sociologic approach.* Hanoi: Social Sciences Publishing House.

CHAPTER 2

Perspectives on Defining Highland Development Challenges in Vietnam: New Frontier or Cul-De-Sac?

A. Terry Rambo

Program on Environment, East-West Center, Honolulu

It is widely recognized that the highlands present a major challenge for Vietnamese development policy. Covering more than 70 percent of the national territory and home for at least one-third of the national population, the highlands are understandably a major concern of the Vietnamese government. Achieving the successful development of these vast areas of mountains and forests is, of necessity, a matter of high priority.

There are, however, two very divergent views of the nature of the development challenge presented by the highlands: one view, which remains the dominant one in official discourse, is that the highland regions represent a new frontier for national development. The highlands are perceived as underpopulated areas containing immense pools of untapped natural resources and vast areas of unutilized lands. From this perspective, the objective of development is to inject settlers and capital into the uplands in order to convert this potential wealth into actual prosperity. The alternative view, one that is shared by many scientists but few policy-makers, is that the highlands are fragile landscapes, already overpopulated and suffering from severe and rapidly worsening environmental degradation with populations locked into poverty and declining quality of life. Seen from this perspective, the main objective of development is to undo past mistakes, restore degraded habitats, and give renewed hope to marginalized peoples. Finding a meeting ground between these divergent views of the highlands as an arena for development is the main challenge before us in this seminar. The purpose of this chapter is to review some of the key issues that make the development of Vietnam's highlands so problematic.

HIGHLANDS DEVELOPMENT IN HISTORICAL PERSPECTIVE

Historically, Vietnamese views of the highlands were ambivalent but weighted toward the negative.[1] Mountain areas were seen as isolated and dangerous, the habitat of fierce wild animals, evil spirits, and savage tribes. Lowland Vietnamese (Kinh) ventured there at no little risk. Diseases, such as malaria, to which the lowlanders had no resistance caused a high mortality among those who attempted to settle the uplands. Conflict with indigenous tribal people, and attacks by bandit gangs and rebels were endemic. Most serious of all, maintenance of a Kinh style of life and adherence to traditional lowland cultural patterns were almost impossible under the very different environmental conditions in the highlands; Kinh who settled there risked being assimilated into the culture of minority peoples as happened with the Kinh mandarins (Tho Ty) who became hereditary leaders of the Tay. Thus, the highlands were generally seen by lowland governments as an area to be kept under quarantine as a possible source of societal destabilization rather than as a frontier waiting to be developed.

Views of the highlands began to change during the colonial period as the French opened up roads into formerly isolated areas, "pacified" the mountain tribes, and created successful plantations of rubber and other commercial crops. The number of lowlanders living in the highlands increased quite rapidly but still remained small in absolute terms before 1954. Following the expulsion of the French, the governments of the north and the south both launched major programs to develop the highland regions economically and to increase the level of control exercised by the state over these zones. In the Democratic Republic of Vietnam (North Vietnam), "autonomous zones" were created in areas of heavy minority settlement. Kinh settlers from the overcrowded provinces of the Red River Delta were relocated in large numbers into the midlands. In the Republic of Vietnam (South Vietnam), the formerly autonomous administration of the Central Highlands (known by the French acronym PMS—*Pays Montagnard du Sud*) was suppressed and the minority areas incorporated into the Kinh-dominated provincial administrative structure. Almost 60,000 Kinh, mostly Catholics who had fled to the south in 1954, were resettled there. Later, many individuals from the Central lowlands were moved into the Diem regime's Land Development Centers. Following national unification in 1975, renewed efforts to develop highland areas and more closely integrate them into the national society were launched. Programs to sedentarize the mountain minorities were accompanied by massive resettlement of Kinh immigrants from the lowlands into new economic zones and large-scale state forestry and plantation agricultural enterprises. The success of these efforts at rapid social and economic development has been decidedly mixed while their environmental impacts have been almost wholly negative (Dang Nghiem Van 1989). Instead of being a bright new frontier, Vietnam's highlands increasingly seem to be a development cul-de-sac.

THE HIGHLANDS AS AN ARENA FOR DEVELOPMENT TODAY

There are several environmental and social attributes of the highlands that make efforts at rapid development difficult and prone to failure. These include geographical remoteness and inaccessibility, a natural environment characterized by low biological productivity and great ecological vulnerability, and high levels of disease pressure. Increasing population pressure, ethnic differentiation, and difficulties of cross-cultural communication contribute further difficulties to development. Most important of all, the highlands are a region of extreme diversity—climatic, edaphic, biotic, and cultural. This diversity greatly complicates the formulation of appropriate development policies. Each of these constraints will be briefly reviewed below.

Remoteness and Inaccessibility

The highlands are remote areas presenting great problems of access. Terrain is frequently steep and broken, making construction and maintenance of roads extremely difficult and costly. Consequently, movement of people and goods is slow and expensive. High transportation costs inhibit production of crops with a low value to weight ratio, even though such crops (e.g., cassava) may be well adapted to cultivation under upland conditions. The attractiveness of opium as a cash crop is in part explained by its extremely high price to weight ratio. In Hoa Binh province, Hmong say they can earn as much cash from one kilogram of opium as from 20 tons of cabbage. The solution may not always be the seemingly direct one—building more roads. Instead, finding systems of production that are adapted to the constraints of distance and expensive transportation should be a high priority in highland development.

Low Biological Productivity

Although often supporting a luxuriant natural vegetation, most of the highlands are characterized by inherently low biological productivity. Net primary productivity is inhibited by climatic factors (low and irregular rainfall, low insolation, and low temperatures) and, especially, problems of soil structure and fertility. Although the basaltic soils of the southern Tay Nguyen are an exception, most mountain zone soils are highly acidic with low fertility. Available nutrients are mostly stored in the biomass, explaining the success of swidden agriculture when sufficient time is allowed for the forest to recover after each period of cultivation. Except in those limited areas where there are adequate water sources to permit construction of wet rice fields, permanent cultivation of cereal crops is unsuccessful on most upland soils. Perennial tree crops such as rubber or coffee and agroforestry systems that mix trees and annual crops together can be more sustainable but are not efficient producers of carbohydrates for human consumption. It is not surprising that the nutritional levels of most highland populations are far below the national average.[2]

Environmental Degradation

Highland ecosystems are relatively fragile and lacking in resilience to recover from human mismanagement. Unfortunately, Vietnam's highlands have had more than their fair share of the latter as a consequence of many years of colonial exploitation, warfare, and poorly conceived development schemes. As a consequence the renewable resource base has already been severely degraded. Soil erosion in areas of agricultural resettlement is a major problem with much of the productive potential of the barren hills of the midlands lost beyond reasonable hope of restoration (Le Trong Cuc, Gillogly, and Rambo 1990). Deforestation due to commercial logging, clearance of agricultural settlements, and shifting cultivation has been extensive and continues to occur at a rate exceeding successful reforestation (Vo Quy 1992, 113).

There is no question but that shifting cultivation, the traditional swidden agriculture practiced by upland ethnic minorities, has in recent years been a major cause of deforestation and environmental degradation. Although viewed as a "backward" system by many Vietnamese government officials, under conditions of low population density (less than 20 persons/km^2), rotational swiddening is actually a highly productive and sustainable system of upland farming (Kunstadter, Chapman, and Sabhasri 1978; Rambo 1980, 1984).[3] Unfortunately, however, population growth in the uplands has in the past twenty years resulted in densities that exceed the carrying capacity of rotational swiddening. As densities increase, more and more land must be put into cultivation. Rotational swidden systems tend to break down as fields are cultivated for longer periods and the fallow period shortened. Thus, where the Tay in Da Bac district of Hoa Binh province formerly used a field for one or two years and then fallowed it for ten years or longer, they are now forced to crop it for two or three years with only a one- or two-year fallow before they again clear it.[4]

Not only does shortening of the fallow cause yields to decline precipitously (500 kg of paddy per hectare is now considered a good harvest), but the forest is permanently destroyed and the rate of soil erosion dramatically increased. Land hunger drives minority farmers to clear fields in "protected forests" in critical watersheds. One can observe swidden fields cleared on 60-degree slopes directly above the reservoir of the Hoa Binh hydropower project. The resulting accelerated soil erosion has shortened the projected working life of this dam from 300 to 80 years. But at present there are no economically viable alternatives to shifting cultivation in many parts of the uplands. So the mountain populations are caught in a downward spiral of worsening environmental degradation and increasing poverty.

Disease and Health Problems

Disease pressure is high in the highlands, not just on the human population but on livestock and crops also. Malaria is perhaps the greatest threat to human well-being resulting in a high mortality among children and sapping the energy that the adult population has available for productive work. The Kinh population is particularly at risk because it lacks the genetic protection provided to many indigenous populations by abnormal hemoglobins (Hickey 1993). Control efforts are increasingly ineffective in the face of evolution of resistance to chemical control agents by both the mosquitos and plasmodia. Unfortunately, demobilized soldiers returning to their native villages after service in Cambodia have introduced the chloroquine-resistant strains of falciparium malaria to many areas in the northern mountains that were formerly free of this deadly variety. Unless control measures are intensified, Vietnam's highlands may face a major health crisis. The debilitating impact of malaria and other infectious diseases is magnified by the often poor nutritional status of the highland populations. Goiter is widespread, reflecting the absence of iodine in the ancient and deeply weathered soils of the northern mountains. This is a particularly insidious disease because it often results in cretinism and lowered intelligence in its victims. Recently, the government has required that all salt distributed in the mountains be iodized, but this may have little benefit, given the low nutritional status of many minority people. Development of tourism into highland areas will inevitably increase the risk of exposure to AIDS, especially if young women from minority populations are drawn into the sexual services sector of the tourist economy as has happened in other Southeast Asian countries.

Population Pressure

Although, when viewed in comparison to the Red River Delta the highlands may seem to still be lightly populated, many areas are in fact already seriously over-populated. This reflects the low biological productivity of highland areas and their consequent low human-carrying capacity. When population density exceeds this capacity, environmental degradation is inevitable. This is particularly evident in the midlands and mountains of northwestern Vietnam where excessive human pressure on the environment has already resulted in almost total deforestation, severe land degradation, and heavy loss of biodiversity (Le Trong Cuc, Gillogly, and Rambo 1990). In areas such as the Da River watershed, the current population density of 200 persons per square kilometer is probably double what is sustainable given the area's low carrying capacity.

The rate of population growth in the highlands is also extremely rapid, both because of high fertility levels of indigenous populations and large-scale immigration. In 1956 the population of Tay Nguyen was 530,000. Thirty years later it was more than 2 million. In the ten years between 1976 and 1986, it increased at an average annual rate of 6 percent per year (Le Duy Dai 1989, 336–37). This is clearly a faster rate of increase than any social system could adequately absorb. As Le Duy Dai (1989, 358) points out, the United States found it necessary to take measures to slow immigration during the nineteenth century when the average yearly rate of increase was only 3 percent.

Most of the increase in the population of the highlands reflects in-migration by Kinh from overcrowded lowland areas. In many areas Kinh have become numerically dominant. Thus, Kinh were only 5 percent of the population of Tay Nguyen in 1940, but they now constitute two-thirds of the total (Dang Nghiem Van 1989, 76). In the mountainous areas of northern Vietnam, Kinh still constitute only about one-third of the total population, but largely as a consequence of massive in-migration have increased at a more rapid rate than the mountain minorities. Thus, in the two decades from 1960 to 1979, the Kinh population increased by 3.3 times in less than twenty years, climbing from 640,000 to 2.1 million. In the subsequent ten years until the 1989 census, it increased by a further 19.3 percent to reach 2.5 million people (Be Viet Dang 1993, 22). This rapid shift in ethnic composition has led to serious competition between indigenous groups and in-migrants for rapidly diminishing land resources. Inequalities in distribution of services and income between the Kinh, who are largely concentrated in towns, and the indigenous people, who are still mostly rural, are growing. These processes have important consequences for the quality of ethnic relations and the process of acculturation in the highlands.

Ethnic Differentiation and Problems of Inter-cultural Communication

The ethnic situation in Vietnam's highlands is everywhere extremely complex. According to the Institute of Ethnology, there are fifty-four distinct minority ethnic groups in Vietnam, with most of these in the highlands.[5] Each of these groups speaks a distinct language, follows different customs, and is characterized by a unique adaptation to its distinctive local environment. Technological and economic innovations that are readily acceptable and highly successful for one group may be complete failures in other contexts. Thus, no two ethnic groups (or even subcommunities within the larger minorities) present exactly the same opportunities and constraints for development projects.

This cultural diversity poses an immense problem for development policy-makers. Formulating policies that are flexible enough to be compatible with the extreme ethnic differentiation in the highlands is an immensely difficult undertaking. It is a challenge that is made even more difficult by the great extent to which policies for highland development reflect the underlying assumptions of Kinh culture rather than being formulated in terms of the cultural logic of the minorities who are expected to implement them.[6] The development process is greatly complicated by problems in communication between populations whose behavior is guided by very different cultural beliefs and values. Finding ways to better incorporate the cultural values of the mountain minorities into the development planning process should be a matter of great concern.

Many Kinh cadre evaluate the development potential of the minorities in terms of the extent to which they conform to specifically Kinh cultural beliefs and practices. Cultural practices of the minorities which diverge from Kinh norms are viewed as "backward." Matrilineal or bilateral kinship systems are seen as inferior to the patrilineal model of the Kinh; houses built on stilts and long houses are seen as vestiges of backwardness; animistic religions and shamanism are considered to be feudalistic superstitions; swidden agriculture is considered a primitive and hopelessly inefficient system of production.[7] Groups that persist in following these practices despite being exposed to Kinh practices are considered to be locked into tradition and resistant to modernization.

Ethnocentrism of this sort occurs in situations of intercultural contact everywhere in the world but is a particularly difficult problem under the specific historical context of ethnic relations in Vietnam's highlands.[8] There, Kinh policy-makers and cadre, whose own cultural system was formed in the conditions of the lowlands, are confronted by indigenous cultures that have evolved over many centuries to become adapted to the specific conditions of the highland environment. Often, this means that the practices of the indigenous people, however bizarre or backward they may seem from the Kinh standpoint, are actually highly adaptive in the context of the upland environment. For example, the building of houses on stilts, having the cooking fire inside the main house, and tethering large livestock under the house—all practices followed by mountain minorities but not by Kinh—may help to protect people from infection with malaria (Le Trong Cuc, Gillogly, and Rambo 1990, 8–14). In planning upland development many mistakes can be avoided if indigenous beliefs and knowledge are taken into full account.

Not all cultural practices of the mountain minorities are necessarily adaptive, however. Some traits may always have been adaptively neutral or even negative. Other traits that were once valuable may no longer be so due to the extensive changes that have occurred in the environment of the highlands over the past thirty years. In suggesting the desirability of viewing minority cultural beliefs and values in a non-ethnocentric manner, I am not suggesting a return to some romanticized image of past cultural perfection. The world in which the mountain minorities live has been forever changed. Their cultures must now undergo a difficult process of readaptation to new conditions. This is an immensely difficult process, especially in the modern world where change occurs in a matter of days or months rather than decades or centuries. Such change adds further to the already incredible diversity that characterizes the highlands.

DIVERSITY AND THE SEARCH FOR NEW HIGHLAND DEVELOPMENT STRATEGIES

The existence of a vast amount of diversity in both ecological and social systems is the greatest and most intractable problem posed by the highlands for development policy-makers. In contrast to the deltas and plains, where the natural environment is relatively homogeneous and the Kinh social system everywhere displays a considerable uniformity in its basic institutions, the highlands present a complex human ecological mosaic. Every region, every province, every village, indeed every field, is somewhat different from every other. In conditions of such high diversity, no single development plan can be broadly applicable, and no single model will prove successful everywhere (Jamieson 1991). Existing knowledge and understanding are simply inadequate to the task of designing such models. I do not, however, propose to end this chapter with the standard scientific refrain that "before anything is done, further research is needed." Yes, further research is needed but given the existing diversity of the highlands and the accelerating rate at which everything there is now changing, there will never be an adequate information base to allow successful central planning of development. Instead, therefore, of trying to formulate a single uniform model for all of the highlands, development planners should be concerned with establishing mechanisms to encourage people in the highlands themselves to generate their own locally adapted strategies for development. If successful, such an approach will yield not one model but a multitude of models, each fitting the needs and aspirations of the local ecological and social systems where it is formulated.

The question that remains is of how to reform the process of development planning for the highlands to achieve this desired outcome. Although it is the current fashion in development studies to advocate decentralized planning and local participation, there are precious few examples of how to actually establish workable mechanisms to achieve these laudable goals. Unfortunately, translation of the rhetoric of "participatory rural development" or "empowerment of marginalized peoples" or "decentralized planning processes" into institutions that can work successfully in the real world is neither easy nor straightforward. And, just as there is no satisfactory model for development of Vietnam's highlands, there is even less possibility of finding a ready-made model for reforming the development planning process itself. Indeed the ultimate challenge of developing Vietnam's highlands is that of inventing viable new institutions and processes for planning that development.

NOTES

1. There is no comprehensive account of the history of development of Vietnam's highlands as a whole. Gerald Hickey's monumental two-volume ethnohistory (Hickey 1982a, 1982b) is an excellent account of the Central Highlands (Tay Nguyen) up to 1975. More detailed ethnographic descriptions of individual ethnic groups are offered in his recently published volume, *Shattered World* (Hickey 1993). Social and economic changes in the Central Highlands since 1975 are discussed in the essays in *Tay Nguyen tren Duong Phat Trien* (Tay Nguyen on the road to development), especially the paper on contemporary social problems by Dang Nghiem Van (1989). I do not know of any equally detailed account of the history of development efforts in the northern mountain areas. McAlister (1966) offers a useful review of colonial relations with the mountain minorities. Le Trong Cuc, K. Gillogly, and A. T. Rambo (1990)

describe the environmental consequences of Kinh resettlement in the midlands of Vinh Phu province.

2. According to an article by Van Cong in *Nhan Dan* (1-30-92, 2), levels of poverty are much higher among the mountain minority populations than among the ethnic Vietnamese (Kinh). In 1990, 9.4 percent of the national population had insufficient food to eat but 15 percent of the people in Lao Cai and Yen Bay, and 20 percent in Dac Lac provinces were undernourished. Among the Muong the rate was 15 percent, Hmong 32 percent, Dzao 37 percent, Thai 58 percent, and the Sedang 78 percent. The average production of staple foods among the mountain people was 240–250 kg/person/yr compared to a national average of 333 kg.

3. Two very different kinds of shifting cultivation are practiced by different ethnic minorities in the highlands of Vietnam. "Rotational swiddening" is a system where a field is cleared, burned, and cultivated for from one to three years before it is fallowed and the forest allowed to regenerate for from five to twenty or more years before the plot is again cleared. As long as population density is below 40 persons/km^2, this system is highly sustainable and does not lead to extensive destruction of forest cover. This is the system employed by groups such as the Rhade (Ede) and Djarai of Tay Nguyen (Hickey 1993). In "pioneering swiddening," fields are cleared from primary forest and cultivated for as long as ten years. They are fallowed only after the decline in soil fertility and loss of topsoil from erosion is so severe that the natural forest cannot recover and the succession is diverted to Imperata grassland. This system, which is highly destructive of forests, is associated with groups such as the Hmong and the Dzao of the northern mountains. It should be noted that Kinh who have been resettled in the highlands also engage in a form of swiddening when they use fire to clear plots for expansion of their permanent field area.

4. The East-West Center, working in cooperation with the Hanoi University Center for Natural Resources and Environmental Studies, is engaged in a long-term study of the human ecology of the Tay and other swidden farming ethnic minorities living in the Da River watershed in Hoa Binh province. Funding for this project is provided by a grant from the John D. and Catherine T. MacArthur Foundation. A preliminary account of research findings about the Tay agroecosystem is given in Rambo (1994).

5. Many foreign ethnologists consider the Institute of Ethnology to hold a conservative position with regard to ethnic classification, tending to "lump" rather than "split" groups that may actually display considerable internal cultural differentiation, although speaking a more-or-less mutually intelligible language. In any case, the highlands are characterized by a very high level of social and cultural diversity.

6. Perhaps the most important factor influencing ethnic relations in Vietnam is the very great numerical preponderance of one group, the Viet or Kinh (lowland ethnic Vietnamese) who constitute almost 90 percent of the national population. All other ethnic groups are minorities, justifying the term *dan toc thieu so* (ethnic groups lacking numbers) used to characterize them by Vietnamese ethnologists. Their numerical inferiority has clear consequences for their relationship to the larger Vietnamese society. Not surprisingly, most policy-makers and cadre are of Kinh origin. No discussion of ethnic relations in Vietnam can ignore this great demographic imbalance between the mountain minorities and the Kinh.

7. Contrary to earlier assumptions about the unidirectional nature of cultural evolution, Western ethnologists now believe that only some cultural traits, primarily those most directly associated with technology and the means of production, can be evaluated as progressive (Rambo 1987, 1991). It is now widely recognized, the earlier views of Morgan and Engels notwithstanding, that

kinship systems are not among the traits subject to progressive evolution. The bilateral nuclear family form of kinship that anthropologists refer to as the "Eskimo" model, because it was first described for this simple hunting society, also happens to be the system that characterizes modern American society. Does that mean that Americans are more backward than the patrilineal Vietnamese? On some occasion after 1975, overzealous Kinh cadre destroyed long houses of the Tay Nguyen minorities (Dang Nghiem Van 1989, 120); yet most urban Kinh and most urban Europeans or Americans live in apartments in high-rise buildings, multistoried long houses if you will. I will not argue that animism is an intellectually viable system in the modern world. But I will note, however, that all societies, regardless of their level of economic development, contain a significant fraction of people who believe in supernatural forces and order their lives accordingly. It is a depressing reality that the most commonly read feature in American newspapers is the astrology column. I suspect the same would be true in Vietnam if newspapers were permitted to run such features. Finally, as has already been discussed, far from being a primitive system, swidden agriculture is a highly evolved system that was well adapted to the environmental conditions of the highlands. Under current conditions of increased population density, it is no longer adaptive; the problem is that there are no suitable alternatives available to take its place in many parts of the highlands.

8. The question of the legitimacy of the traditional cultural beliefs and values of the mountain minorities is probably the issue on which there will be most disagreement between Vietnamese and Western participants in this meeting. We each bring to this discussion certain assumptions and beliefs about cultural systems that reflect our own cultural traditions. Many Western scholars but few Vietnamese belong to a scientific tradition that is built on the philosophy of *cultural relativism*, the view that there is no privileged position from which to judge the merit of different cultures. It is thus inappropriate to judge the practices of one culture to be inferior to that of another. Most Vietnamese, on the other hand, reflect a different tradition, that of progressive cultural evolution as incorporated in Marxist thought. From this perspective, cultures can be evaluated as being "backward" or "progressive" according to the extent to which they conform to certain assumptions about relations between the means of production, the social relations of production, and the ideological superstructure. In our discussions, we should recognize the existence of these different assumptions, but we will be unrealistic if we expect to fully resolve them.

BIBLIOGRAPHY

Be Viet Dang, ed. 1993. *Nhung bien doi ve kinh te - van hoa o cac tinh mien nui phia bac* [Some changes in the economy and culture of northern highland provinces]. Hanoi: Social Sciences Publishing House.

Dang Nghiem Van. 1989. *Nhung van de xa hoi hien nay o Tay Nguyen* [Some contemporary social problems in the Central Highlands]. In *Tay Nguyen tren duong phat trien* [The Central Highlands on the development road], ed. Vietnamese Social Sciences Committee, 67–151. Hanoi: Social Sciences Publishing House.

Hickey, Gerald Cannon. 1982a. *Sons of the mountains: Ethnohistory of the Vietnamese Central Highlands to 1954.* New Haven: Yale University Press.

Hickey, Gerald Cannon. 1982b. *Free in the forest: Ethnohistory of the Vietnamese Central Highlands, 1954–1976.* New Haven: Yale University Press.

Hickey, Gerald Cannon. 1993. *Shattered world: Adaptation and survival among Vietnam's highland peoples during the Vietnam war.* Philadelphia: University of Pennsylvania Press.

Jamieson, Neil L. 1991. *Culture and development in Vietnam.* Honolulu: East-West Center Indochina Initiative Working Paper No. 1.

Kunstadter, Peter, E. C. Chapman, and Sanga Sabhasri, eds. 1978. *Farmers in the forest: Economic development and marginal agriculture in northern Thailand.* Honolulu: University Press of Hawaii.

Le Duy Dai. 1989. *Qua dac diem dan cu thu ly giai may van de kinh te-xa hoi* [Using population characteristics to test theories of socio-economic problems]. In *Tay Nguyen tren duong phat trien* [The Central Highlands on the development road], ed. Vietnamese Social Sciences Committee, 335–61. Hanoi: Social Sciences Publishing House.

Le Trong Cuc, Kathleen Gillogly, and A. Terry Rambo. 1990. *Agroecosystems of the midlands of northern Vietnam.* Honolulu: East-West Center Environment and Policy Institute Occasional Paper No. 12.

McAlister, John T., Jr. 1966. Mountain minorities and the Viet Minh: A key to the Indochina war. In *Southeast Asian tribes, minorities, and nations*, ed. Peter Kunstadter, 771–844. Princeton, NJ: Princeton University Press.

Rambo, A. Terry. 1980. Fire and the energy efficiency of swidden agriculture. *Asian Perspectives* 23(2):309–16.

Rambo, A. Terry. 1984. Why shifting cultivators keep shifting: Understanding farmer decision-making in traditional agroforestry systems. In *Community forestry: Some aspects*, 73–81. Bangkok: Food and Agriculture Organization.

Rambo, A. Terry. 1987. Black flight suits and white *ao dais*: Borrowing and adaptation of symbols of Vietnamese cultural identity. In *Borrowing and adaptations in Vietnamese culture*, ed. Truong Buu Lam, 115–23. Honolulu: University of Hawaii Center for Southeast Asian Studies Paper No. 25.

Rambo, A. Terry. 1991. The study of cultural evolution. In *Profiles in cultural evolution*, ed. A. T. Rambo and K. Gillogly, 23–109. Ann Arbor: University of Michigan Museum of Anthropology Anthropological Papers No. 85.

Rambo, A. Terry. 1994. Feudal social systems in the mountains of northern Vietnam: The human ecology of the Tay Tho of Hoa Binh province. Paper presented at the Association for Asian Studies Meeting, Boston, 25 March.

Vo Quy. 1992. Environment and development in Vietnam. In *The challenges of Vietnam's reconstruction*, ed. N. L. Jamieson, Nguyen Manh Hung, and A. T. Rambo, 110–26. Fairfax, VA: George Mason University Indochina Institute.

CHAPTER 3

Natural Conditions and Resources of the Tay Nguyen Highlands

Nguyen Tran Cau
Institute of Geography, Hanoi

INTRODUCTION

Vietnamese geographers divide the national territory of Vietnam into eight geographical regions: the Northeastern mountains, the Northwestern mountains, the Red River Delta, the Northern Truong Son mountain range, the Southern Truong Son mountain range, the Thanh-Nghe-Tinh coastal plain, the Southeastern midlands, and the Mekong River Delta. Each of these regions has distinct characteristics defined by its natural conditions and resource potential. The Institute of Geography has a study program for each of these natural regions. This paper concerns one of these regions, the Southern Troung Son range, known to most Vietnamese as the Tay Nguyen and to most non-Vietnamese as the Central Highlands.

NATURAL CONDITIONS OF THE TAY NGUYEN

The Tay Nguyen is an area composed of mountain plateaus bracketed by high mountain chains. As a region, it takes in all of Gia Lai, Kon Tum, Dac Lac, and Lam Dong provinces, as well as small areas of several bordering provinces (Map 3.1). Its area, at more than 50,000 square kilometers, covers about 17 percent of the national territory.

In recent years, the diverse resources of the Tay Nguyen have become the object of intensifying development pressure, much of which has been unplanned and uncontrolled. The results have been serious resource depletion and degradation. In response, Vietnamese research institutions have undertaken three five-year research programs, beginning in 1976, on the natural conditions, resources, and environmental protection of the Tay Nguyen. This research has focused on seven program areas, including the geological structure of the Tay Nguyen, its geomorphology, climate and climatic regimes, water resources, soil regimes and soil suitability analysis, biotic resources, and the differentiation of integral subregions. The results of these programs are being used to plan for the rational and sustainable utilization of the region's natural resources.

Minerals

The geological structure and tectonic characteristics of the Tay Nguyen suggest the presence of abundant mineral resources. To date, a wide variety of economically important minerals have been found. These include iron, nickel, lead, zinc, tin, arsenic, bauxite, gold, and gemstones such as opal, sapphire, and tektite. In addition, a number of nonfer-

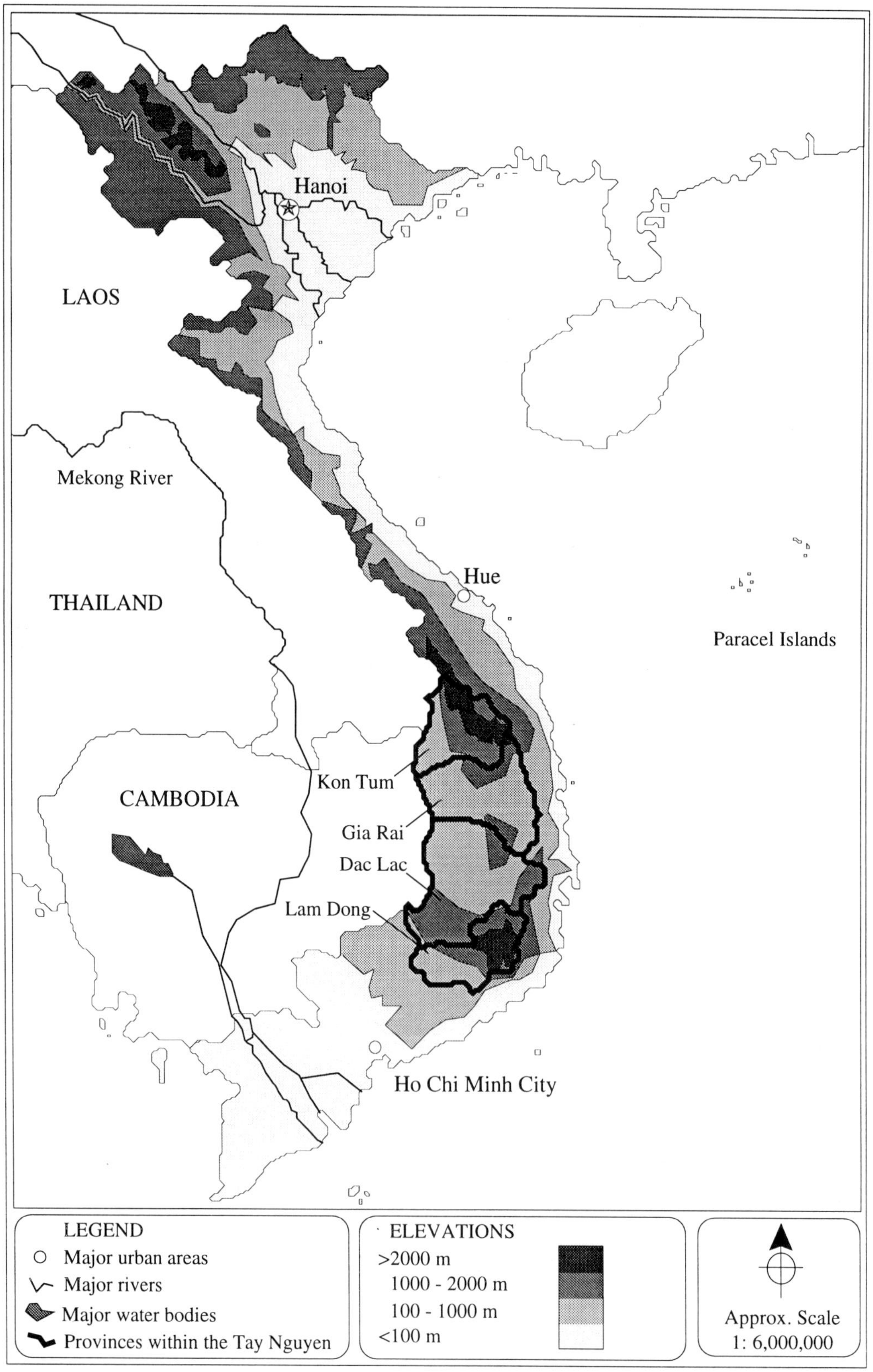

Map 3.1 The Tay Nguyen (Central Highlands) of Vietnam

rous minerals important to the construction industry—pyrite, dolomite, calcium carbonate, and graphite—have been found.

To date, exploitation of these mineral resources has not been carried out on a large scale. Bauxite, for example, though locally abundant, has not been exploited due to lack of power and production technologies. Other minerals, such as gold, have been exploited through small-scale hand mining. Small mines that require the use of toxic chemicals to process ore, particularly the gold mines operated by fortune hunters from the lowlands, have caused significant and potentially long-term environmental damage to the Tay Nguyen.

Climate

The Tay Nguyen has the high-average temperatures and high, but seasonal, levels of solar radiation and rainfall typical of a tropical monsoonal climate. The total amount and intensity of solar radiation reaching the region is higher than any other region within the country. Temperatures, at between 800 and 1,000 meters above sea level, range from 19° to 21° C with a temperature amplitude of only 3° to 5°. The average temperature for eight to nine months of the year is 20° C. The absolute lowest temperatures recorded in the Tay Nguyen are from 4° to 6° C, though these temperatures generally prevail only in high mountain areas. Rainfall is high, averaging more than 2,000 mm per year. Between 80 and 90 percent of this rainfall occurs within the rainy season. Thus, although extreme weather conditions such as typhoons, frosts, and desiccating winds are rare, the long and severe dry season limits the region's agricultural potential.

Nevertheless, in high mountain areas such as Dalat (1,500 meters) and Ngoc Linh (2,000 meters), cool temperatures make it possible to grow a variety of temperate crops including cabbage, cauliflower, tomatoes, strawberries, peaches, pears, plums, and apples. Major cities in the coastal zone and Mekong Delta such as Ho Chi Minh city, Bien Hoa, Vung Tau, and Nha Trang provide steady markets for these crops. Ornamental plants and flowers, exported to the lowlands and sold locally to tourists, have become a particular high-income earning specialty of the Tay Nguyen.

Water Resources

The Tay Nguyen's water regime is rigidly divided between wet and dry seasons. Rainfall is heavy during the six- to nine-month wet season, resulting in average annual rainfall in excess of 2,000 mm. The dry season, which normally lasts from three to four months between February and May, is equally marked. Under such conditions, large-scale field agriculture is severely limited. Nevertheless, because geomorphological conditions mitigate some of these extremes, a number of areas with less severe seasonality may be used for the production of staple grains such as rice or corn.

The surface waters of the region are drained by a hydrological system composed of twenty-two large rivers and lakes. Although hydrological density is not high (0.5 km/km^2), because of the region's large size and high precipitation rate, approximately 50 billion m^3 of water, or 80 percent of the total yearly rainfall, are transported through the river system each year.

Given the extremes in seasons, underground water in the Tay Nguyen is extremely important for agricultural production and for the maintenance of life. Fortunately, basaltic formations in the region absorb and maintain large stores of high-quality water. These waters are, however, threatened due to the reduction of recharge capacity through upland clearing, timber exploitation, and deforestation.

The Tay Nguyen is also very rich in mineral water and geothermal springs that can be used for drinking, hydrotherapy, and energy production.

The eastern slope of Tay Nguyen also has great hydroelectric potential. A few hydroelectric stations, such as Ya Ly and Thac Mo, have already been built here. Experience at these sites underscore that this great potential can be developed only if the surrounding forest is protected. As forests are cleared, the water retention and regulating functions of forest cover are lost, erosion becomes a critical concern, and hydroelectric dams become subject to the twin forces of rapid fluctuations in water level and siltation.

Soil Resources

Soils of the Tay Nguyen are generally divided into eight groups:[1] alluvial soils, gray degraded soils, eroded soils, black soils, ferrallitic soils (< 1,000 m elevation), humic red-yellow mountain soils (between 1,000 m and 2,000 m elevation), humic mountain soils, and podzols. The most important of these soils are those that have basaltic parent material. These are the black soils, ferrallitic soils, and humic red-yellow mountain soils. About two-thirds of the basaltic soils in Vietnam occur in Tay Nguyen where they cover 27 percent of the region.

Biotic Resources

Vegetation Natural and anthropomorphic vegetation zones within the Tay Nguyen fall into four large groups: dense forest, open forest, scrub, and meadows. Dense forests are further divided into tropical evergreen forests (humid, seasonal, semi-deciduous, bamboo, coniferous, and swamp) and deciduous forests (dipterocarp and nondipterocarp). Foreign botanists working in the years prior to re-unification[2] identified 3,400 vegetation types within these vegetation zones. After 1975, Vietnamese biologists added to this list through the discovery of hundreds of unrecorded species. For example, Le Kim Bien added 45 unrecorded chrysanthemum to the pre-liberation list of 85 types (Nguyen 1985). As a result of these investigations, more than 200 new species of higher plants have been identified. Among the current total of 3,600 plant species, woody plants occupy 1,200 species in 223 families. The most economically important among these are various *Pinus* species. In addition, 250 species of Orchidaceae and 219 species of rice have been identified within the Tay Nguyen. The region is also home to many endemic species, some of which, like the Nepenthaceal species; illustrate the characteristics of proto-tropical flora. All told, Vietnamese researchers suggest that the Tay Nguyen may hold as many as 4,500 plant species, among which the greater majority would include fern, woody climber, areca-nut palm, chrysanthemum, pine, and rice species.

In the absence of human activities, the Tay Nguyen would be covered by dense evergreen and semi-deciduous rain forest. Because of human exploitation, however, the landscape has been transformed and ancient forests are now quite rare. Secondary growth, such as deciduous forest, bamboo, scrub, and meadow, is predominant. The Tay Nguyen's remaining forests are continuously being impoverished through human exploitation. Government policy must limit this exploitation by protection of remaining forests and reforestation of barren lands in order to reconstruct natural ecological systems and wildlife habitats.

Zoological Resources The Tay Nguyen, with its diversity of natural conditions, contains a rich variety of animal species including 80 species of freshwater fish, 25 species of frog, 50 species of reptile, 370 species of birds, and 100 species of mammals. Among these are many rare animals such as tiger, elephant, gaur (*Bos gaurus*), and rhinoceros (*R. sondaicus*), as well as rare peacock (*Pavo muticus*) and pheasant (*Rheinardia ocellata*) species. Many of these animal species are threatened by the activities of humans. As forests are exploited, natural ecosystems are transformed and only those animals that can tolerate the presence of humans or live in these transformed environments can survive. The most threatened of these species, the rhinoceros, could face extinction despite official protection.

CONCLUSION

The Tay Nguyen's central plateau, formed of basaltic parent material, contains high-quality soils which, despite hydrological limitations, show very good agricultural and silviculture potential. However, up to now, use of these lands has been irrational and difficult to regulate. Detailed research is required to prepare a plan for resource protection and rational utilization. Legal procedures also need to be established to govern natural resources exploitation.

Planning for the Tay Nguyen should be carried out not only by individual economic branches of the state sector but by related branches through integrated study projects. The agriculture, forestry, communications, energy, and labor departments should cooperate on the most functional plans for land utilization and infrastructure development.

Various models of socioeconomic development have been tried in the Tay Nguyen. These include VAC (garden, pond, and pen) in lowland areas as well as agroforestry, forest gardens, silviculture, and social forestry on sloping lands. Each of these models has its advantages and disadvantages. Further study is needed to match the specific characteristics of these models to local physical and social conditions within the Tay Nguyen. In this way, appropriate interventions can be designed.

Most ethnic minorities within the Tay Nguyen continue to practice shifting cultivation. Although this practice is decreasing, further efforts are needed to bring it to an end. Where shifting cultivation is practiced, land cannot be rationally utilized. In an effort to end deforestation and land degradation, the movement from shifting cultivation to fixed cultivation and settlement should be accelerated. Strategies for this transition, developed and supported at the national level, should be solidified through local planning.

The biological resources of Tay Nguyen are diverse and abundant but they are not limitless. Due to rapid and ecologically irresponsible exploitation, many rare and endangered animal and plant species currently face extinction. A strategy is needed to promote sustainable use of the Tay Nguyen's rich resources, which also preserves the region's diverse habitats and life forms, especially those most endangered.

NOTES

1. Following Vietnamese and Dokutraev soil classification systems.
2. M. Smid (1962 and 1974). Quoted in Nguyen (1985).

BIBLIOGRAPHY

Nguyen Van Chien, ed. 1985. *Tay Nguyen: Cac dieu kien tu nhien va tai nguyen thien nhien* [Tay Nguyen: Its natural conditions and resources]. Hanoi: Science and Technology Publishing House.

Nguyen Van Chien, ed. 1986. *Cac vung tu nhien Tay Nguyen* [The natural regions of Tay Nguyen]. Hanoi: Science and Technology Publishing House.

Phan Trinh Chuc, ed. 1986. *Nong nghiep Tay Nguyen* [Agriculture in Tay Nguyen]. Hanoi: Science and Technology Publishing House.

Social Sciences Committee of Vietnam. 1988. *Ve kinh te-xa hoi Tay Nguyen* [Concerning the socio-economy of Tay Nguyen]. Report presented at the Third Scientific Conference of the Social Sciences Committee of Vietnam. Hanoi: The Authors.

PART TWO

The Impact of Large-Scale Development on the Highlands

CHAPTER 4

From Highland Hamlet to Regional Capital: Reflections on the Colonial Origins, Urban Transformation, and Environmental Impact of Dalat

Robert R. Reed
University of California, Berkeley

During the nineteenth and early twentieth centuries, a thin line of Westernized hill stations[1] marked the leading edge of imperial conquest and permanent European settlement along the highland frontiers of South and Southeast Asia. Some of these outposts had been grafted onto already substantial indigenous villages, but most were new colonial foundations which originated as strategically sited military garrisons that housed small hospitals or highly specialized health resorts sponsored by government. Their well-documented proliferation between 1820 and 1930 represents a fascinating chapter in the urban and social history of tropical Asia. Then continued evolution in the post-colonial era is of equal interest.

In recent decades the Asian hill station[2] has attracted a good deal of attention among historians and social scientists. Some scholars are curious about the colonial genesis and functional evolution of highland towns, as well as their comparatively rapid transformation into exclusive sanitaria and centers of Western tourism (Mitchell 1972; Spencer and Thomas 1948). Others have concentrated on the cultural, political, and economic roles of hill stations during the heyday of European dominion (Aiken 1987; Butcher 1979, 68–79, 157–66, 225; Edwardes 1969, 86–95; King 1976, 156–79; Voon and Khoo 1980). At the same time many individuals with interests in local history are today publishing both scholarly works and delightful popular essays that focus on the development of individual highland settlements, and especially on the emergence of the renowned "summer capitals" of South and Southeast Asia (Barr and Desmond 1978; Buck 1979; Bührlein 1991; Clay 1928; Gokhale 1988; Kanwar 1984, 1990; Panter-Downes 1967; Price 1908; Pubby 1988). In the past decade a number of writers have also initiated investigations on the latter-day emergence of hill stations as centers of domestic tourism (Ballabh 1967; Reed 1979; Saini 1964; Sasikumar 1967; Senftleben 1973) and urban growth poles in underdeveloped mountain areas (Reed 1976a). While earlier generations of researchers virtually ignored the multifaceted impacts of rapidly expanding towns and cities on fragile upland ecosystems, a few concerned scholars recently began to highlight the significance of hill stations as powerful instruments of environmental transformation (Dar 1989; Manahan 1989; Singh 1980). Collectively these studies have produced a convincing image of Western settlement, colonial society, and politico-economic outreach in the highlands of South and Southeast Asia before World War II.

PRELUDE TO HIGHLAND CONQUEST: COLONIZATION IN TROPICAL ASIA BEFORE AND AFTER 1800

Prior to 1800 effective European dominion in South and Southeast Asia was essentially confined to geographically compact lowland regions, narrow coastal possessions, a few deltaic areas, and several island strongholds. The few far-flung colonies established by various Western powers were loosely structured through nascent urban systems consisting of a comparatively cosmopolitan primate city[3]—which served at once as an entrepôt, the capital, and a major military garrison—and scattered towns, strategically located forts, trading posts, and missions (in certain Portuguese and Spanish dependencies) where smaller communities of European merchants, administrators, priests, and soldiers promoted imperial interests while avoiding exhausting wars and unnecessary entanglements in the affairs of indigenous states (Basu 1979; Broeze 1989; McGee 1967, 42–75; Meilink-Roelofsz 1962; Murphey 1969; Reeves, Broeze, and McPherson 1989). Such "pin-prick imperialism" (Emerson 1967, 66)[4] clearly reflected the limited commercial goals of the Westerners, who were primarily interested in exotic goods of great value and little bulk that could be obtained without a significant expansion in their colonial holdings or the costly cmployment of civil and military officialdoms. Accordingly few Europeans called for additional territorial expansion along the littoral or into interior lowlands. By the same token they completely ignored the heavily forested and almost inaccessible hill and mountain sectors of mainland Asia and the larger islands (Kalimantan, Java, Sri Lanka, and Sumatra).

During the early decades of the nineteenth century neither the Dutch, the English, nor the Spaniards, who each by then controlled substantial lowland territories in the Asian tropics, had effectively penetrated the uplands of their respective realms. It is true that a few short-lived trading posts, army encampments, and mission centers testified to the periodic dispatch of Western expeditions into previously uncharted hill and mountain regions. However, such ventures usually failed because of the stubborn hostility of fiercely proud indigenous peoples and the excessive human and financial costs required to maintain dependent European communities in the densely forested, rugged, and sparsely settled highlands. While certain adventurous individuals, occasional hunters, and dedicated missionaries continued to reconnoiter the flanks of hill zones and mountain chains, these exploratory enterprises seldom resulted in formal colonization through the permanent occupation of territory and subsequent European settlement (Cobban 1971, 136–43; Panter-Downes 1967, 19–39; Reed 1976b, 554–55).

As decades wore on during the nineteenth century, changing political and economic conditions in the West began to herald a new imperial order in Asia. With increasing industrialization, the nations of Europe inevitably experienced a growing appetite for imported raw materials and insistent public demands for secure markets abroad in the form of new and larger colonies. During the resulting competition for overseas possessions, South and Southeast Asia were almost completely partitioned by the Western powers. Throughout their newly acquired territories, the Europeans acted quickly to construct infrastructures that would ensure their bureaucratic control over dependent peoples, promote the easy exploitation of resources, and facilitate integration into the emerging world economy. Western officialdoms systematically built modern transportation and communications systems, orchestrated the development of towns and cities, offered potentially lucrative land and mineral rights to Western investors, and organized strong military structures and police forces to guarantee peace (Cady 1964, Pts. 3–6; Hall 1968, Pts. 3–4; Steinberg 1987, Pts. 2–4; Tate 1971). Predictably these mutually supportive imperial efforts not only fostered economic development in most colonies, but also triggered a significant growth in the population of European sojourners in Asia.

As the number of European colonists increased dramatically in South and Southeast Asia during the middle and late decades of the nineteenth century, so did their individual complaints and shared concerns about widespread health hazards and persistent "tropical fatigue" in the hot and humid environments of Asia's coastal and riverine plains.[5] While continuing to suffer disease and discomfort throughout their workaday lives in the Asian lowlands, many of these Western settlers were soon to find welcome respite from both debilitating and life-threatening illnesses—as well as psychological relief following traumatic bouts of heat stress or struggles with loneliness and depression—in newly explored hill and mountain regions of most colonies.

HILL STATIONS IN SOUTH AND SOUTHEAST ASIA: ORIGINS AND FUNCTIONS

Although some Europeans settled permanently in South and Southeast Asia without undue discomfort and seldom succumbed to sickness, the majority of colonists apparently believed that prolonged residence in monsoonal Asia always increased personal health risks and invariably led to the progressive deterioration of body and mind (Balfour 1923; Carthew 1927; Fayrer 1881, 1882; Lind 1811; Renbourne 1963; Ward 1931, 557–76). While sadly accepting the real and perceived mental perils of long duty assignments in tropical climes, most Western settlers particularly feared the clearly agonizing deaths associated with the ubiquitous wasting illnesses (dysentery, local or systemic infections, hookworm, leprosy, and simple diarrhea) and the frightening specter of unpredictable epidemic diseases (malaria, smallpox, typhoid, and cholera). Indeed the majority of settlers were convinced that serious diseases, mental disorders, and emotional fatigue could be prevented only through early retirement or lengthy vacations in cooler mid-latidudinal countries of the West or northeast Asia. But with the extension of imperial authority into the highland interiors of various Asian colonies, the Europeans soon discovered mountain habitats that seemed relatively free of the more fearsome health hazards and not unlike the comfortable environments of their temperate homelands. Western colonists were thus presented with an alternative to the long, often disruptive, and sometimes career threatening overseas furloughs. Almost all European sojourners who visited the pleasantly cool highlands experienced a marked emotional renewal and some even testified to miraculous recoveries from fevers, intestinal diseases, depression, and other assorted maladies (Mitchell 1972, 13–55).

Western military doctors were probably the first to advocate the systematic development of government sanitaria and supportive recreation facilities in the highlands of South and Southeast Asia. During the course of their work, these medical practitioners noted and chronicled the rapid recovery of sickly and despondent soldiers who had been assigned to mountain camps following extended service in pestiferous lowland cantonments situated near rivers or swamps. In time certain physicians began to treat assorted health problems among European troops by simply transferring the invalids to highland posts for recuperation and rest.[6] Some of these highland compounds were gradually transformed into small military hospitals or convalescent facilities that later evolved into hill stations (Reed 1976a, 39–55). Civil servants, merchants, planters, missionaries, and others who suffered from real and imagined ills soon followed the soldiers to such mountain retreats, thereby transforming the nascent health resorts into fairly complex colonial communities.

Even before 1850 increasing numbers of Europeans were beginning to trek to the emerging hill stations of South and Southeast Asia while in perfectly good health (Map 4.1). Some Westerners were convinced that periodic vacations in the mountains actually enhanced their internal defenses against endemic diseases and decreased their vulnerability to psychological problems (Aiken 1987; Fayrer 1900; Spencer and Thomas 1948; Ward 1931, 557–61, 573–76). Other colonists and many Eurasians simply enjoyed the invigorating climate of the highlands, welcomed the opportunity to relax with families and friends in relative isolation, and were happy to be temporarily freed from their professional and domestic responsibilities in the sweltering lowlands. Before long the hill stations of South and Southeast Asia evolved into specialized outposts of empire where the collective social life, recreational pursuits, and cultural activities of a rather large European citizenry intertwined to foster a romantic milieu that always evoked memories of the West. These sojourner communities were effectively integrated through daily rounds of teas, competitive sports, traditional religious celebrations, community concerts and dramatic presentations, endless gossip, and informal evening promenades, all of which were played out on a cultural landscape that featured European architectural forms, well-maintained groves of pine, cedar, or eucalyptus, golf courses, and other recreational fields, and gardens brimming with fruits, vegetables, flowers, and ornamental plants imported from northern lands (Edwardes 1969, 86–95; King 1976, 156–79; Reed 1976b). For Europeans stationed in the Asian tropics, the hill stations offered cool and comfortable refuge in secure and vibrant enclaves of metropolitan culture that remained closed to almost all indigenous peoples.[7]

Colonial authorities in both South and Southeast Asia soon recognized the utility of hill stations as health resorts, as well as their emerging role as pivots of European social life. Accordingly Western officialdoms proved quite willing to commit substantial public funds to facilitate their development and to popularize the annual trek of Europeans from the plains to the highlands during the dry season. By systematically pacifying hostile indigenous peoples in the mountains and by financing essential infrastructural projects, Western military and civil leaders acted in concert to pave the way for private investments in summer cottages, boarding houses, hotels, churches, recreational complexes, schools, and various businesses essential to the urban growth and functional elaboration of major upland settlements. Some hill stations—such as Simla (India), Buitenzorg (Netherlands East Indies), Maymyo (Burma), and Baguio (Philippines)—were actually transformed into temporary seats of administration in their respective colonies when European governors-general and their supportive bureaucracies shifted the government to these "summer capitals" for a period of three to six months each year (Kanwar 1990; Reed 1976a, 1976b). These annual migrations during the dry period and early weeks of the wet

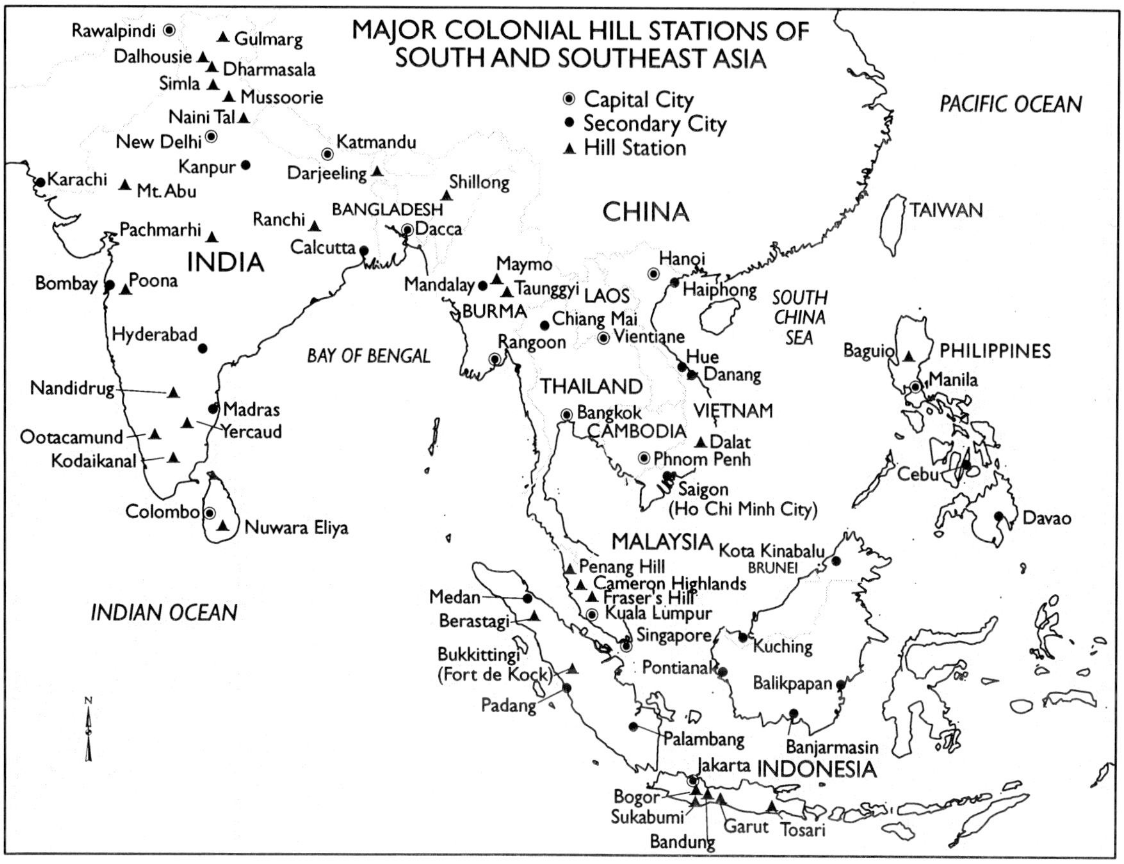

Map 4.1 Major hill stations in South and Southeast Asia, c. 1940

monsoon involved the transfer of ranking civil and military officials with their families, domestic servants, and essential clerical staffs, as well as an even more numerous community of Western colonists (business people, professionals, educators and missionaries, plantation owners, foreign diplomats, and European retirees) who required easy access to government offices and enjoyed the elite social season in the highlands. Despite its rather late foundation, Dalat had been transformed into one of the foremost "summer capitals" in tropical Asia by the 1930s.

ON THE ORIGIN OF FRENCH *STATIONS D'ALTITUDE*: HIGHLAND-LOWLAND RELATIONSHIPS

When the French began their colonial penetration of the southern Central Highlands of Vietnam, these heavily forested territories remained a preserve of many indigenous minority groups (Rhadé, Mnong, Sre, Maa, Chru, Roglai, Bahnar, Lat, and others) who lived by a combination of swidden cultivation, subsistence fishing and hunting, and the exploitation of diverse forest resources for small-scale barter with itinerant Vietnamese (Kinh) traders (*lái buôn* or *các lái*) from towns and cities along the coast.[8] Despite this centuries old and mutually beneficial commerce with the more politically complex and culturally sophisticated societies of the lowlands, the mountain peoples had always proved resolute in guarding their independence by rejecting excessive demands for taxes and tribute imposed by imperial authorities; by repulsing occasional Vietnamese military incursions into their rugged homelands; and by resisting the ongoing encroachment of pioneering agriculturists from the plains who opened fields, planted irrigated rice, and founded new villages along riverine corridors reaching into the uplands.[9] The resultant frontier separating highland and lowland peoples effectively marked two distinctive regions in terms of physical geography, society, polity, economy, and culture. Never precisely demarcated nor permanently fixed in form, this narrow and sinuous borderland was frequently reshaped through recurrent clashes resulting from attempts by the majority Vietnamese to permanently project their sovereignty into the mountains and predictable counterattacks by marauding bands of upland warriors against small or otherwise vulnerable lowland communities on the periphery of the mountain realm (Hickey 1982, 144–89).

As recently as the nineteenth century, continuing conflicts between pioneering Vietnamese settlers and often hostile minority peoples forced the imperial officialdom in Hue to reorganize its system of security in parts of the piedmont zone where the highlands abutted the plains. In the 1820s Gia Long initiated this process by building an impressive wall called the Truong Luy—more than 90 kilometers long and complete with ditches, hedge growths, closely spaced fortlets, and attendant militias—designed to shield an especially vulnerable section of Tran Man (lit., barbarian province). This special frontier district between Quang Nam and Binh Dinh consisted mainly of hilly and mountainous territories, embraced many tribal groups, and remained for decades an area of periodic ethnic discord. It was ultimately secured only by innovative constructions such as the defensive wall and scattered military strongholds that provided some degree of protection for agricultural settlers from the lowlands. By the 1850s the Nguyen rulers also maintained a lengthy chain of more than 150 major army outposts north and south of Quang Ngai in order to define and stabilize a boundary line separating the mountaineers from the majority Vietnamese. Such garrisons not only helped to prevent intermittent raids on lowland communities by highlanders but also served to contain localized warfare born of disagreements over matters of trade, taxes, resource rights, and conflicting customs. Individually and collectively these military structures also testified to an abiding Vietnamese contempt for the mountain minorities, which was reflected in royal ordinances that prevented intermarriage, in unequal social and economic relationships, and in language that fostered a deprecatory image of highlanders (Hickey 1982, 154–55, 164–68, 181–89).

Although successive generations of minority chieftains were generally successful in defending their traditional mountain strongholds against Vietnamese intruders, at the same time they seemingly acknowledged the suzerainty of the Hue court by obeying periodic demands for tribute and the annual *hóa-mai*.[10] But such compliance should not necessarily be viewed as an explicit or convincing symbol of submission. Indeed it may be fairly inferred that the actual levies in kind were proffered by the mountaineers as peace offerings designed to keep the more numerous and powerful Vietnamese at bay and so preserve the political autonomy, functional independence, and cultural integrity of highland communities. By the middle of the nineteenth century, or right before the dawn of French rule, such military, political, and economic sparring between uplanders and lowlanders had resulted in an effective territorial standoff. Accordingly it is apparent that the mountain peoples were still holding firm as various Nguyen emperors attempted to extend their authority into the western mountains through military force, commercial monopolies, agricultural trailblazing, traditional tribute, new taxes, and other administrative mechanisms (Hickey 1982, 154–89, 196–97). Much of the southern Central Highlands, including Dalat and its salubrious environs, thus remained a *terra incognita* to most Vietnamese even in the latter half of the nineteenth century.

Not surprisingly the formal inauguration of French sovereignty in Indochina, which was ratified in 1862 through the Treaty of Saigon that transformed the Mekong Delta into the colony of Cochinchina, did not result in an immediate occupation of the southern Central Highlands. Nor did the subsequent conversion of northern (Tonkin) and central (Annam) Vietnam into French protectorates stimulate a rapid advance into the highlands. For almost two generations, Western colonization in fact remained geographically synonymous with lowland and coastal provinces where French colonists were almost totally involved in the creation of Westernized military forces and bureaucratic organizations, the construction of modern urban and rural infrastructures, the reorganization of taxation and land tenure systems, the proselytizing of Catholicism, and the orchestration of a multifaceted process of economic change designed to effectively integrate Vietnam into the world market (Murray 1980; Osborne 1969). As in other Southeast Asian colonies, most European colonists lived and worked in lowland commercial, military, and administrative centers (Hanoi, Haiphong, Saigon [Ho Chi Minh city], Nhatrang, Hue, Tourane [Danang], and other key provincial capitals), or along agricultural frontiers in the lowlands where they were starting to develop extensive tropical plantations.

Although the French between 1876 and 1898 launched at least ten official and unofficial expeditions into the highlands, these exploratory efforts remained but a prelude to systematic conquest and politico-economic incorporation of the mountainous hinterlands of southern, central, and northern Vietnam during the early decades of the twentieth century. Only then did the colonial government establish a network of permanent garrisons in the highlands and encourage a small cohort of French, Chinese, and Vietnamese pioneers to settle in embryonic highland towns (Hickey 1982, 207–320).

Even while the French were still consolidating their recent acquisitions of territory in Indochina at the turn of the twentieth century, a few farsighted individuals inside and outside of the officialdom began to recognize the potential of the newly explored uplands for the development of colonial sanitaria and so advocated the foundation of *stations d'altitude* (hill stations) within the easy reach of major lowland cities. Distressed by the serious medical problems, persistent malaise, crippling mental depression, and general difficulties of acclimatization experienced by many European settlers and sojourners in the lowlands of Vietnam and Cambodia, they argued that rest and recreation complexes were essential to any long-term imperial enterprise in the tropics (Bernard 1901, 281–92; Doumer 1902, 112–15, and 1903, 363–69). In time such expressions of concern prompted some French officials to seriously evaluate the utility of hill stations as health resorts, to initiate systematic exploration designed to pinpoint appropriate settlement sites in the mountains, and to successfully establish seven *stations d'altitude* (Bach Ma, Bana, Ba Vi, Bokkor, Chapa, Dalat, and Tam Dao) during the four decades from 1893 to 1933 (Gouvernment Général de l'Indochine 1930, 1–23; Hickey 1982, 278, 318–19, 334; Les Guides Madrolle 1928, 156–58, 192–95, 257–63; Taboulet 1956, 589; Teston and Percheron 1931, 224–26, 512–13, 554–56). In its formative design, and ultimately in its multifunctional role, Dalat easily ranked foremost among the colonial hill stations of Indochina.

The Origins of Dalat (1893–1900): Yersin and Doumer

Nestled high in the southern Central Highlands of the Truong Son Mountains (Annamite Chain), Dalat is located approximately 100 kilometers from the South China Sea in the contemporary confines of Lam Dong province. Since the settlement sits on an undulating sector of the Lang Bian Plateau, which is comprised mainly of shale, quartzite, and metamorphosed conglomerate, measured points of elevation within the city limits range widely between 1,300 and 1,600 meters. Dalat's rolling landscape—marked by gently rising hills, deeply etched but still small valleys, sinuous ridges, and localized basins—not only guarantees countless scenic vistas that bring pleasure to visitors and residents alike, but also provides its citizenry with thousands of fine building lots that offer a sense of privacy and even isolation. Nearby the overshadowing granitic and rhyolitic peaks of the Lang Bian massif rise to heights of almost 2,200 meters and so provide a truly imposing backdrop for Vietnam's premier hill station. Still quite densely clothed by pine trees (predominantly three-needled *Pinus khasya* with some two-needled *Pinus merkusii*) enfolding small meadows at the time of French colonial contact, even today after nearly a century of urban and agricultural development, Dalat is justly famed for the extensive groves of conifers within its municipal boundaries (70 square kilometers) and in the immediate environs of the modern city (Consigny 1937; Naval Intelligence Division 1943, 21–22, 84; Neveu 1937, 22; Nguyen 1992, 19–22, 59; Parsons 1967, 1–5; Tardif 1949, 141–43). Favored by nature in the melding of these primary ingredients of site and situation, the uneven topography and temperate forests of Dalat have continued to impress countless foreign and domestic tourists during the past century.

Revealed to the French in 1893 through the explorations of Dr. Alexandre Yersin,[11] Dalat and its surrounding region seemed to possess the key environmental ingredients of a successful Asian hill station: a fairly high elevation, mild temperatures in all seasons, dense pine forests, sufficient building space for a major urban community, ample water supplies, a hinterland rich in resources, and spectacular mountain vistas. Following discussions with Yersin in 1897 on the possibility of establishing a *station d'altitude* somewhere in the southern sector of the Central Highlands with secure transportation linkages to Saigon and Nhatrang, Governor-General Paul Doumer dispatched two military missions to the highlands to select the most promising site for the new sanitarium and to chart the best routes for bridle paths, roads, and railways reaching from the lowlands.

The first French expedition (October 1897 to September 1898) to reconnoiter potential sites for the new colonial hill station, which was led by a French artillery officer (Captain Thouard), resulted in a detailed geographical record of the area between Nhatrang and the

Lang Bian Plateau. It also resulted in the foundation of a small gardening facility at Dankia (about 10 kilometers from Dalat) that later evolved into a major agricultural experimentation station specializing in the adaptation of mid-latitudinal vegetables, fruits, and ornamental plants to conditions in the Vietnamese uplands for subsequent distribution to local farmers (D'Andrè 1902). A second exploratory mission under the command of Captain Paul Guynet set out late in 1898 and by November 1899 had constructed a rough access road from Phan Rang to the base of the mountains and a mule trail from there to the Monts du Lang Bian overlooking Dalat (Hickey 1982, 276–78).[12] Guynet was accompanied by one Dr. Etienne Tardif, who strongly endorsed the idea of a colonial sanitarium and submitted a persuasive report to Doumer on the physiography, climate, hygienic conditions, natural resources, locally available construction materials, likely town sites, best routes of approach from the lowlands, and considerable agricultural potential of Dalat and its immediate environs (Tardif 1946, 141–63). With findings of the exploratory missions in hand, the Governor-General himself visited several likely town sites on the Lang Bian Plateau in March 1899 before deciding on the most desirable location for the proposed French *station d'altitude*. Rejecting Yersin's recommendation of Dankia, Doumer ultimately followed the advice of Tardif and authorized the establishment of a combined sanitarium and resort complex at Dalat (Mollaret and Brossolet 1985, 117–18; Pineau 1937, 59–61, and 1939, 30–31; Tardif 1949, 127–29, 217–28).

Informed and impressed by the utility of highly segregated hill stations as health facilities, vacation centers, and Western social enclaves in British India, the Dutch East Indies, and other tropical Asian colonies, Doumer moved quickly to initiate the development of a major *station d'altitude* at Dalat, together with several smaller sanitaria elsewhere in Indochina. The activist Governor-General not only hoped to construct a multifunctional hill station on the Lang Bian Plateau in the mold of such famed highland cities as Simla (India), Nuwara Eliya (Sri Lanka), and Buitenzorg (Java), but also approved the creation of a regional resort at Bana to serve the somewhat isolated European communities posted in the coastal cities of central Vietnam. Additionally he hoped to find an appropriate site for a third highland retreat somewhere along the mountainous periphery of the Red River watershed (Map 4.2). However, his ambitious designs for Dalat (let alone other *stations d'altitude*), which included general proposals for integral urban planning in addition to road and railway links with Saigon (Doumer 1902, 112–15, and 1903, 363–69; Gouvernement Général de l'Indochine 1930, 14–17), proved abortive. Doumer was recalled to France in 1901 and, in the absence of a strong executive commitment, the process of hill station development as a many faceted and high priority project of the imperial government was effectively curtailed for more than a decade.

An Embryonic Hill Station (1900–20): From Sarraut to Long

Despite the apparent indifference of Doumer's immediate successor Governor-General Paul Beau, Dalat did in fact begin to grow and acquire distinctive elements of morphology during the early decades of the twentieth century: albeit at a very slow pace. Although the military in 1903 seriously considered designs for a specialized cantonment with sanitarium facilities in the new *station d'altitude* capable of accommodating 3,500 to 4,000 European troops, the colonial government at that time remained unwilling to commit the

Map 4.2 Hill stations in French Indochina, c. 1940

sizable financial resources required for such a large undertaking.[13] By the same token in 1906 a comparatively generalized urban plan—delimiting large public and private spaces, a municipal center, sites for key civic buildings, a railway station, a large military camp, and the commercial area—was fashioned by Paul Champoudrey (a military surveyor and Dalat's first French administrator) to guide the anticipated urbanization process (Pineau 1937, 60–62, and 1939, 31–35). But these highly tentative proposals failed to serve as binding outlines for formative city growth.

In reality most of the early improvement efforts in Dalat were largely informal and remained unregulated by official decree or urban code. Without strong and steady formal endorsement by the Governor-General and other ranking authorities, let alone corollary financial support from their various bureaucracies, minor local and regional officials were compelled to improvise on basic infrastructural undertakings and depended almost entirely on private investors to generate even minimal economic change in and around the embryonic town. In light of such conditions few entrepreneurs displayed much interest in Dalat since its shallow base of patronage consisted only of occasional hunters, small groups of adventurous tourists, French officials on inspection tours, and a few ambitious Western planters who had been attracted to the highlands by the promise of generous land concessions. At the end of the first decade of the twentieth century, the still neglected *station d'altitude* embraced little more than several brick buildings occupied by a few Europeans, an informal marketplace, scattered vegetable fields, a modest hotel constructed on piles, a tiny post office, several clusters of thatched huts belonging to indigenous mountain people, and about a dozen wooden houses owned by Chinese and Vietnamese pioneers who had recently migrated from the lowlands in search of their fortunes along the mountain frontier (Duclaux 1941a, 1941b).

The appointment of Albert Sarraut as Governor-General of Indochina marked the real start of Dalat's evolution into one of Southeast Asia's foremost hill stations. Early in 1912 this new executive inaugurated an ambitious road construction program designed to connect the southern Central Highlands with Saigon and the major coastal cities of Annam and Cochinchina. At the same time he guaranteed the release of public funds for essential building projects within the municipal bounds of the nascent *station d'altitude*. By 1915 Dalat was effectively linked to the steadily spreading lowland highway system and so became easily accessible year-round to lowlanders by carriages and carts as well as the earliest motorcycles, automobiles, and buses. Almost immediately the still tiny town began to attract a growing clientele of French colonists and other Westerners who relished the opportunity for rest and relaxation in a pleasantly cool and forested mountain milieu; who were recuperating from tropical fatigue, malaria, dysentery, and other debilitating illnesses; who enjoyed hunting or other invigorating outdoor sports activities; and who sought general psychological relief from their day-to-day responsibilities in lowlands (Munier 1941, 6; Petite Guide 1930, 6–7). They were soon followed by numerous Vietnamese and Chinese migrants from the lowlands, as well as by a small number of upland peoples, who clearly recognized the proliferating employment opportunities in Dalat and thus sought work as clerks, civil servants, gardeners, porters, carpenters, cooks, household help, general craftsmen, firewood cutters, fodder collectors, petty merchants, curio-vendors, and common laborers.[14]

Testifying to its functional elaboration, population growth, and strategic location in the geographic context of the southern Central Highlands, the emergent hill station was named provincial capital of the newly formed Lang Bian province in 1916 and thereby assumed a key and enduring regional administrative role in an extensive mountain realm. As might be expected, these various factors of development soon entwined to stimulate economic and urban growth along with a quickening process of landscape change during the difficult but prosperous years of World War I (Berjoan 1943, 2; Nguyen 1954, 39; Pineau 1937, 61–62; Tessan, 1923a, 1923b).[15]

Colonial Florescence of Dalat (1920–39): Growth and Change

Anticipating Dalat's continued rapid growth and functional diversification in the years following World War I, the newly appointed Governor-General Maurice Long in 1921 commissioned Ernest Hébrard to prepare a comprehensive urban blueprint for the increasingly popular *station d'altitude*.[16] Admired at the time throughout Europe for his recent planning accomplishments in Greece, Hébrard served the French colonial government for six years (1921–26) as chief architect and city designer in the Department of Urbanism.[17] While he built numerous public buildings that grace the urban landscapes of Vietnam even today and prepared detailed schemes for the commercial and industrial sectors of Hanoi, Haiphong, Saigon, and other cities, Hébrard apparently considered Dalat his favorite and most rewarding project in Indochina (Wright 1991, 201–33).

Despite Champoudrey's tentative site plan and subsequent development during World War I, Dalat in the early 1920s was still a small and loosely ordered town, thereby remaining a comparatively blank slate for the planner. Consequently Hébrard enjoyed fairly free rein in composing a scheme that conformed to the natural terrain and seemed to minimize the human impact on environment. Recognizing the formative functions of Asian hill stations, he de-emphasized industrial and commercial districts while providing ample spaces for a health complex (hospitals, clinics, and recuperation bungalows), hotels and tourist facilities, a cantonment and administrative structures (private compounds for the governor-general and other ranking colonial officials), extensive residential districts for the French elite and compact quarters for the Vietnamese, sports areas (golf, tennis, swimming beaches, and playing fields), schools and religious retreats, and general leisure activities (clubs, gardens, walking and riding trails, and municipal forests).

Hébrard clearly attempted to limit population densities, to prescribe fair and binding zoning guidelines, to separate ethnic groups and classes, to provide for both civil and military communities, to establish reasonable building guidelines (regularized lot sizes, height limits, types of material, construction standards), and to guarantee an overall harmony (Munier 1941, 7; Pineau 1937, 62–63; Tessan 1923a, 156; *L'Urbanisme* 1933, 170; Wright 1991, 230–33). Although the Hébrard Plan of 1923 (Figure 4.1) was not without critics and certainly did not impose an immutable morphological order on the mountain capital, it did incorporate a widely shared vision of Dalat as a city of leisure and suggested that the urban development process required fairly strict regulation to guarantee the preservation of environment for residents and visitors alike. Late in the 1930s when Louis-Georges Pineau in his role as consulting architect and urban planner for the Govern-

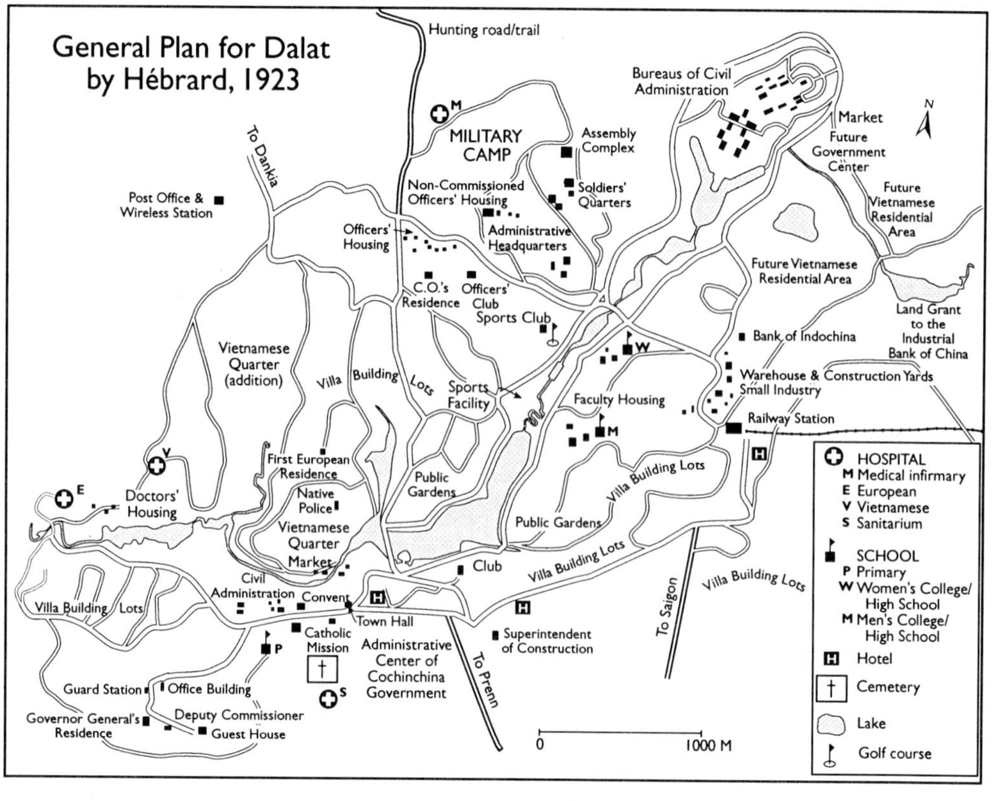

Figure 4.1 Hébrard Plan of 1923 (based on Tessan 1923a, 156)

ment of Indochina modified the Plan of 1923, he clearly echoed Hébrard's call for carefully controlled and ecologically appropriate development that preserved the forests, environmental integrity, and natural beauty of Dalat (Pineau 1939, 38–49).

Around 1920 the promotion and expansion of Dalat began in earnest as the colonial officialdom systematically endorsed the development process through substantial and continuing investments in essential infrastructure, through adoption of Hébrard's detailed urban plan, and through frequent personal vacations in the ever more popular *station d'altitude* of Lang Bian province. Their institutional and capital support, together with individual and collective patronage, in turn helped to promote interest in Dalat throughout the Western community and fostered increasing curiosity among certain members of the Vietnamese elite. Unlike contemporary lowland towns and cities, which were then being transformed into powerful instruments of economic exploitation, political control, religious change, and cultural transformation, the French from the outset clearly envisioned Dalat as a dual purpose urban center designed primarily as a European health and recreation resort and secondarily as an instrument for regional administration.

Described even by the earliest Western residents and tourists as the *"City of Eternal Spring"* or the *"City of Flowers,"* Dalat's generally mild temperatures, fresh air, pine-clad hills, gardens and parks, and picturesque residential areas coalesced to form the linchpin that secured its early development while an increasingly significant political and economic role was clearly defined during the two decades between the world wars. Throughout this time the new *station d'altitude* grew in population, became ever more functionally diverse, evolved in an orderly fashion along the general lines of a comprehensive urban plan, and emerged as the urban keystone of the southern Central Highlands. By 1940 Dalat was a provincial center of education and political administration, an important religious retreat and nexus of Christian missionary activities, a primary hub of transportation and communications, and a strategic market town where forest products, handicrafts, and exotic mid-latitudinal vegetables and fruits produced by highland peoples and Vietnamese migrants were assembled for shipment to Saigon and other lowland cities.

Marking the beginning of Dalat's colonial florescence, the Langbian-Palace Hotel—which still stands as one of the most enduring, widely recognized, and monumental landmarks of the city—was dedicated in 1922 following several years of slow, expensive, and exacting construction.[18] Functioning almost immediately as the nerve center of proper Western colonial society in the highlands, this famed structure with its fine architecture, well-appointed rooms, excellent dining facilities, extensive grounds, impressive hillside site, and panoramic views from almost every window at once validated the French perception of Dalat as the perfect setting for a first-class health and vacation resort. There is no doubt that the imposing Palace Hotel served to signal a growing collective confidence in the future of the mountain city. Other public building projects, infrastructural improvements, private ventures, and enterprises by charitable organizations followed in rapid succession.

Predictably government spearheaded the systematic transformation of the premier French *station d'altitude* throughout the 1920s and 1930s. Functioning separately and in tandem, local, regional, and national authorities systematically enhanced Dalat's urban infrastructure by extending and surfacing both primary and secondary roads within the city; constructing an electric power plant (1919) as well as subsequently expanding and improving hydroelectric facilities when demand increased; building a large hospital complex and a Pasteur Institute; inaugurating a municipal water system (1920) while also improving sewerage disposal, garbage collection, and surface drainage as necessary; laying out a sprawling cantonment and convalescent camp for army and navy personnel along with summer retreats for the governor-general and other ranking French officials in Indochina; establishing schools for Europeans and indigenous peoples; gracing roadsides and parks with ornamental trees and flower gardens; and fashioning a magnificent artificial lake at the heart of the emerging hill station (Anonymous Author 1928; Berjoan 1943, 2–3; Gouvernment Général de l'Indochine 1930, 13–14; Nguyen 1954, 39; Petite Guide 1930, 7, 13–16; Tessan 1923a, 157–58). Additionally various branches of the colonial bureaucracy further contributed to the growth of Dalat by promoting tourism, managing divers, public services, encouraging market gardening and floriculture, and fostering plantation agriculture in surrounding areas.

Testifying to a growing popularity of the hill station project, successive governors-general for more than ten years continued to lavish scarce national funds on an undeniably important yet extremely costly traction and cog railway from Phan Rang that opened in 1933 and capped the project with construction of a fine municipal station (1938) in Dalat. This rail line ultimately guaranteed easy access to the highlands and an increasing passenger traffic comprised of tourists, residents, and temporary workers (Map 4.3). At the same time it greatly facilitated the transport of machinery, cement, pipes, brick, and other heavy building materials from the lowlands and the reverse shipment of steadily increasing tonnages of mid-latitudinal vegetables (green beans, carrots, cabbage, lettuce, cauliflower, and potatoes) and fruits (apples, apricots, peaches, pears, and figs), plantation

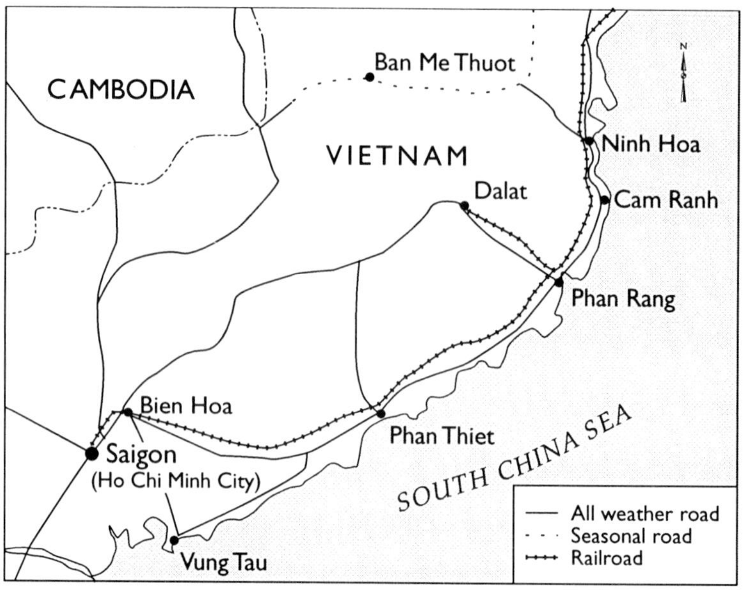

Map 4.3 Transportation links to Dalat, c. 1940

products (coffee and tea), flowers, and lumber from the uplands to Saigon and other urban destinations along the coast (Gouvernment Général de l'Indochine 1930, 10–11; Lefèvre 1937; Teston and Percheron 1931, 225; Tran 1941, 92–94).

While government orchestrated the metamorphosis of Dalat from highland hamlet to multifunctional hill station-cum-regional capital, individual colonists, Western companies, and charitable institutions played an expanding role with each passing year in actualizing the process of urbanization and in forging an internally integrated urban community. Symbolized by the stately Sacred Heart basilica (1942) that still towers over the city, the Catholic Church systematically intervened in the cultural matrix of the hill settlement through interlinked religious, social, and educational systems that were formally expressed in the organization of at least three parishes, several convents, a seminary, and private schools for wealthy European and Vietnamese children and the Eurasian sons of Western military personnel: all before 1940. Equally important were the French settlers and summer sojourners who served as essential journeymen in the process of urban transformation through hundreds of independent and collective investments in hotels, restaurants, and other touristic enterprises, various commercial undertakings, professional offices, clubs and social organizations, and both modest summer homes and imposing villas (A. N. I. 1937; Munier 1941). They also provided wage work and helped generate secondary employment opportunities for thousands of Vietnamese and Chinese migrants together with occasional laborers from the lowlands whose muscles, assorted skills, entrepreneurial impulses, and cultural inheritance contributed fundamentally to the economic and social dynamics of the Lang Bian *station d'altitude*.

Summer Capital of Indochina (1940–45): Adaptation During World War II

By the onset of World War II, Dalat had been transformed into one of the foremost hill stations in tropical Asia and was functioning as the "summer capital" of Indochina.[19] Even while French authority was beginning to erode in the southern Central Highlands as the flames of nationalism swept Vietnam (Hickey 1982, 321–84), Dalat seemed destined to grow and prosper. From a hamlet of several hundred people in 1910 and town of 1,500 permanent residents in 1920, it had become a small city embracing more than 13,000 inhabitants—including at least 3,000 Europeans—by the outbreak of war in Southeast Asia late in 1941. Four years later the citizenry of Dalat exceeded 20,000 with the permanent population of Europeans totaling around 5,000 men, women, and children. The fact that Vietnamese and Chinese residents comprised some 75 percent of the urban population (Berjoan 1943, 3; Nguyen 1954, 39; Pineau 1937, 69) evidently failed to neutralize a widely held vision of Dalat as a model French provincial city.

In a process that seemed to give substance to the then prevailing image of Dalat, Western settlers completely transformed many ridges and hillsides of the highland capital between 1940 and 1945 through the construction of family villas. Large houses in a Swiss alpine mold had in fact been a familiar element of landscape in the hill station since around 1913 when a dozen such structures served as both permanent residences and summer retreats of European *colons* (Pineau 1939, 32). Scores of additional houses in the expansive chalet form were built during and immediately after the first boom period of World War I. By

1930 several hundred so-called "French villas" graced the hills of the growing *station d'altitude* and in 1940 they totaled 530. Only two years later the number had reached 730 and by 1945 the figure easily exceeded 1,000 (Berjoan 1943, 3; Nguyen 1954, 39). Although a few of the villas constructed during the incredible residential building boom of the war years belonged to wealthy Vietnamese, most were owned by European families who found themselves effectively stranded in Indochina during World War II. A majority of these Western-style structures were situated on hill crest lots in accordance with a "garden city" scheme conceived during the wartime administration of Governor-General Jean Decoux (Sauveplane 1942). Collectively the picturesque villas of Dalat served to evoke fond memories of France and to generate a persistent nostalgia for home.

Post-Colonial Development (1946–94) and the Future

Despite dire predictions that the hill stations of Southeast Asia would decline and even disappear with the ultimate demise of colonialism, these highland settlements have actually grown in population and in functional diversity since independence. Dalat is no exception even though the rate of its urban development was undoubtedly slowed during more than a generation of continuing warfare. Still the city's infrastructure remained comparatively undamaged throughout the French and American wars, and the settlement was never abandoned.

In fact it is easy to summarize the primary role of Dalat during the years of conflict and peace since 1946. The social utility and functional form of the mountain city as a resort center persisted even after departure of the European *colons*. Preserving its essential mix of health and recreational activities, Dalat continued as a favorite destination of the elite. But it also began to attract increasing numbers of ordinary people. Indeed the ethnicity of patrons underwent profound changes following 1946 as the French retreated, the Americans came and went, and the Vietnamese claimed Dalat as their own vacation center. What was formerly a strictly segregated and socially exclusive *station d'altitude* became in time a national playground for people of many regions and cultural backgrounds.

Reflecting the democratization of tourist patronage, Dalat's citizenry also changed as Westerners disappeared completely from the urban scene to be replaced by lowland Vietnamese from both the North and the South. In the mid-1950s many of the settlers were Catholics who had fled from Hanoi and other places in the Red River Delta. Predictably these migratory flows served to fuel continuing population growth. At the end of World War II, Dalat was home to about 20,000 people. By 1955, this number had at least doubled and in 1960 the city embraced approximately 50,000 residents. Still growing steadily, the population of Dalat reached 80,000 in 1970, 100,000 in 1975, and probably exceeds 150,000 today if circular migrants are included in the total (Parsons 1967, 11; Thrift and Forbes 1986, 124).

Predictably Dalat's substantial population increase has effectively reinforced the original multifunctional urban character of the colonial highland capital that evolved during the 1920s and 1930s. Dalat thus retains a comparatively balanced mix of functions. In addition to its diverse touristic activities, the city is at once the hub of a developing agricultural realm; an important regional focus of trade and commerce; a medical complex and research facility (with a small nuclear reactor); a center of major educational and cultural institutions; a military pivot; and a seat of religious administration (and minor pilgrimage). Still firmly anchored by tourism, Dalat clearly commands a sizable highland hinterland and displays the character of a flourishing regional capital of the Third World.

One of the most rapidly growing secondary cities in Vietnam, Dalat is beginning to display many characteristics of an urban environment under serious stress. It appears today not unlike other major hill stations in South and Southeast Asia—Maymyo, Baguio, Simla, Naini Tal, or Shillong—some twenty or thirty years ago, or before each of these health resorts experienced periods of massive tourism and ever more rapid urbanization.

Despite prohibitions against cutting, the municipal forests of Dalat are being destroyed at an alarming rate through selective and secretive cutting for fuel and lumber. In almost all residential areas the densities of population already exceed reasonable limits defined in the formative Hébrard Plan of 1923 and in Pineau's revision, and much of the recent construction has surpassed established building height limits. Some areas and pine groves set aside as parks, gardens, and other public spaces have been converted to vegetable gardens in a process that obviously compromises the essential natural beauty of the hill station and sometimes produces serious localized erosion. The now substantial central business district of Dalat is becoming seriously overbuilt through a melding of business, warehousing, residential, and light industrial uses. With a foreign investment of more than US$40 million, a complete re-development of the city golf course has not only produced widespread erosion and soil loss along its flanks but also significant siltation in Xuan Huong Lake. In an even more ambitious venture, Strategic Development International Corporation (Hong Kong) plans to invest US$150 million in Dalat's infrastructure (roads, electrical system, and water supplies) in exchange for the right to create a 200-hectare tourist complex on the outskirts of the city (Reuters, February 21, 1994). There can be no doubt, therefore, that Dalat will continue to grow and that its landscape will be transformed during the next few decades. But at what environmental cost?

NOTES

1. The pioneering comparative essay on the origin, distribution, and imperial role of hill stations in Asia was published nearly fifty years ago by Spencer and Thomas (1948).

2. Although few colonial hill stations flourished outside tropical Asia, some were in fact established in Africa and the Caribbean. For a commentary on one such highland retreat, consult Frenkel and Western (1988).

3. Students of comparative urbanism were introduced to the idea of the primate city by the geographer Mark Jefferson (1939). In his seminal article published more than five decades ago, he observed that the largest city in many nations remains dominant over the centuries not only in demographic terms, but also in its diversity of functions and broad national influence.

4. Unlike Europeans elsewhere in South and Southeast Asia, the Spaniards were strongly committed to continuing acquisition of new territories in the Philippines from the onset of colonization in 1565. Their system of direct territorial rule—which was designed to facilitate the Christian conversion and cultural transformation of Filipinos—rested on the notion that all conquered lands were ultimately vested in the Spanish Crown and

thus immediately subject to the administration of Hispanic civil, military, and religious officialdoms in Manila (Corpuz 1989; Phelan 1959).

5. For a fine commentary on Western perceptions of health hazards in the Asian tropics, see Savage (1984, 141–87). An historical survey of health and disease in Southeast Asia is offered in Owen (1987). Mitchell (1972, 13–55) has thoroughly reviewed the prevailing patterns of disease distributions in monsoonal Asia during the heyday of Western imperialism. A broader geographic perspective on pestilence in tropical colonies of both the Old and New Worlds, as well as a stimulating discussion of military and civilian hygiene, is presented by Curtin (1989).

6. The practice of sending sickly troops to mountain garrisons for cure and convalescence was apparently routinized in British India by the 1850s (Curtin 1989, 47–50; Martin 1861, 278–90) and soon diffused to Western colonies in Southeast Asia.

7. A fictionalized version of social life and Western cultural forms in the archetypal hill station of Simla has been constructed by Farrell (1981).

8. Among the forest products collected by the mountaineers for trade, as well as for the taxes, tribute, and gifts exacted by Vietnamese imperial authorities, were the following: betel, beeswax, areca nuts, elephant tusks, tobacco, honey, resin, indigo, animal pelts, honey, rhinoceros horns, precious metals, various foods, oils, eaglewood, cinnamon, ebony, and other precious woods. In exchange the lowlanders offered silk garments, high-quality muslin, domesticated animals, small ingots of gold and silver, salt, crystal ware, brass items, coins, jewelry, porcelain objects, and other manufactured goods (Hickey 1982, 160, 162–63, 169–81, 185–89).

9. Some Vietnamese settlements established by the court of Hue on the periphery of the mountains included not only landless lowlanders, but also vagabonds, army deserters, social misfits, criminals, prisoners of war, political exiles, and other undesirables. Their banishment to the frontier apparently helped to guarantee peace and tranquillity in both rural and urban areas throughout the kingdom (Hickey 1982, 162–63).

10. A form of exploitation marked by the monopoly control and purchase of designated highland products by local Vietnamese officials for delivery to the imperial court in Hue (Hickey 1982, 185).

11. Dr. Alexandre Yersin was a remarkable man who is still remembered with deep affection by the Vietnamese. Among the pioneers who introduced Western medicine to Southeast Asia, he was born in Switzerland in 1863 and studied at Lausanne and Marburg before serving with Louis Pasteur in Paris. While at the Pasteur Institute, Yersin and Pierre Roux collaborated in discovering the diphtheria toxin. In 1890 he traveled to Indochina as a ship physician and entered the colonial health service two years later. While working and traveling widely in French Indochina, he considered himself a permanent resident of Nhatrang and maintained a laboratory, library, and home in that coastal community until 1943. Renowned during his lifetime in Vietnam and abroad, it would be difficult indeed to exaggerate Yersin's contributions to the public health of his adopted country. During a half-century of labor in Asia, he organized Pasteur Institutes in various Vietnamese cities; acted as the national director of these institutions; founded the College of Medicine in Hanoi; pursued trailblazing research on a variety of tropical diseases; and gained international fame by identifying the bacterium of bubonic plague (*Pasteurella pestis*) during an outbreak in Hong Kong (1894). One year later he introduced a serum that proved effective in combating the disease. A scholar of wide ranging interests, Yersin also made original contributions to the fields of meteorology, oceanography, geography,

forestry, and anthropology. While launching his brilliant professional career in Nhatrang during the 1890s, this amazing scientist somehow found time also for pathfinding and sometimes extremely dangerous geographical explorations in the mountains of Annam. In 1893 he journeyed through the forests, fields, and savanna of the Lang Bian Plateau and was overwhelmed by the beauty and temperate weather of the area. Convinced of the utility of hill stations as health resorts and recreation centers, he later advocated establishment of a *station d'altitude* somewhere in the shadow of Lang Bian massif (Bernard 1922, 1944, and 1955; Mollaret and Brossolet 1985; Nguyen and Le 1992).

12. For a detailed account of Guynet's expedition, consult Tardif (1949).

13. The commission, which proposed this project, was led by Général de Beylié (Pineau 1937, 61) and was probably informed by the model of certain British army settlements in the mountains of India such as Ranikhet, Wellington, and Landour. These specialized hill stations were conceived as triple-function hospital facilities, recreation centers, and training camps designed to accommodate sick and debilitated European soldiers from pestiferous lowland garrisons (Mitchell 1972, Chapters 1–3).

14. Although the individual and collective stories of Vietnamese and Chinese settlers in Dalat are yet to be told, the growing indigenous presence in colonial hill stations has been well documented in other mountain cities where Asians sometimes outnumbered the Europeans by a factor of ten to one (Kanwar 1990, 130–45; Reed 1976a, 168).

15. Curiously Gwendolyn Wright in her wide ranging survey on *The Politics of Design in French Colonial Urbanism* asserts that a "continued lack of rail service [to Dalat] meant that the fledgling town was abandoned at the time of World War I" (1991, 232) . Obviously such was not the case. In fact the recently opened road to the lowlands stimulated considerable growth during the wartime period in the newly proclaimed provincial capital. However it is undeniable that the railway linkage to the coast, which was finished sixteen years later, helped to intensify the development process by facilitating a marked increase in shipments of heavy and bulky goods at reasonable prices.

16. Most hill stations apparently developed without a formal and formative plan. But in a few cases Western colonial officials requested the professional services of leading architects and urban designers from the metropole to fashion detailed and integrated plans for major hill stations. In the Philippines, for example, the famed architect and city planner Daniel H. Burnham developed the city plan for Baguio (Hines 1979, 197–216; Reed 1976a, 119–27).

17. For summary accounts of Hébrard's work, consult Lavedan (1933), Pottier and Picard (1933), *L'Urbanisme* (1933).

18. This substantial structure apparently replaced the original wooden building with its encompassing verandah and sheet metal roof (Hickey 1982, 312; Nguyen 1954, 39).

19. In terms of morphology, functions, demographic profile, and general pattern of development, Dalat clearly mirrored and was often compared in popular and official literature with the Philippine city of Baguio in the Cordillera Central of Luzon (Pineau 1937, 62; Tessan 1923a, 156). Both places were acknowledged products of Western enterprise and were designed by influential and internationally renowned architects and urban planners of the period; both retained identities born of their formative colonial communities of the nearly 5,000 French and Americans who steadfastly preserved their Western lifestyles even while residing in Asia; both embraced supportive resident populations of approximately 15,000 to 17,000 migrants from the lowlands who provided essential labor and skills and greatly outnumbered indigenous minority peoples settled within the urban bounds; both offered a substantial array of health

services and recreational activities to permanent residents together with a rapidly growing tourist clientele that numbered in the tens of thousands each year; and both had evolved into the foremost upland hubs of regional development (lumbering, market gardening, floriculture, and some plantation agriculture) in their respective highland hinterlands. Furthermore, both Dalat and Baguio served as "summer capitals" and so were the effective seats of political authority in their respective colonies for much of the year.

BIBLIOGRAPHY

Aiken, S. R. 1987. Early Penang hill station. *The Geographical Review* 77:421–39.

A. N. I. 1937. Physionomie de Dalat en 1937. *L'Asie Nouvelle* (Saigon) 56:11–14.

Anon. 1928. La salubrité de Dalat. *Bulletin Economique de l'Indochine* (Nouvelle Série) III, 193:229–31.

Balfour, A. 1923. Sojourners in the tropics. *The Lancet* 204:1329–34.

Ballabh, C. 1967. Nainital: A resort town study. Summer Study Report in Planning. New Delhi: Department of Town and Country Planning, School of Planning and Architecture (typescript).

Barr, P., and R. Desmond. 1978. *Simla: A hill station in British India.* New York: Charles Scribner's Sons.

Basu, D. K., ed. 1979. *The rise and growth of the colonial port cities in Asia.* Santa Cruz: Center for South Pacific Studies, University of California.

Berjoan, A. 1943. L'effort Français en Indochine. *Indochine* 126:2–5.

Bernard, F. 1901. *L'Indo-Chine: Erreurs et dangers—un programme.* Paris: Bibliothèque-Charpentier.

Bernard, N. 1922. *Les institutes Pasteur d'Indochine: centenaire de Louis Pasteur, 1822–1895.* Saigon: Imprimerie Nouvelle.

Bernard, N. 1944. Alexandre Yersin (1863–1943). In *Yersin et la peste: Ouvrage publié pour le cinquantenaire de la découverte du microbe de la peste,* edited by P. Hauduroy. Lausanne: F. Rouge & Cie S.A.

Bernard, N. 1955. *Yersin: pionnier-savant-explorateur (1863–1943).* Paris: Editions du Vieux Colombier.

Broeze, F. 1989. Introduction: Brides of the sea. In *Brides of the sea: Port cities of Asia from the 16th–20th centuries,* edited by F. Broeze. Honolulu: University of Hawaii Press.

Buck, E. J. 1979 (orig. 1904). *Simla past and present.* Delhi: Sumit Publications.

Bührlein, M. 1991. *Nuwara Eliya: "Hill station" und zentraler ort im hochland der insel Ceylon (Sri Lanka),* Beiträge zur Südasienforschung (Südasien-Institut, Universität Heidelberg), Band 146. Stuttgart: Franz Steiner Verlag Wiesbaden GMBH.

Butcher, J. G. 1979. *The British in Malaya, 1880–1941: The social history of a European community in colonial South-East Asia.* Kuala Lumpur: Oxford University Press.

Cady, J. F. 1964. *Southeast Asia: Its historical development.* New York: McGraw-Hill Book Company.

Carthew, M. 1927. The aetiology and prophylaxis of mental irritability in Europeans in the tropics. *The Journal of Tropical Medicine and Hygiene* 30:112–17.

Clay, J. M. 1928. *Naini Tal: A historical and descriptive account, 1927.* Allahabad: The Superintendent, Government Press, United Provinces.

Cobban, J. L. 1971. Geographic notes on the first two centuries of Djakarta. *Journal of the Malaysian Branch of the Royal Asiatic Society* 44:110–50.

Consigny. 1937. Le pins de Dalat. *L'Asie Nouvelle* (Saigon) 56:29–30.

Corpuz, O. D. 1989. *The roots of the Filipino nation*. 2 vols. Quezon City: AKLAHI Foundation, Inc.

Cruz, G. 1988. 1986 survey of economic establishments in Baguio City. CSC Working Paper No. 9. Baguio City: Cordillera Studies Center, University of the Philippines College Baguio.

Curtin, P. D. 1989. *Death by migration: Europe's encounter with the tropical world in the nineteenth century*. Cambridge: Cambridge University Press.

D'Andrè, A. 1902. Note sur les cultures de la station sanitaire du Lang-Bian. In *Situation de l'Indo-Chine (1897–1901): Rapport par M. Paul Doumer, gouverneur général*, by P. Doumer. Hanoi: F. H. Schneider.

Dar, R. K. 1989. Industrial development in a hillside city of the Himalayas: A case study of Nainital, Uttar Pradesh, India. Paper presented at the International Conference on Hillside Cities (Focusing on the Revitalization of Medium-Sized Cities), United Nations Centre for Regional Development, Nagasaki, Japan, November 3–7.

Davis, W. G. 1973. *Social relations in a Philip pine market: Self-interest and subjectivity*. Berkeley and Los Angeles: University of California Press.

Dickason, D. G. 1975. The Indian hill station. *The Geographical Review* 65:115–17.

Doumer, P. 1902. *Situation de l'Indo-Chine (1897–1901): Rapport par M. Paul Doumer, gouverneur général*. Hanoi: F. H. Schneider.

Doumer, P. 1903. *L'Indochine Française (Souvenirs)*. 2nd ed. Paris: Vuibert et Nony.

Duclaux, P. 1941a. Le Dalat de 1908. *L'Indochine* 39:2–5.

Duclaux, P. 1941b. Le Dalat de 1908. *L'Indochine* 40:7–11.

Edwardes, M. 1969. *Bound to exile: The Victorians in India*. London: Sidgewich and Jackson.

Emerson, R. 1967. *Malaysia: A study in direct and indirect rule*. New York: The Macmillan Company.

Farrell, J. G. 1981. *The hill station: An unfinished novel and an Indian diary*, ed. John Spurling. New Delhi: Vikas Publishing House.

Fayrer, (Sir) J. 1881. *Tropical dysentery and chronic diarrhoea and on health of European children and others in India*. London: J. & A. Churchill.

Fayrer, (Sir) J. 1882. *On the climate and fevers of India: Being the Croonian lectures delivered at the Royal College of Physicians in March, 1882*. London: J. & A. Churchill.

Fayrer, (Sir) J. 1900. The hill stations of India as health resorts. *The British Medical Journal* 1:1393–97.

Frenkel, S., and J. Western. 1988. Pretext or prophylaxis? Racial segregation and malarial mosquitoes in a British tropical colony: Sierra Leone. *Annals of the Association of American Geographers* 78:211–28.

Gokhale, B. G. 1988. *Poona in the eighteenth century: An urban history*. Delhi: Oxford University Press.

Gouvernment Général de l'Indochine. 1930. *Stations climatiques de l'Indochine*. Publication de l'agence economique l'Indochine, No. 25. Paris: Imprimerie A. Tournon.

Hall, D. G. E. 1968 . *A history of South-East Asia*. 3d ed. rev. London: Macmillan and Company.

Hickey, G. C. 1982. *Sons of the mountains: Ethnohistory of the Vietnamese Central Highlands to 1954*. New Haven and London: Yale University Press.

Hines, T. S. 1979. *Burnham of Chicago: Architect and planner*. Chicago and London: The University of Chicago Press.

Kanwar, P. 1984. The changing profile of the summer capital of British India: Simla 1864–1947. *Modern Asian Studies* 18:215–36.

Kanwar, P. 1990. *Imperial Simla: The political culture of the Raj*. Delhi: Oxford University Press.

Kincaid, D. 1938. *British social life in India, 1608–1937.* London: Routledge & Kegan Paul.

King, A. 1976. *Colonial urban development.* Boston: Routledge and Paul.

Lavedan, P. 1933. Ernest Hébrard. *L'Architecture* 46:109–12.

Lefèvre, F. 1937. Le chemin de fer du Langbian. *L'Asie Nouvelle* (Saigon) 56:8–9.

Les Guides Madrolle. 1928. *Manuel du voyageur en Indochine du sud.* Paris: Librairie Hachette.

Lind, J. 1811. *An essay on diseases incidental to Europeans in hot climates.* Philadelphia: William Duane.

L'Urbanisme. 1933. 2:142–72. Special issue on Ernest Hébrard.

Manahan, G. V. 1989. Planning and development in a highland city: The case of Baguio, the Philippines. Paper presented at the International Conference on Hillside Cities (Focusing on the Revitalization of Medium-Sized Cities), United Nations Centre for Regional Development, Nagasaki, Japan, November 3–7.

Martin, J. R. 1861. *Influence of tropical climates in producing the acute endemic diseases of Europeans.* London: John Churchill.

McGee, T. G. 1967. *The Southeast Asian city: A social geography of the primate cities of Southeast Asia.* New York: Frederick A. Praeger, Publishers.

Meilink-Roelofsz, M. H. P. 1962. *Asian trade and European influence in the Indonesian Archipelago between 1500 and about 1630.* The Hague: Martinus Nijhoff.

Mitchell, N. 1972. *The Indian hill-station: Kodaikanal,* Research Monograph No. 141. Chicago: Department of Geography, The University of Chicago.

Mollaret, H. H., and J. Brossolet. 1985. *Alexandre Yersin, le vainqueur de la peste.* Paris: Librairie Arthème Fayard.

Moore, W. J. 1886. *A manual of the diseases of India with a compendium of diseases generally.* London: J. & A. Churchill.

Munier, P. 1941. Dalat. *Indochine* 28:2–5.

Murphey, R. 1969. Traditionalism and colonialism: Changing urban roles in Asia. *Journal of Asian Studies* 29:67–84.

Murray, M. J. 1980. *The development of capitalism in colonial Indochina (1870–1940).* Berkeley and Los Angeles: University of California Press.

Naval Intelligence Division. 1943. *Indo-China,* B.R. 510, Geographical Handbook Series, Naval Intelligence Division of the Admiralty. Cambridge: H. M. Stationery Office at the University Press.

Neveu, A. 1937. La Végétation du Langbian. *L'Asie nouvelle* (Saigon) 56:22.

Nguyen P. Q. and Le Phuong (Rédacteurs). 1992. *Alexandre Yersin (1863–1943): un demi-siècle au Vietnam.* Publication No. 83. Hanoi: Département de Publication de Ministère de la Culture, de l'Information et des Sports.

Nguyen T. D. 1992. *Geography of Vietnam: Natural-human-economic.* Hanoi: Foreign Languages Publishing House.

Nguyen T. N. 1954. Dalat, ville de rêve. *Indochine: Sud Est Asiatique* 30:36–41.

Osborne, M. E. 1969. *The French presence in Cochinchina and Cambodia: Rule and response (1859–1905).* Ithaca and London: Cornell University Press.

Owen, N. G., ed. 1987. *Death and disease in Southeast Asia: Explorations in social, medical and demographic history.* Asian Studies Association of Australia, Southeast Asia Publications Series, No. 14. Singapore: Oxford University Press.

Panter-Downes, M. 1967. *Ooty preserved: A Victorian hill station in India.* New York: Farrar, Straus and Giroux.

Parsons, R. M. 1967. Dalat water supply facilities: A study for the Ministry of Public Works, Republic of Vietnam. Los Angeles and Saigon: The Ralph M. Parsons Company (typescript).

Petite Guide. 1930. *Petite guide illustré de Dalat, Indochine Française, 1930.* Illustre Hanoi: Imprimerie d'Extrême-Orient.

Phelan, J. L. 1959. *The Hispanization of the Philippines: Spanish aims and Filipino responses, 1565–1700.* Madison: The University of Wisconsin Press.

Pineau, L.-G. 1937. Dalat, capital administrative de l'Indochine? *La Revue Indochinoise Juridique & Economique* 2:45–81.

Pineau, L.-G. 1939. Le plan d'amenagement et d'extension de Dalat. *La Vie Urbaine* 49:29–49.

Pottier, E., and C. Picard. 1933. Ernest Hébrard (1875–1933). *Revue Archéologique*, Series 6, 1:148–50.

Price, (Sir) F. 1908. *Ootacamund: A history.* Madras: Government Press.

Pubby, V. 1988. *Simla then and now: Summer capital of the Raj.* New Delhi: Indus Publishing Company.

Reed, R. R. 1976a. *City of pines: The origins of Baguio as a colonial hill station and regional capital.* Research Monograph No. 13. Berkeley: Center for South and Southeast Asia Studies, University of California.

Reed, R. R. 1976b. Remarks on the colonial genesis of the hill station in Southeast Asia with particular reference to the cities of Buitenzorg (Bogor) and Baguio. *Asian Profile* 4:545–91.

Reed, R. R. 1979. The colonial genesis of hill stations: The Genting exception. *The Geographical Review* 69:463–68.

Reeves, P., F. Broeze, and K. McPherson. 1989. Studying the Asian port city. In *Brides of the sea: Port cities of Asia from the 16th–20th Centuries,* edited by F. Broeze. Honolulu: University of Hawaii Press, pp. 29–53.

Renbourne, E. T. 1963. Seasoning fluxes and fevers of acclimatization: An introduction to the history of tropical adaptation. *The Journal of Tropical Medicine and Hygiene* 66:193–203.

Reuters News Service. 1994.

Saini, N. S. 1964. Mussoori: Study of a resort town. Thesis for the Post-Graduate Diploma in Town and Country Planning. New Delhi: Department of Town and Country Planning, School of Planning and Architecture (typescript).

Sasikumar, S. 1967. Study of resort towns: Coonoor (Madras State). Summer Study Report in Planning. New Delhi: Department of Town and Country Planning, School of Planning and Architecture (typescript).

Sauveplane, J. 1942. La cité 'Admiral-Jean-Decoux': Dalat, 1942. *Indochine* 94:9–11.

Savage, V. R. 1984. *Western impressions of nature and landscape in Southeast Asia.* Singapore: Singapore University Press.

Senftleben, W. 1973. Some aspects of the Indian hill stations: A contribution towards a geography of tourist traffic. *Philippine Geographical Journal* 17:21–29.

Singh, J. P. 1980. *Urban land use planning in hill areas: A case study of Shillong.* Delhi: Inter-India Publications.

Spencer, J. E., and W. L. Thomas. 1948. The hill stations and summer resorts of the Orient. *The Geographical Review* 38:637–51.

Steinberg, D. J., ed. 1987. *In search of Southeast Asia: A modern history.* 2d ed. rev. Honolulu: University of Hawaii Press.

Taboulet, G. 1956. *La geste Française en Indochine.* Vol. 2. Paris: Adrien-Maisonneuve.

Tardif, E. 1949. *La naissance de Dalat (Annam), 1899–1900 (capitale de l'Indochine, 1946).* Vienne: Editions Ternet-Martin.

Tate, D. J. M. 1971. *The making of modern South-East Asia: Volume one, the European conquest.* London: Oxford University Press.

Tessan, F. de. 1923a. Une station d'altitude en Indochine: a 250 kilomètres au nord est de Saïgon. *l'Illustration* 4172:156–59.

Tessan, F. de. 1923b. Une station d'altitude: le Langbian. In *Dans l'Asie que s'éveille: essais Indochinois,* Chap. 9. Paris: La Renaissance du Livre.

Teston, E., and M. Percheron. 1932. *L'Indochine moderne: encyclopédie administrative, touristique, artistique et économique.* Paris: Librairie de France.

Thrift, N., and D. Forbes. 1986. *The price of war: Urbanization in Vietnam, 1954–1985.* London: Allen and Unwin.

Tran, V. T. 1941. *Les chemins de fer de L'Indochine.* Paris: Librairie L. Rodstein.

Truong, P. A., and N. Diep. 1993. *A hundred years history of Dalat.* Dalat: Dalattourist (Lam Dong Combined Culture Company).

Voon, P. K., and S. H. Khoo. 1980. Upland development and settlement in Malaysia. *Malaysian Journal of Tropical Geography* 1:43–56.

Ward, R. D. C. 1931. *The acclimatization of the white race in the tropics.* Annual Report of the Board of Regents of the Smithsonian Institution. Washington, D.C.: Government Printing Office.

Wright, G. 1991. *The politics of design in French colonial urbanism.* Chicago and London: The University of Chicago Press.

CHAPTER 5

Some Issues of Fixed Cultivation and Sedentarization of Ethnic Minority People in Mountainous Areas of Vietnam

Le Duy Hung
Department for Fixed Cultivation and Settlement, Hanoi

GENERAL BACKGROUND

Mountainous areas of the Socialist Republic of Vietnam, which are the home of most ethnic minorities in the country, possess a rich diversity of the many natural resources necessary for regional and national development. Despite this considerable potential, highland societies, cultures, and economies remain comparatively underdeveloped, particularly in areas where minority groups depend on shifting cultivation.

According to recent reports, over 3 million minority people living in the thirty-four mountain provinces of Vietnam are practicing migratory swidden or fixed subsistence agriculture. Each year as many as 100,000 hectares of forests are destroyed for food cultivation, leading to extensive soil erosion and the substantial loss of forest resources. For these and other reasons, biological and landscape protection measures in mountainous areas are seriously needed.

Although not all of this destruction can be attributed to the indigenous minority peoples of the Vietnamese highlands, it cannot be denied that the most populous groups of shifting cultivators are the Hmong (with a population of roughly 520,000), the Dzao (360,000), the Thai (350,000), the Gia Rai (250,000), the Ede (200,000), and the Bana (130,000).[1] In addition, numerous minority groups with populations under 1,000, such as the Brau (only 216), Romam (225), and Ruc (200), continue to practice shifting cultivation. Sadly these latter groups live under very poor conditions and are today in serious danger of extinction as specific cultural groups. Their individual and collective disappearance would represent an irretrievable loss of a rich but localized cultural-ecological heritage.

Each minority group is distinct in its settlement patterns, architecture, cultural traditions, cultivation methods, and social structure. Despite these differences, highland minorities share commonalities in their poor and unstable living conditions, dependence on limited micro-regional resources, and resultant susceptibility to localized famines. In some areas, rice shortages often last three to four months per year. As a result, the incidence of nutrition-related illnesses such as goiter, child malnutrition, and diarrhea remains widespread while diseases such as malaria are endemic.

At present, half of all highland communes are not accessible by road, relying rather on paths and mountain trails. Even today some of these localities are three or four days walking distance from main transport lines. Such isolation has clearly contributed to the preservation of many long-established and perhaps obsolete customs. By the same token, village elders—as representatives of ancient clan lines—are highly respected and exert a powerful conservative influence in the majority of minority communities. As a result, certain archaic customs and persistent superstitions, which seem to have a negative impact on the people's daily life, work, and educational standards, continue to contribute indirectly to the underdevelopment and regional inequalities characteristic of the highlands.

GOVERNMENT POLICIES

The sedentarization of people engaged in migratory shifting cultivation has been supported by a number of (interdependent mutually supportive) state policies since 1968. More recently, it has become a priority in the Vietnamese government's initiatives for socioeconomic development in highland areas. In brief, sedentarization and fixed cultivation policies have been promoted in an effort to:

- substantially increase the participation of ethnic minority people in forest rehabilitation, protection, and replanting campaigns;
- steadfastly assist ethnic minority people in transitioning from unstable, autarkic livelihood strategies dependent on swidden to stable, diversified strategies of integrated bio-agricultural commodity production; and
- help promote the development and modernization of rural-mountainous areas, eradicating poverty, famine, diseases, and illiteracy even while attempting to preserve unique and highly valued ethnic characteristics.

Sedentarization and transition to fixed cultivation provide an effective means of protecting Vietnam's remaining forest resources, creating favorable conditions for local people to replant the forests on barren lands, and using highland resources sustainably, appropriately, and effectively.

PROGRAM IMPLEMENTATION

The program for fixed cultivation and sedentarization is a comprehensive socioeconomic development scheme for ethnic minority people carried out through small-scale projects at the commune level. Specific projects seek to create conditions for sustainable development and have been oriented toward a combination of agriculture and forestry in accordance with local ecological conditions. Projects are conceived at the village level with households operating as autonomous economic units. The allocation of lands and forest management contracts are thus granted to households in conjunction with the selection of local project officers charged with monitoring the implementation of project guidelines. State funds are channeled to the projects as direct cash payments or interest-free loans to households contracted for protection and restoration of forests, management of afforestation areas, and care of windbreaks. Assistance is also given to households reclaiming new lands or preparing paddy fields for intensive permanent cultivation. If households elect to participate in a fixed cultivation and sedentarization project, they must move to a project site. They are then given a six-month supply of food, compensation for moving costs, and essential funds for home construction. Interest-free loans are also provided to households involved in the cultivation of industrial crops, traditional specialty products, fruit trees, or raising improved animal breeds.

Households that have been contracted to oversee an area of protection forest are paid for their services and are authorized to collect secondary forest products. A maximum of 30 hectares of protected or special-use forest can be allocated to individual households. Where protected or special-use forests remain unavailable for assignment, households can also be employed to manage barren lands in preparation for reforestation. Each household contracted to manage protection forest, special-use forest, or barren land also receives 1 hectare for the production of grain, 1 hectare for tree crops, and one-half hectare for home gardens.

At the community level, funds are allocated for the construction of roads, schools, health-care stations, water supply systems, irrigation infrastructure, and hydropower development. Efforts are made by the authorities to support communities through a variety of extension services, including the application of agricultural and forestry research through assistance in selecting high-yielding cultivars (both local and improved) suitable to local ecological conditions, adoption of the latest scientific and technological advances for the production and processing of agricultural and forest commodities, and construction of model farms.

PROGRAM RESULTS

During the past twenty-five years of program implementation, deforestation in project areas has generally diminished or stopped while the highland minorities themselves have been increasingly integrated into the national society through better roads, modern education, improved health care, and ongoing cultural exchange. Since inception of the program, as many as 660,000 people in some 378 project communes have ceased practicing shifting cultivation and have taken up fixed cultivation. Forests in these areas are no longer destroyed for food crop production. Rather, 47,000 hectares of new forest has been planted in such project areas. In addition, 70,900 hectares of industrial tree plantations[2] and 140,000 hectares of permanent food crop land have been established. In many sites, the local economy has passed from one in which production was largely for subsistence use to one in which households engage in production for sale on commodity markets, a process of transformation due in part to the construction of road access to project sites. All project sites have schools, health stations, and safe water supplies, and in many, small-scale hydropower generators supply electricity for lighting. Social centers or culture houses provide opportunities for the organization of ethnic dance and visual arts groups. Finally, tens of thousands of local cadres have been trained in management techniques or have taken part in study tours to enrich their experience and gain new knowledge.

Successful projects exist in every highland province. Khoc Lo village in Via Son commune, Yen Bai province, provides a case in point. This village of 500 people in 81 households has planted 200 hectares of cinnamon. Villagers are able to harvest 17 tons of dried cinnamon bark from this area annually. Income from the sale of cinnamon has had a beneficial effect on the community. Currently, 30 percent of the households are considered wealthy by local standards while 70 percent possess a radio and television and 40 percent own a motorbike or live in a two-story house.

Examples of failed projects also exist. Cao Thuong, a Hmong village in Cao Bang province, provides a clear illustration of such failures. In an effort to settle this population of shifting cultivators, 200 hectares of swidden fields were converted to pine tree cultivation and an additional 100 hectares were planted in *mu* oil trees. The project seemed successful, but because of high transport fees for products obtained from these plantations, villagers decided to cut the trees for fuel and use the land for food crop cultivation.

PROGRAM COST

The program for fixed cultivation and sedentarization is financed by the state through its annual plan. The Department of Fixed Cultivation and Sedentarization submits approved projects to the state annually. When assessing a proposed project for submission to the state, the department director takes into account both the state's contribution and the contribution of local people. In most cases, this will be a labor contribution rather than a financial one. According to national policy, the state's contribution for fixed cultivation and sedentarization projects will not exceed 20 million *dong* (US$2,000) per household. Half of this investment must go to households for use in increasing production capacity. The remainder is invested, as necessary, in infrastructure improvement, social welfare services, and moving costs. These finances are allocated through the state planning system. The Ministry of Finance then disburses authorized funds through its provincial offices to local project directors.

PROGRAM BENEFITS AND CONSTRAINTS

Successful extension of the program for fixed cultivation and sedentarization will result in the settlement of 3 million people and the end of forest destruction due to shifting cultivation in highland areas. The output per capita of highland people will increase through the development of agroforestry, allowing for increased incomes, opportunities for local self-development and participation in mainstream society. Forest coverage will gradually increase from 9 or 10 percent to between 25 and 40 percent, depending on the region, by the year 2000.

Despite sustained efforts by national and regional authorities, the pace of program implementation over recent years has been somewhat slow and limited in scale. For the most part, projects have focused on those communes that are either easily accessible by road or whose products can be sold on commodity markets. Progress in more remote localities has been limited. In part, this simply results from problems of access. Projects can only be initiated where conditions for their successful implementation prevail. But the limited reach of fixed cultivation and sedentarization projects has also been due to a number of cultural features. Vietnamese minority groups are diverse, each with its own psychological features, traditions, material inheritance, and cultural practices. For many, current states of extreme backwardness require tremendous efforts and financial inputs to improve their socioeconomic situation. Our earlier awareness of the problem, which did not adequately comprehend these complexities and difficulties, assumed that socioeconomic change could be completed in a few years. As a result, the institutional and financial frameworks for projects were too often too short and too underfunded.

CONTINUING NEEDS

Despite the numerous achievements of this sedentarization program, the number of shifting cultivators still remains quite large (over one million) and most live in fairly disadvantaged communities situated in geographically remote localities. Among those who have been resettled, 70 percent require continued and substantial state support. Unfortunately, government inputs into the program are quite limited and are likely to continue to be so in the foreseeable future. As a result of severely limited financial resources, national officials remain unable to expand the program's outreach while still maintaining previously resettled communities. To expand this effort in settling shifting cultivators, protecting remaining forests and transforming highland societies, Vietnam will require the sustained support of international teams of scientists, foreign governments, and NGOs.

NOTES

1. Data and case studies presented in this chapter are drawn from documents of the Department of Fixed Cultivation and Sedentarization.
2. Coffee, tea, cinnamon, cashew, star anise, and various tropical fruits.

CHAPTER 6

Hydro Versus Gas—Getting It Right: Implications for Highland Developments in Vietnam

Charles J. Johnson
Program on Resources: Energy and Minerals, East-West Center, Honolulu

INTRODUCTION

Economic reforms since the late 1980s have put Vietnam on a high economic growth path with GDP now growing at about 8 percent per year. Electricity consumption is growing at an average of about 10 percent per year, but could increase to 12–15 percent per year during the last half of the 1990s.[1] The energy sector is expected to remain a leading sector for foreign investments and multilateral bank loans over the next decade. The government can save hundreds of millions of dollars by ensuring that the most economic projects are developed first, and then moving to higher cost energy options. In addition, some of the higher cost energy options have substantial environmental and social costs that need more attention.

RESOURCE POTENTIAL

Map 6.1 shows the distribution of energy resources in Vietnam. At least two-thirds of Vietnam's hydropower potential is located in the north along with over 90 percent of the coal potential. At least two-thirds of the natural gas and oil potential is located offshore in the south.

Historically, the Vietnamese government has given priority to hydropower projects and coal-fired power plants, most of which are located in the north. The largest power project in the country is the recently completed 1,920 MW Hoa Binh hydropower plant. Excess electricity from the Hoa Binh plant is now being transferred to the south over the recently completed 1,400-km north-south electricity transmission line.

ELECTRICITY FORECASTS

Hanoi and Ho Chi Minh city are Vietnam's two main demand centers for electricity, with limited demand in the middle of the country. The combination of widely separated electricity demand centers (separated by 1,400 kilometers) and uneven distribution of energy resources complicates long-term energy planning in Vietnam.

Electricity generating capacity is projected to grow at 8–10 percent per year over the 1995–2010 period. Assuming an average of 9.0 percent per year growth, capacity will increase from approximately 3,700 MW at the beginning of 1995 to 13,500 MW in 2010.

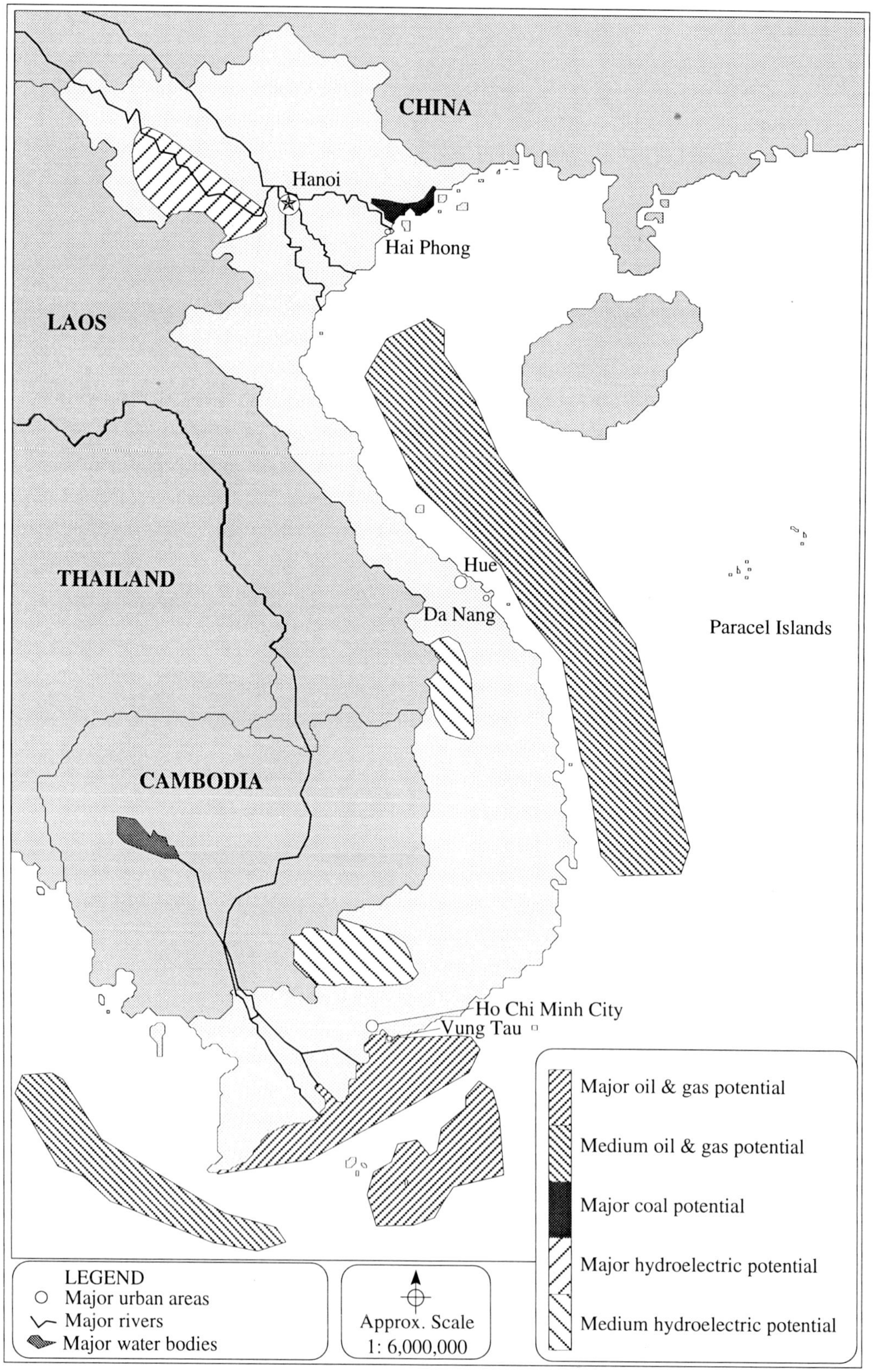

Map 6.1 Distribution of Vietnam's major energy resources

HYDROPOWER POTENTIAL

Vietnam has ambitious plans to rapidly expand its electricity generating capacity to meet the projected high growth in demand. Hydropower potential could be as high as 10,000–15,000 MW; however, 5,000 to 7,500 MW appears to be a more plausible range for development over the 1995–2010 period. Hydropower projects have the following three primary purposes: to meet future electricity demand, to control periodic flooding, and to provide water for the agriculture sector.

The problem with hydropower projects is that capital costs are much higher than for gas-fired plants, and the construction period is two to three times longer.

HYDROPOWER AND COAL

Historically, the two main domestic energy resources were hydropower and anthracite coal. Due to a combination of technical and management problems, coal has had difficulty competing with hydropower. To date, coal's place in Vietnam's energy mix has been assured by the characteristics of hydropower. Due to annual variations in river volumes and the limited storage capacity of dams, back-up coal or diesel capacity is necessary for the dry periods when hydropower plants have to reduce their electricity output by more than 50 percent in some cases.

NATURAL GAS POTENTIAL

Since 1988, active oil exploration has resulted in the discovery of large amounts of natural gas (gas). The technical and economic problems in developing gas markets are much greater than for oil. Companies are cautious in announcing proven gas reserves, prior to concluding secure agreements with the government on terms and conditions for developing gas discoveries. Given these reservations, Figure 6.1 shows estimates of gas reserves and total gas potential based on discussions with petroleum company geologists and exploration results to date. As shown in Figure 6.1, reserves are in the range of 6 trillion cubic feet (tcf), far below the potential of 10 to 30 tcf. For long-term energy planning purposes, 15–20 tcf is suggested as reasonable at the present stage of exploration. For comparison purposes, a combined cycle 1,000 MW power plant consumes about 0.8–1.0 tcf of gas over the life of the power plant.

Domestic gas demand, including demand from the electricity sector, is very difficult to estimate at the present early stage of development of the market. A medium–high estimate of gas demand is 5–10 tcf over the next 20 years, well below the likely gas potential. Therefore, exports of gas appear likely to the energy-deficient market in Thailand and perhaps to southern China.

HYDROPOWER VERSUS GAS

Preliminary financial analyses of hydropower versus gas-fired power plants have shown that electricity from gas-fired power plants is likely to have lower total costs than the majority of the hydropower projects in Vietnam. Hydropower developments have numerous technical, financial, and social risk factors that require careful examination prior to commitments to these projects. Gas developments take two to four years and can often be

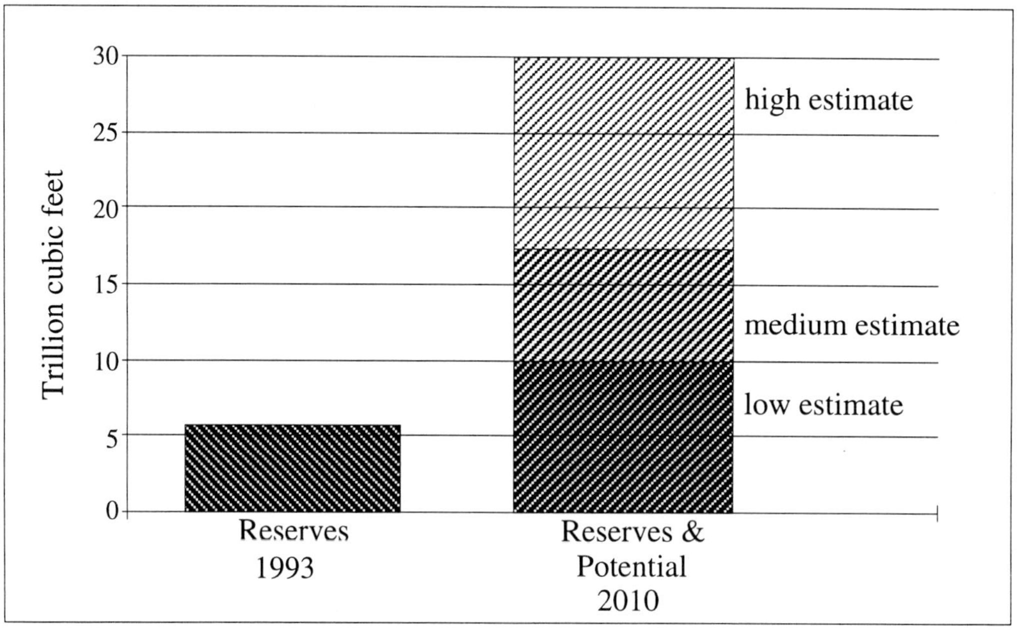

Figure 6.1 Vietnam's gas potential

fully financed with private capital. In contrast, large hydropower developments require construction periods of six to nine years and usually require major government financial commitments and loan guarantees.

The optimal energy mix strategy should be the result of careful and consistent financial and economic analyses of the major energy options. It is essential to use discount rates that reflect the true cost of capital to the government—a minimum rate of 10 percent and probably higher. Low discount rates, as used in the past, will encourage investment in capital-intensive projects with long construction periods (i.e., hydropower).

Figure 6.2 shows a comparison between gas and hydropower for electricity generation. In Figure 6.2, hydropower projects are the lowest cost option when the cost of natural gas and the capital costs of hydropower intersect above the diagonal line. Conversely, hydropower projects are the lowest cost option for intersections below the line. Most hydropower projects in Vietnam are expected to cost more than $1,100/kW.

In Figure 6.2 it can be seen that gas is competitive with $1,100/kW hydropower up to about $3.40/1000 cubic feet of gas. The costs of supplying large quantities of natural gas to southern Vietnam is between $2.00 and $3.00/1000 cubic feet; therefore, natural gas is likely to be the lowest cost option in southern Vietnam. The costs of gas supplies in the north are more speculative but may be in the range of $2.50–$3.50/1000 cubic feet. It is possible that the existing north-south transmission line could be used in the future to transfer electricity from the south to the north.

The available information on costs of electricity supplies from hydropower, gas, and coal suggests that the lowest cost and less risky development strategy is to accelerate gas

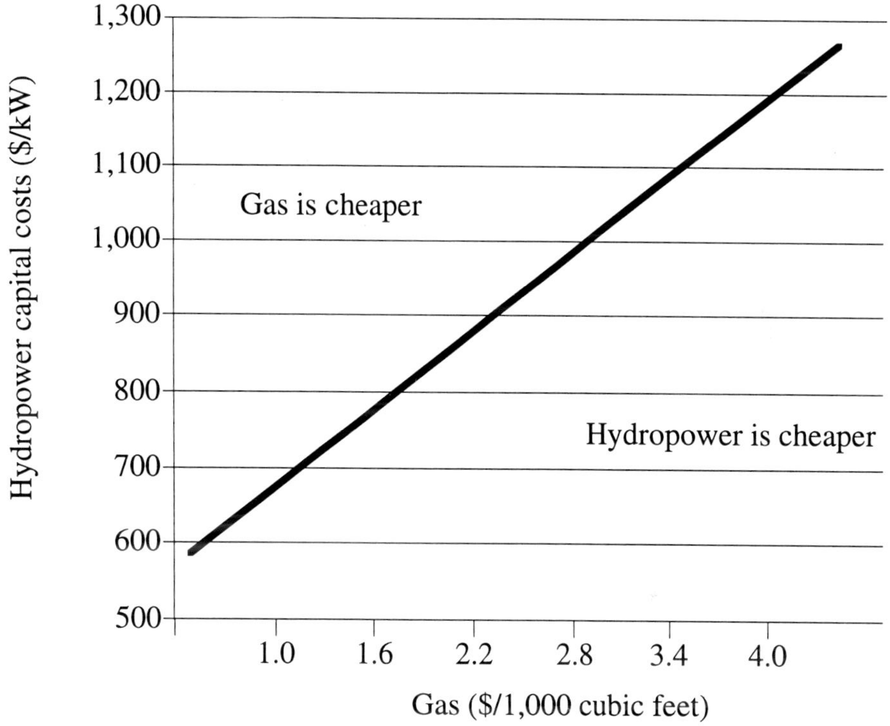

Figure 6.2 Comparison of the total costs per kWh for a hydroelectric versus a gas-fired plant

developments in the early years (1995–2005), and phase in higher cost, higher risk hydropower projects gradually (2005–15).

IMPLICATIONS FOR THE HIGHLAND AREAS

Highland areas can benefit substantially from a shift toward greater emphasis on gas. The extra five to ten years of breathing space before commitments to the larger hydropower developments provide time to fully evaluate the technical aspects of hydropower developments (including rates of siltation of reservoirs) and to examine options to reduce the social problems associated with displaced communities.

A "gas first" strategy gives government more time to consult with the impacted communities and to develop strategies to minimize the long-term disruptive social impacts of large hydropower developments.

It is recognized that hydropower projects have a role to play in meeting Vietnam's electricity needs over the long term. Vietnam has the advantage of multiple energy options that, if carefully developed using sound financial and economic analysis, can provide greater economic and social benefits to the nation and reduce unintended environmental and social damages.

NOTE

1. Much of the information in this chapter has been abstracted from the author's chapter, "Vietnam's Energy Sector" in *In Search of the Dragon's Trail: Economic Reform in Vietnam*, edited by D. Dapice, D. Perkins, and J. Haughton. Boston: Harvard Institute for International Development, forthcoming.

PART THREE

Developing Human Resources

CHAPTER 7

Activities of the Agricultural University No. 3 in the Development of the Northern Highlands of Vietnam

Nguyen Khanh Quac, Tu Quang Hien, Hoang Van Phu
Agricultural University No. 3, Bac Thai Province, Vietnam

BRIEF HISTORY

Agricultural University No. 3 (AU3), located in Thai Nguyen, the administrative capital of Bac Thai province, was established by the Ministry of Agriculture in 1960 as a three-year college offering degrees in agriculture and forestry. In 1970, it was declared a university by the Ministry of Education and Training. With this change in status, its duties were expanded to include the training of professionals in animal husbandry, silvaculture, and agricultural economics, agricultural research, and the transfer of new agricultural and silvacultural technologies into production throughout the midland and mountainous regions of northern Vietnam. In 1993, the university launched a graduate degree program offering a Master's degree in crop production, animal husbandry, and agricultural economics.

At present, AU3 has 181 lecturers[1] and 148 service staff working in five faculties (Basic Science and Part-time Training, Crop Production, Animal Husbandry and Veterinary Medicine, Agricultural Economics, and Forestry), two research centers (Agro-forestry Research and Development Center for the Northern Mountain Region and the Mountain Resource and Environment Center), and an experimental farm.

CONSTRAINTS ON DEVELOPMENT IN THE NORTHERN MOUNTAINOUS REGION

General Characteristics

The Northern Mountainous Region (NMR) consists of thirteen provinces, covering approximately 102,937 square kilometers, or 31.1 percent of the national territory of Vietnam. It is divided into two ecological zones, the highlands (including Lai Chau, Son La, Hoa Binh, Yen Bai, Lao Cai, Ha Giang, Tuyen Quang, Cao Bang, Lang Son, Bac Thai, and Quang Ninh provinces) and the midlands (including Vinh Phu and Ha Bac provinces). The population of the NMR is about 11.2 million (16.9 percent of Vietnam's population), of which about 5 million (45 percent) are ethnic minority peoples (General Statistical Office 1992). Tables 7.1, 7.2, and 7.3 present background data on ecological and social characteristics of the NMR.

Climate In general, the region has a tropical monsoon climate with high summer temperatures and humidity. The average yearly temperature ranges between 21°C and 27°C. In the winter, however, prevailing cold winds from southeast China lower tempera-

Table 7.1 Comparison of highland resources, Vietnam and the NMR

	The Highlands of Vietnam		Northern Mountainous Region			
			Northern Mountains		Northern Midlands	
	Total	% of nation	Total	% of highlands	Total	% of highlands
Area (1,000 ha)	23,930.0	72.4	8,890.9	37.1	1,373.2	5.7
Total number of districts	249.0	47.5	99.0	39.7	35.0	14.0
Mountain districts	62.0	–	38.0	61.2	–	–
Total pop. (millions)	19.0	29.5	6.3	37.1	3.9	20.5
Labor force (millions)	7.0	26.5	2.6	37.1	1.6	22.8
Ag. land (1,000 ha)	5,360.0	–	1,688.2	31.5	561.9	10.4
Cultivated (1,000 ha)	3,484.0	–	1,172.2	33.6	436.4	12.5
Upland rice (1,000 ha)	537.7	25.3	217.4	37.9	67.4	12.5
Double rice (1,000 ha)	766.1	23.3	122.8	16.0	127.5	27.3
Field crops (1,000 ha)	1,427.7	95.0	164.5	11.5	180.1	12.6
Perm. crops (1,000 ha)	510.0	59.0	98.3	19.2	55.3	10.8
Grasslands (1,000 ha)	297.7	92.3	183.4	61.6	23.7	6.6
Arable land not in use (1,000 ha)	1,876.0	74.8	518.0	27.6	125.0	10.9
Designated forest land (1,000 ha)	8,160.3	83.5	1,734.4	21.2	890.0	4.7
Percent forest coverage	29.2	–	20.5	–	20.1	–

Source: Xuan (1992).

Table 7.2 Land distribution in Bac Thai, Cao Bang, and Lang Son provinces, 1992

	Bac Thai		Cao Bang		Lang Son	
	Total	% of total	Total	% of total	Total	% of total
Total area (km^2)	6,502.90		8,444.60		8,167.20	
Agriculture (1,000 ha)	117.80	100.00	70.16	100.0	95.48	100.0
Rice (1,000 ha)	50.00	42.44	28.46	40.6	37.79	39.6
Field crops (1,000 ha)	33.00	28.01	27.69	39.5	13.41	14.1
Fruit trees (1,000 ha)	11.00	9.34	0.65	0.9	16.85	17.7
Ponds (1,000 ha)	1.40	1.19	–	–	0.69	0.7
Pasture (1,000 ha)	12.20	10.36	12.29	17.5	16.99	17.8
Potential (1,000 ha)	10.20	8.66	1.07	1.5	9.74	10.2
Forest land (1,000 ha)	404.00	100.00	565.50	100.0	634.06	100.0
Forested (1,000 ha)	196.20	48.56	185.00	32.7	142.62	22.5
Coverage (%)	< 19.00	–	< 17.00	–	< 17.00	–
Reforested (1,000 ha)	6.70	1.66	2.50	0.44	–	–
Non-forested (1,000 ha)	207.83	51.44	380.50	67.3	491.44	77.5
Other (1,000 ha)	160.00		208.81		89.19	

Source: Phu (1993).

tures to between 8°C and 13°C, a condition that seriously affects both crop and animal production.

As with temperatures, rainfall varies with the seasons. Average rainfall in the NMR is between 1,400 and 2,200 mm per year with the rainy season occurring between May and September and the dry season between November and April. Between 75 and 85 percent of total annual precipitation falls in rainy season. The number of wet days ranges from 135

Table 7.3 Population characteristics of Bac Thai, Cao Bang, and Lang Son provinces, 1992

	Bac Thai	Cao Bang	Lang Son
Population (1,000s)	1,060.40	581.20	624.30
Minorities (%)	31.50	95.97	84.75
Kinh (%)	68.50	4.03	15.26
Tay (%)	–	43.86	33.92
Nung (%)	–	32.85	43.86
Dzao (%)	–	10.68	3.54
Other (%)	–	8.40	1.41
Households (1,000s)	253.68	75.34	78.91
Ag. laborers (1,000s)	355.73	215.67	235.05
Ag. Pop. (1,000s)	861.90	531.40	545.50
Urban Pop. (1,000s)	198.50	49.80	78.80
Male (1,000s)	519.60	283.30	304.10
Female (1,000s)	540.80	297.90	320.10
Population growth rate (%)	2.10	2.40	2.30
Population density (person/km^2)	163.00	69.00	76.00

Source: Phu (1993).

to 150 per year (Phu 1993), depending on the province. Water loss by run-off is substantial, particularly on sloping lands, resulting in soil erosion during the rainy season and lack of water in the dry months.

From February to April, cold air from southeastern China interacts with warmer tropical air over the Gulf of Tonkin to produce high humidity and periodic light rains over much of northern Vietnam. While these rains do not generally saturate soils, they provide some water to the uplands during part of the dry season.

Nevertheless, water remains a major limiting factor in agricultural development in the NMR. Lack of water during the dry season generally restricts farmers to the production of only one crop per year.

Soil While the inability to produce a dry season crop is a major factor in the region's characteristically low annual yields, it is not the only factor. The productivity of the region's annual crop is limited by soil fertility as well. Most of the region is covered by ferrilized red or yellow soils with low pH values (pH 4.0–5.5), poor fertility, and comparative low levels of organic matter. These natural conditions, however, have been exacerbated through the inadequate use of soil conservation practices in farming. As a result, at least 78 percent of the steep lands in the NMR have been degraded.

Ecological Problems

Deforestation, soil erosion, and soil degradation are the overriding ecological problems in the NMR. Most inhabitants of the NMR practice mixed swidden or swidden mono-crop subsistence farming. Fires used to clear field plots have destroyed large areas of grassland, natural forest, and forest plantations. As noted, these practices not only result in deforestation but also cause serious problems of soil erosion. The improper use of chemical fertilizers and pesticides has further contributed to ecological difficulties by degrading water supplies for human consumption.

In the past, research for development of the NMR has received low priority, most investigations being concentrated on the varietal adaptation of rice, coffee, and tea, and the application of irrigation methods for high-yield wet rice production in terraces.[2] In almost all the provinces surveyed by Xuan (1992), however, farmers practiced mixed subsistence farming. Upland rice was either directly broadcast or hand planted into furrows. Some farmers then intercropped with corn, peanuts, mung beans, sesame, millet, or cassava. Others mixed cultivated crops with exotic trees (cassava and tea with cinnamon trees)[3] rather than rice.

More recently, government efforts have been concentrated in assisting indigenous people in their traditional practices of mono-cropping upland rice, cassava, yam, sweet potato, peanut, and mung bean. These crops are highly adapted to the climatic and soil conditions of the uplands. At the same time, despite their low output, they meet upland farmers' requirements for self-sufficiency.

As the centrally planned economy has gradually given way to a market economy, the main focus of agricultural production has shifted from cooperatives and state farms to individual farming households. Since 1989, the new policies of agriculture and economic management have given individual land-use rights to farmers. This has, in turn, resulted in higher levels of farm output throughout much of the country. Nevertheless, food production in the NMR is only 198.0 to 238.9 kilograms per person per year (Xuan 1992) and poverty is common. Furthermore, with the break-up of the cooperatives, as every farming family tries to maximize its human and natural resources, resources are being unconsciously, and even intentionally, degraded or destroyed for short-term gain. Hundreds of thousands of hectares of forest have already been lost in this way.

These ecological problems are all the more serious given that the survival of the region's people will continue to depend on the sustainability of agricultural and rural resources for quite some time into the future. Effective management of these resources involves issues related to population growth, poverty, current patterns of resource use, and environmental degradation. Unfortunately, there are indications of unsustainable trends in agricultural and rural development in the NMR. Deforestation, declines in farm production, decreasing bio-diversity, increasing competition in the use of natural resources, and demographic imbalances are all on the rise. If these trends continue unchecked, they will result in increasing poverty, malnutrition, and political instability, with regional and national impacts.

CONSTRAINTS ON HIGHLAND DEVELOPMENT

Socioeconomic Constraints

High population growth rates,[4] health problems, and illiteracy are the main socioeconomic constraints in highland regions, particularly in remote areas. Infrastructure in the uplands is totally inadequate. Roads, health care centers, educational facilities, markets, and communication channels are all poorly developed.

Like the physical characteristics of the region, these social characteristics negatively affect agricultural production. Fertilizers and pesticides, for example, are much more expensive in the highlands than the lowlands. When combined with lack of capital and inadequate knowledge of their appropriate use, highland farmers generally shun them. Rather, they continue with their traditional practices, such as shifting cultivation, which produce reliable but low levels of output at minimum financial cost.

In the past, to stop deforestation due to swidden farming, the government attempted to resettle ethnic communities to lowland areas. It was thought that resettlement to the lowlands, where better irrigation was available, would benefit highlanders since it would enable them to produce more food. This policy did not, however, gain popularity among minority peoples. For a number of reasons, highland minority groups prefer to continue their traditional practices in the environment with which they are familiar over the potential gains in agricultural production possible in the lowlands. More recently, to assist people of the region, the government has subsidized food, capital, and technology and prioritized policies to facilitate highland development *in situ*.

ROLES AND ACTIVITIES OF THE UNIVERSITY IN THE DEVELOPMENT OF VIETNAM'S HIGHLANDS

Labor Force Training

Agricultural University No. 3 is mandated to provide both the region and the nation with high-quality undergraduate and graduate training in agriculture; to promote, undertake, and coordinate research related to the needs and problems of the region, and to disseminate the findings of this research and experimentation. It has carried out this mandate through a variety of long-term, short-term, and part-time training courses, as well as workshops and seminars.

Content of Training The faculty of AU3 have designed training courses with the special natural and social characteristics of the NMR in mind. These include courses in methods to increase crop, animal, and forest yields, methods to organize production for increased efficiency, methods to develop the household economy, methods to protect and improve soil, water, and other natural resources, and agricultural policy analysis.

Students The University has especially focused on training the more promising young people from ethnic minority groups. Since minority students come from the hill and mountain areas, they understand the natural, economic, and social difficulties present in such environments. Their experiences, communicated through such vehicles as short-term training courses, provide essential links between AU3 and local extension workers, technicians, decision makers, and farmers.

Research and Extension Activities

The research and field study activities of AU3 have contributed both to its training and agricultural development missions and its prestige in the region. The University's research activities can be divided into four main groups:

Crop Production Over the years, AU3 has been involved in a variety of efforts aimed at increasing crop production in the NMR. At a regional level, the university has classified lands in the Northern Highlands for specific uses. At the level of individual farms, it has been involved in the selection of crop varieties, research into methods of increasing crop production through integrated pest management, fertilizer use and water management, and investigation into means of reducing erosion. The outgrowth of this research has been the construction of an integrated rural development model. The model, which has been developed with the Vietnamese Farming Systems Network, has produced good results at Trang Xa village, Von Hai district, Bac Thai province.

Animal Husbandry Much of the university's work in animal husbandry has been focused on the improvement of local livestock lines through cross-breeding with exotic varieties. Along with this work, AU3 has introduced methods of artificial insemination and the use of mixed feeds.

Forestry The university has done considerable work in introducing and improving agroforestry, afforestation, and reforestation methods through the use of indigenous species, some exotic species such as eucalyptus and acacia, and in the case of agroforestry, tea. AU3 has also been involved in the allocation of forest land to farmers and communities.

Agricultural Economics Over the years AU3 has been engaged in the field of agricultural economics through analyses of the economic efficiency of particular crops, analyses of the productive efficiency of agricultural households, and the organization of agricultural production and marketing. It has more recently been involved in an analysis of changes in economic policies and their effects on agricultural development in the region.

SUCCESSES AND OBSTACLES

Successes

From the time of its establishment, the university has continued to contribute significantly to the development of its proximate highland region through training and research and extension activities.

Training The university has produced more than 4,700 bachelors in agronomy (crop production, animal husbandry, forestry, and economics). It also provided instruction in SALT (Sloping Lands Agricultural Technology) methods, as well as the organization and management of agricultural production for 600 extension workers and farmers. Additionally AU3 has trained 200 farmers to be agricultural extension workers and produced 85 agricultural accountants.

More recently, AU3 began to systematically update its training courses to match the current situation of market orientation and new economic policies. In addition, formal courses are beginning to include the results of the university's own farming systems research and development experiments. The concepts and practices of sustainable agriculture, with an emphasis on bottom-up approaches, have been of particular importance in the emerging curriculum.

Research and Extension The university has achieved positive results in its research and extension work, experimenting with and introducing high-yielding rice and crop varieties to several nearby highland provinces. With these new crops, AU3 is also attempting new methods of crop production, such as integrated pest management, and soil conservation, such as SALT. Finally, AU3 has been quite involved in developing the agricultural markets needed to distribute surpluses generated by these changes in crops and production techniques.

In the area of forestry, AU3 has been successfully engaged in the allocation of forest land to farmers and farming communities, as well as the introduction of policies of social and community forestry. These policies have had a positive impact on forest conservation efforts throughout the north.

Obstacles

Despite the range of successes with which the university's activities have met, there still remains a number of obstacles. Most farmers in the NMR, for example, hold less than 1 hectare of agricultural land and are barely able to meet their household consumption needs. Agricultural production for the market, apart from occasional surpluses, is largely out of the reach of most cultivators. Yet even if they were able to produce marketable surpluses, infrastructure in the region remains so poor that they would probably be unable to get their excess production to market. At the same time, because highland infrastructure is so badly developed, farmers rarely have access to the agricultural inputs, new technology, and information that could enable them to increase production.

This isolation has had another effect as well. Environmental awareness and an understanding of the need to conserve resources rarely incorporate a larger scientific and geographical context. As such, locally abundant species of plants and animals may be exploited excessively, with no knowledge of overriding conservation issues and ecological linkages to other regions of Vietnam.

In another vein, there is a whole set of obstacles presented by the recent change from centrally planned to market allocation of resources. Since most highlanders have lived in either traditional communities or socialist cooperatives, few possess the skills required for success in market-oriented agricultural management. As the highlands are integrated into the cash economy, those skills will become increasingly important and lack of them will put highlanders at a great disadvantage.

TRAINING AND RESEARCH PLAN

Training

The university's major training goal is to promote the concepts, methodologies, and study materials of sustainable agriculture. AU3 has added courses in sustainable agriculture for rural development to its curriculum. Sustainable agriculture will also be taught in workshops and short training courses, as well as through graduate student research, case study analysis, and lectures by specialists.

Research and Extension

Research for sustainable rural development should be systems-oriented and interdisciplinary. Technical impact assessments must incorporate environmental and sociocultural factors. General systems analysis, agroecosystems analysis, rapid rural appraisal, and economic evaluation are methods that the university will study and disseminate in the region further.

In agricultural extension, AU3 will steadily move to farmer-based approaches. Farmers and communities will be systematically incorporated at all stages of project cycles. Research and extension will seek the integration of technological change and sociocultural continuity. As such, rather than imposing new technologies on highlanders, AU3 will concentrate on introducing and improving highland farmers' traditional technologies.

Some of the research and extension activities proposed or under way by the university are listed below.

- *Crop production*
  Select suitable food crops (rice, corn, beans, etc.), fruit trees (litchi, apricot, small apple, etc.), and green tea varieties for production in the Northern Highlands.
  Research integrated tea production.
  Research and select suitable species for soil cover and reforestation in the Northern Highlands.
  Research limiting factors in rice soil in lowland areas.

- *Animal husbandry*
  Crossbreed Bach Thao and local goat varieties.
  Research the use of artificial insemination in crossing local and exotic cattle for meat production.
  Research the use of artificial insemination in crossing F1 pigs.
  LXDE with F1 breeding line DBxMC.
  Research the production of lean pork for export.

- *Forestry*
  Reclaim degraded forestry through silvacultural practices.
  Research effective policies aimed at the development of agroforestry.
  Research and extend local multipurpose trees in reforestation.

- *Agricultural economics*
  Study effective economic measures and development policies for integrated agroforestry production in Bac Thai.
  Set up agricultural marketing strategies for three tea enterprises in Bac Thai, Tuyen Quang, and Yen Bai provinces.
  Study effects of renovation policies on Vietnamese farmers' living standards.
  Commercialize cassava processing in northern Vietnam.

- *Agroecosystems*
  Construct high productivity agroforestry models for sustainable development in the NMR.
  Research integrated farming systems.
  Improve methods of soil and water conservation.

Study improvement of farmers' traditional practices in highland areas.

Study the physical and sociocultural constraints in technology transfer in the highlands.

INTERNATIONAL COLLABORATION IN THE DEVELOPMENT OF THE NMR

The AU3 has established cooperative programs with several governmental and nongovernmental organizations, universities, and international agencies. These cooperative activities have included both exchanges and research projects.

Exchanges

Annually, the university sends many of its staff abroad to study and attend training courses, workshops, and seminars. In turn, it welcomes many foreign specialists to visit the university and conduct research in the region. AU3 shares research experiences through the exchange of publications and materials with interested parties and agencies.

Joint Research Projects

The highlands of Vietnam are similar to the tropical and sub-tropical highlands of many countries in the Southeast Asian region. Results of scientific work done in Vietnam can thus be tested at other comparable sites. Similarly, research in the uplands of other countries in the region can be tested in Vietnam. Joint research projects offer one means of exchanging such experiences. These projects, however, require the support of international and national funding agencies and research institutions.

Training Exchange

AU3 has been pursuing a goal of being the center for agroforestry science and technology in the NMR. To accomplish this goal, the university has set up the necessary regional, national, and international institutional linkages to continually develop and enrich its agricultural and forestry research programs. The ultimate aim, however, is to help farmers increase their living standards while maintaining and protecting environmental resources.

To attain and maintain this position and this goal will require the efforts of a well-trained staff. The university is interested in developing a joint academic program for Master's and Ph.D. degrees in agriculture and English language training for its staff.

To promote the functions of the university will require further strengthening of existing institutional linkages and creation of new ones among regional, national, and international institutions.

NOTES

1. A total of 20 percent hold a Ph.D. or M.S. degree.
2. Compared with lowland rice yield in terraces, which yield between 3.0 and 5.0 tons per hectare per year, upland wet rice yields appear low, between 0.7 and 1.5 tons per hectare per year. These low annual yields are partly due, however, to climatic factors. Due to a lack of irrigation water in the dry season, only one crop of wet rice, which yields 2.5 to 3.0 tons per hectare, is produced each year (Phu 1993).

3. In Bac Thai, Quang Ninh, and Lang Son provinces.

4. About 2.4 percent per year (General Statistical Office 1992).

BIBLIOGRAPHY

Anon. 1985. *Annual report.* Agricultural University No. 3. Thai Nguyen, Bac Thai: Authors.

Anon. 1990. *Annual report.* Agricultural University No. 3. Thai Nguyen, Bac Thai: Authors.

Anon. 1993. *Annual report.* Agricultural University No. 3. Thai Nguyen, Bac Thai: Authors.

General Statistical Office. 1992. *Statistical data of the Socialist Republic of Vietnam.* Hanoi: Statistical Publishing House.

IBSRAM. 1990. Work progress in Vietnam. In *Management of sloping lands for sustainable agriculture in Asia.* Asialand annual report. Chang Mai, Thailand: Authors.

Phu H. V. 1993. Evaluation of cropping systems on sloping lands in the Northern Mountainous Region of Vietnam. M.S. thesis. Chiang Mai University, Thailand.

Xuan V. T. 1992. Upland farming systems development in Vietnam. In *Report of the regional expert consultation on farming systems development in upland areas.* RAPA report 1991/23. Chiang Mai, Thailand.

Xuan V. T. 1993. Agricultural extension in Vietnam: Gaps and needs. In *Proceedings of the first Southeast Asian workshop on the formulation on technology transfer on major food crops production.* University of Agriculture and Forestry, Thu Duc, Ho Chi Minh city.

PART FOUR

Approaches to Sustainable Development

CHAPTER 8

Biodiversity Conservation and Sustainable Land Use in the Da River Watershed

Le Trong Cuc

Center for Natural Resources and Environmental Studies, Hanoi University

The Da River watershed is a mountainous area extending from the fringes of the Red River Delta well into China. Due to the great diversity of ecological conditions prevailing in this watershed area, its biological and cultural diversity is quite pronounced. Such cultural, environmental, and biological complexity has resulted in considerable variation in land-use practices. This paper will examine these practices as they relate to biodiversity conservation.

BIOPHYSICAL CHARACTERISTICS

The Da River watershed, located between 20°37' and 22°49' latitude and 102°11' and 105°25' longitude, occupies most of Lai Chau and Son La provinces, one district in Lao Cai province, two districts in Yen Bai province, and portions of Hoa Binh (Map 8.1). The watershed is bounded on the north by China and the west by Laos.

Topography

The topography of the area is oriented northwest to southeast. A limestone karst range runs through the center. There are numerous river valleys, formed by secondary and tertiary streams, where the majority of the regional population is located. The limestone mountains are sometimes isolated and surrounded by irrigated rice fields. The Hoang Lien Son mountain range in the east, with peaks greater than 3,000 meters above sea level, is sharply dissected with slopes over 45 degrees. On average, however, more than 50 percent of the area is between 800 and 2,000 meters above sea level, with slopes ranging between 30 and 35 degrees. Slopes below 700 or 800 meters, adjacent to the river valleys, are frequently used for cultivation.

Climate

The territory drained by the Da River is influenced mainly by a tropical monsoon climate. But because of geography and the diversity of relief, it also displays several somewhat unique climatic patterns. Since the Hoang Lien Son range effectively bars the northeast monsoon, which brings continental winds from southeast China during the winter, the cold season in the Da River watershed is somewhat warmer than in the nearby Northeastern Highlands. In the early summer the annual wind reversal of the southwest monsoon

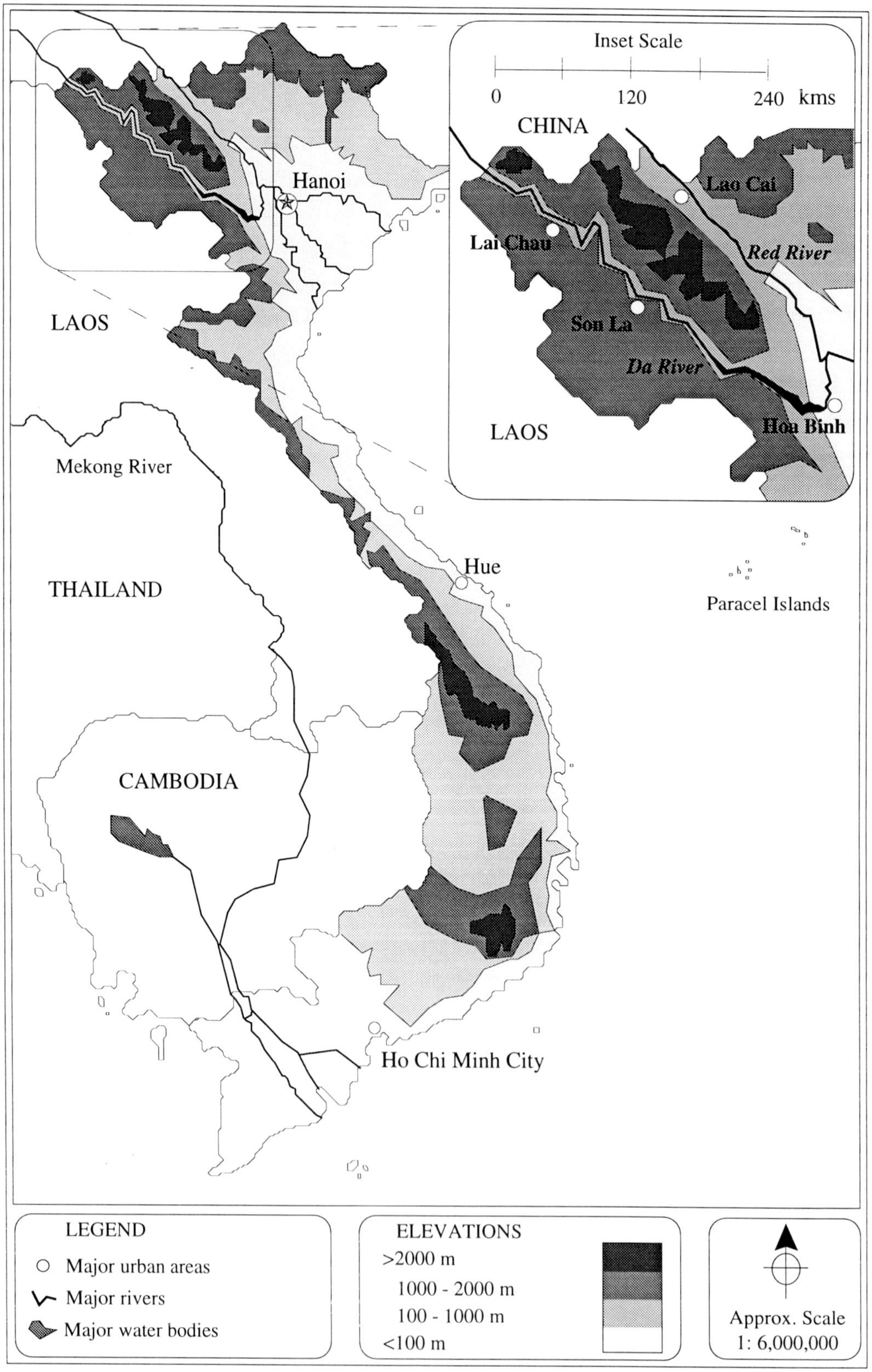

Map 8.1 The Da River watershed

brings hot and dry weather as it bridges the high mountain ranges of upper Laos, creating a localized rain shadow.

Predictably temperature depends heavily on elevation. In general, the mean annual temperature in the region at elevations of less than 700 meters ranges from 20 to 23°C; between 1,500 and 1,600 meters, it is around 16°C; and at greater than 1,600 meters, the temperature always remains less than 16°C.

Annual average rainfall within the watershed varies between 1,300 mm and 3,600 mm, increasing from west to east and from south to north. The rainy season lasts for six or seven months, from April to September or October, with the amount of rain falling in the rainy season equal to more than 90 percent of total annual rainfall in the north and over 85 percent in the south.

Soil

Most soil in the Da River watershed has been transformed through ongoing processes of ferralization, but with decreasing impact at higher elevations. As a result, the majority of soils are quite acidic and have very low nutrient content. Still the amount of humus generally increases with altitude. This is due to the increased likelihood of forest cover on slopes situated at higher elevations.

According to the National Institute of Agricultural Planning and Projection (NIAPP), there are twenty-one types of soil in the region defined by the Da River, eighteen of which are located on slopes of more than 25°. But in general the soils prevailing in this watershed can be divided into six major types. These are, as follows:

- *Red yellow soil and red humic soil on claystone and metamorphic rocks.* These soils are formed on steep slopes, are strongly weathered, and have a loamy to clay loam texture. Soil depth usually exceeds 50 cm. Soil fertility remains poor (pH 4.0–4.5). Widely distributed in territories along the course of the Da River and its tributaries, these soils cover about 42 percent of the total area of the watershed.
- *Lightly yellow soil and lightly yellow humic soil on sandstone.* Soils of this sort are formed mainly on steep slopes and display a loamy to sandy loam texture. The fertility of such soil is low (pH 4.0–4.5). Quite significant in terms of area and broad distribution, such soils cover about 27 percent of the total watershed.
- *Yellow red humic soil on acid magma* is found mainly in the highly mountainous areas that define the upper reaches of the Da River domain. They have sandy loam texture with a soil depth of around 50 cm. Such soil is low in potassium and phosphorus and moderate in humus and nitrogen content. This soil covers approximately 15 percent of the total watershed area.
- *Brown red soils and brown red humic soils on limestone* are found mainly below 900 meters above sea level.
- *Alluvial soils* are distributed on lower hillsides. They have a sandy loam texture and are moderately fertile.

- *Soil formed under irrigated rice cultivation* is found on impounded terraces. This soil has a clayey texture and moderate-to-high fertility.

Today agricultural land occupies 9.4 percent of the watershed area. Yet only 64 percent of the land suitable for agriculture is in use. Production remains divided among wet rice (17 percent), upland rice (36.4 percent), short-term industrial and food crops (40.2 percent), long-term industrial crops (4.8 percent), pasture (0.7 percent), and water surfaces (0.9 percent).

DEMOGRAPHY

According to the national census of 1989, the total population living in the watershed of the Da River was 973,282. The density of population was 37 persons per square kilometer and human distribution remained uneven. Predictably the highest population densities are to be found along Highway 6, the main road. In general, however, higher population densities are associated with the presence of irrigated lands.

Some twenty-three ethnic groups live in the watershed area (Table 8.1). The greatest diversity of ethnic communities can be found in Lai Chau province, home to over seventeen different groups. The main peoples here are Thai (42.5 percent), Kinh (18 percent),

Table 8.1 Ethnic composition of the Da River watershed

Ethnic group	Total	Percent
Thai	410,361	42.53
Kinh	174,344	18.07
Hmong	170,609	17.68
Muong	93,146	9.65
Dzao	47,273	4.90
Tay	12,916	1.34
Ha Nhi	9,874	1.02
Xa	8,947	0.93
Giay	6,786	0.70
Kho Mu	6,421	0.67
Sinh Mun	6,046	0.63
La Hu	5,297	0.55
Lu	3,808	0.39
Xi Mang U	3,334	0.35
Khang	1,618	0.17
Lao	1,326	0.14
Hoa	1,139	0.12
Coong	840	0.09
Xa Phang	810	0.08
Nung	19	0.0020
Ta Oi	14	0.0015
Lo Lo	9	0.0009
Puoc	–	–
Total	964,937	100.00

Source: Central Census Steering Committee (1991).

Hmong (17.7 percent), Muong (9.7 percent), and Dzao (4.9 percent). Together these five ethnic groups comprise 92.8 percent of the whole population of Lai Chau.

The Thai, with a population of 410,361, are the largest ethnic group in the watershed of the Da. They migrated to northwestern Vietnam from southwestern China some 700 to 800 years ago. The Thai are divided among a number of sub-groupings, the two main ethnic communities being the Black Thai and the White Thai. Thai farmers have usually settled in fertile valleys where they practice wet rice cultivation. Other crops include corn, cassava, sweet potato, squash, beans, cotton, and indigo. The Thai are skilled weavers, and they also practice sericulture in many places. About three-fourths of the Thai population in the Da River watershed live in Son La province.

The Kinh, with a population of 174,344, comprise the second largest group in the watershed area. They are concentrated in the provincial capitals of Son La and Lai Chau, as well as in the areas with state or provincial agricultural and forestry enterprises. Most are migrants from the Red River Delta—especially from populous provinces like Thai Binh—who have participated in resettlement schemes to develop upland areas.

The Hmong are said to have started an ongoing emigration from southern China to Vietnam some 300 years ago, with the bulk of their migration occurring within the past 200 years. There are 170,609 Hmong people concentrated in the higher mountains and most isolated parts of the region. The Hmong in Vietnam are divided into five sub-groups: Black Hmong, White Hmong, Red Hmong, Blue Hmong, and Flowered Hmong. All are well known for their practice of swidden, or shifting cultivation, in hill-slope situations. Their main crops and food staples are corn and rice, but opium poppies are also grown during the winter. In 1993, government authorities attempted to destroy all the poppy fields, which were to be replaced by locally appropriate cropping combinations of maize, sugarcane, groundnut, and fruit trees.

There are 93,146 Muong in Da River watershed. The majority are concentrated in the southern part of the riverine basin. The Muong are said to be related to the Kinh in terms of their place of origin and language, and to the Thai in their cultural and social features. While the Muong prefer irrigated rice agriculture, they also practice upland cultivation through systems of shifting cultivation.

The Dzao are said to be similar to the Hmong, not only belonging to the same language group, but, through intermarriage, to the same clans. There are some 47,273 Dzao spread throughout the highland and midland areas of the Da River watershed. They generally practice a rotating field form of swidden farming, although some Dzao groups also cultivate paddy in areas where the construction of irrigated fields is possible. The staple crops are upland rice, maize, and cassava.

Concentrations of other ethnic minorities may be found in specific localities. For example, more than 12,916 Tay people are living in Da Bac district, Hoa Binh province.

LAND USE

Land use within the watershed is divided into forest and agricultural categories (Table 8.2).

Forest Land

Total land area of the Da River watershed is about 2,606,500 hectares, of which 2,261,909 hectares (or 86.7 percent) is classified as forest land. Only 282,296 hectares (10.7 percent) of the total amount of land classified for use as forest land is actually covered with some type of forest. The remaining 1,979,573 hectares (76 percent), classified as non-forested forest land, is covered with grass, shrubs, and scattered trees, or is under cultivation.

Agricultural Land

The 150,374 hectares of land within the watershed designated for agricultural production are divided into four sub-groups. Approximately 93,581 hectares of sloping land (61 percent of the total agricultural land) presently serve for the production of secondary food crops such as maize, upland rice, and cassava. Another 48,032 hectares (32 percent) are utilized for the production of irrigated rice; some 3,686 hectares (2.5 percent) have been earmarked for industrial crops; and at least 7,075 hectares (4.5 percent) are assigned as grazing lands. No agricultural land has been designated for the use of swidden farmers. Instead, lands now in use for shifting cultivation have been described as non-forested forest lands.

At least three major agricultural land-use systems can be distinguished in the Da River watershed: shifting cultivation on slopes, irrigated rice cultivation, and the cultivation of industrial crops.

Table 8.2 Land use in the Da River watershed

Land use	Area in hectares	Percent
Total land area	2,606,500	100.0
Forest land	2,261,909	86.7
Forest	282,296	10.7
Timber	177,709	6.8
Bamboo	26,157	1.0
Mixed	6,217	0.1
Forest on rock	66,212	2.6
Plantation	5,991	0.1
Non-forested	1,979,573	76.0
Grassland	587,544	22.5
Shrubs	638,317	24.5
Scattered trees	537,339	20.6
Shifting cultivation	216,373	8.3
Agricultural land	150,374	5.8
Upland food crops	93,581	3.5
Irrigated rice	48,032	1.9
Grazing land	7,075	0.25
Industrial crops	3,686	0.15
Other land	205,028	7.9

Source: Nguyen and Van der Poel (1994).

Shifting cultivation has been characterized as the production of food crops on slopes. In migratory swidden agriculture, a whole village moves from one place to another as fields are exhausted. In sedentary shifting cultivation, swidden fields are rotated within a fixed area. Throughout the Da River watershed, most of the shifting cultivation practiced is sedentary and is mainly associated with the Hmong, Dzao, and Kho Mu people. The Thai, Muong, and Tay cultivate irrigated rice but, due to limited availability of irrigated fields, have increasingly begun to practice swidden on sloping lands as well. Both shifting cultivation systems are appropriate for the production of upland rice, maize, and cassava.

Irrigated rice cultivation is the primary agricultural activity of the Thai, Kinh, Muong, and Tay. Most of the narrow valleys in the Da River watershed have been made suitable for irrigated rice cultivation. On hill slopes, terraced paddies have been incorporated into some of the flatter lands along the sides of streams. The people have long been able to fashion irrigation systems through the use of *phai*, *muong*, *lin*, and *con*. *Phai* are dams, usually created near water sources, that supply water to irrigation canals (*muong*). Water is also led from streams and dams to paddy fields through bamboo pipes (*lin*). Many Thai, Muong, and Tay communities also use water wheels (*con*) to lift water from streams into irrigation canals.

The cultivation of industrial crops occupies the smallest portion of land designated for agriculture. Tea and sugarcane are widely grown on state farms in the more accessible areas, particularly the highland plateaus that are relatively easy to cultivate on a large scale (Moc Chau, Mai Son, Phong Tho districts). A majority of the people working on these farms are Kinh. State farms are presently allocating land to laborers on a contract basis, allowing them to cultivate food crops and establish small home gardens in addition to their contracted output of industrial crops.

IMPACT OF HYDROPOWER PROJECTS ON THE DA RIVER WATERSHED

The Hoa Binh hydroelectric dam, near the town of Hoa Binh, is the most significant project in the Da River watershed. It is important not only in terms of the energy it delivers, but also in terms of its impact on social and ecological systems. The dam has a maximum head of nearly 100 meters, with an eventual maximum generating capacity of 1,920 MW of electricity. The reservoir behind the dam has a normal maximum level of 115 meters, though the water level could eventually reach 120 meters. The normal maximum level creates a reservoir extending 230 kilometers upstream from the dam, with a surface area of 200 square kilometers and a volume of 9.5 billion cubic meters.

Some 58,000 people belonging to 9,305 households in nine districts of two provinces have had to move as a result of inundation from the dam. Approximately 11,000 hectares of agricultural land were flooded, including 4,000 hectares of wet rice fields. Most of the people displaced were ethnic minorities who had long been residents in the area.

As a result of relentless population growth, the area of agricultural land per capita in the Da River watershed has been drastically reduced over the past several decades, as has the extent of substantial forest cover. People displaced by the dam have put even greater pressure on already limited natural resources and social services. The Ministry of Forestry estimates that, in their efforts to sustain themselves through swidden agriculture on steep slopes around the reservoirs and in surrounding districts, displaced people continue to destroy around 2,000 hectares of forest per year.

Meanwhile, although some 10,000 people dislocated by the Hoa Binh dam are still not resettled, plans already exist for a second dam farther up the Da River near Son La. If this proposed dam is constructed to an elevation of 265 meters as presently envisaged, the reservoir it creates will flood an area of 58,277 hectares consisting of 14,192 hectares of agricultural land, 42,026 hectares of forest land, and 2,059 hectares of residential land. An estimated 120,500 people will have to be resettled.

THE AGRICULTURE AND FORESTRY POLICY FRAMEWORK

The institutional and policy framework within which agriculture and forestry are operating in Vietnam has undergone dramatic changes since the beginning of the 1980s, when the introduction of the contract system began giving the family unit an independent economic role within the predominantly cooperative and state farm structures. The economic reforms that were initiated in 1986, and that in a sense culminated with the adoption of the new land law in July 1993, have restored the family farm as the primary producer and the market as the foremost distribution channel of agricultural goods.

In the forestry sector, land belonging to state farms and cooperatives has gradually been allocated to households since 1988, a process which is still in progress. The Forest Resources Protection and Development Act adopted in 1991 provides the main judicial framework for this reorganization, while the first Vietnamese Forest Policy enacted by the National Assembly outlines the strategy. In a more recent and proactive development, the government in 1993 found it necessary to severely restrict logging and export of forest products.

Specific Programs and Policies

A number of specific government policies and programs, as well as some major internationally supported projects in the agriculture and forestry sectors, have or are likely to be of great influence on the development of land use in Vietnam. Most of them have transfer-of-technology components that may come to influence the direction of future extension efforts.

Fixed Cultivation and Settlement The Program for Fixed Cultivation and Sedentarization was initiated in 1968 by the creation of a separate department in the Ministry of Forestry. Since 1990 the department has reported to the Office for Ethnic Minorities and Mountainous Areas, under Office of the Government. This effort was expected to be completed within three years. But in spite of a substantial investment and considerable political pressure during the past twenty-five years, less than half of the more than two million swidden cultivators registered in 1968 have been settled. Sadly even fewer have abandoned shifting agriculture.

Development of Mountain Agriculture A policy for the development of mountain agriculture was announced by the Prime Minister on September 23, 1993, followed by a set of instructions for social and economic development of the uplands issued by the Prime Minister in November. The government program sets out several specific tasks and targets related to agriculture to be reached by 1995.

Most of these designated targets imply further steps away from subsistence farming to commodity production, and there is a heavy emphasis on agricultural production for export. The instructions issued by the Prime Minister explicitly abandon the long-established goal of local food security in stating that "Industrial crop and fruit tree plantations must be established on a massive scale. It has become obvious that upland areas cannot progress through food production."

Decree 327 A program for covering the barren hills was initiated through Decree 327, issued by the Council of Ministers in September 1992. Guidelines were issued by the Ministry of Finance for provision of credit on April 7, 1993; for the allocation of land by the General Department of Land Management on May 8, 1993; and on actual implementation by the Ministry of Forestry on June 9, 1993.

The stated tasks of the program, which are to be achieved within ten to fifteen years, include re-greening of degraded hills and re-utilization of barren hill lands. It incorporates the Fixed Cultivation and Sedentarization Program and seeks to improve prevailing economic conditions in the New Economic Zones. In agriculture, concentration will be on industrial crops such as tea, coffee, rubber, and mulberry, as well as on certain commercial food crops, medicinal plants, livestock, and the breeding of wildlife.

PAM-Project (World Food Programme) Between 1989 and 1993, PAM-Project 3352 established thousands of hectares of forest plantations in the Northwestern Highlands, many of them in the Da River watershed. These plantations are intended to reduce erosion and soil degradation by providing ground protection, as well as to produce timber and pulp. Such forest plantations were established with Pinus, Eucalyptus, Acacia, Melia, Stirax, and bamboo species.

PROJECT ON BIODIVERSITY CONSERVATION AND SUSTAINABLE LAND USE IN THE DA RIVER WATERSHED

Because the overall situation in the Da River watershed is highly complex and rapidly changing, as well as insufficiently documented, there is an urgent need for basic information. This information will permit the development of a common base of knowledge, a necessary starting point for future research and development activities. To obtain the necessary information, the project is carrying out baseline studies, mainly through the execution of biodiversity, agro-economic and agro-ecological farm household surveys, as well as market surveys. The project is being conducted by the Center for Natural Resources and Environmental Studies (CRES) at Hanoi University in cooperation with the Program on Environment (ENV) of the East-West Center (EWC), the Southeast Asian Universities Agroecosystem Network (SUAN), and Winrock International.

The purpose of the project is to contribute to improving sustainable land use in the upland areas through an improved understanding of the relationship between biodiversity conservation and sustainable upland development. Such understanding can be of immediate benefit to education, research, and development activities in Vietnam.

We may hypothesize a relationship between diversity of composition and complexity of structure in agroecosystems. Multiple networks within an agroecosystem may stabilize and enhance the overall performance of the system. They may provide flexibility for coping with future change. Biodiversity may be related to the system properties of stability, resilience, and sustainability by means of providing greater structural complexity. The project considers biodiversity conservation for sustainable development from several perspectives. This includes a major emphasis on increasing the scope and reliability of current knowledge regarding biodiversity conservation in swidden agroecosystems of both traditional and transitional shifting cultivators.

The project employs an interdisciplinary, multi-sectoral approach. Concepts and concerns from many fields (ecology, sociology, economy, forestry, agriculture, population, and public health) are integrated into research, training, and community-based planning activities.

Biodiversity Research

Biodiversity refers to the variety of and variability among living organisms and the ecosystems of which they are integral components. Biodiversity includes diversity within species (genetic diversity), between species, and between ecosystems. Until recently, the dominant development model in Vietnam focused on control of nature through science for maximum production, and large-scale monocropping based on the principle of "comparative advantage" in international trade. This resulted in diminished cultural diversity, as well as a loss of genetic diversity in the inventory of plants and animals. The systems that once operated in a reasonable balance with resources are quickly being replaced by systems that earn more money in the short term at the cost of depleted resources.

Research is now being focused on biodiversity within different ecosystems that are related to the activities of swiddeners. This includes primary forests, secondary forests, swidden fields, fallow fields in different stages of the succession, paddy or terraced fields, tree gardens, and home gardens. For each system we seek to identify:

- The composition of wild and cultivated species, varieties of plants and animals, cultural practices, knowledge, beliefs and preferences regarding species of economic use (for food, timber, fodder, medicinal and commercial purposes).
- Interaction between biological, cultural, and socioeconomic diversity including population growth, public policy, traditional knowledge, marketing, and communication. The relationship between cultural and biological diversity remains relatively unexplored, as do the technical, social, and economic interventions appropriate and necessary to ensure that indigenous peoples (as primary stakeholders) become key decision-makers in the process to conserve and sustainably use local resources.

Farming Systems Research

A farming systems theory recognizes agriculture as a complex bio-economic operation where resources and inputs are manipulated and managed according to well-defined principles in response to the physical, biological, and socioeconomic environment and in accordance with the household's goals, references, and resources. Thus a farm household system is not simply a collection of crops, trees, and animals to which one can apply one input or another to one component to predictably achieve a single change in output without affecting or taking into account other components. Rather, it is an extremely complex interwoven network of soils, plants, animals, tools, workers, other inputs, and environmental influences that must be managed by the farm family under natural, economic, social, cultural, and technological influences according to goals and references. Farming systems in the uplands of the Da River watershed are swidden-based agroecosystems.

Shifting cultivation in the Da River watershed is no longer in its incipient stage of slashing and burning. It has evolved into various systems of much greater complexity. As population increased and forest land decreased, the time-tested traditional swidden practices could no longer meet the needs of the people. Different groups of people, and different households within groups, have employed various means of intensifying production. The initial and most widespread response has been a steady shortening of the swidden cycle. Fallow periods are no longer enough to enable forests to regenerate. Some people have also introduced new technology into their shifting cultivation (i.e., the use of hoes and plows). When local conditions and household resources permitted, some people have also added new elements to their agroecosystems, including terraced paddy fields, tree gardens, home gardens, and fishponds.

Generally, swidden plots in the Da River watershed have shifted from simple slash-and-burn cultivation to nomadic farming and then to settled swiddening. Many villages and hamlets have been settled for hundreds of years. In addition to shifting cultivation, their primary mode of production, farmers gather many products from natural ecosystems to consume, exchange, or sell in the market. They have developed a settled and diversified agricultural system to improve and maximize land use, raise productivity, increase income, and stabilize their lives.

Yet slash-and-burn farming remains an integral and important part of the agroecosystems of the Da River watershed. Thirty years of strenuous efforts to eliminate systems of swidden adaptation have failed to significantly reduce the number of people who depend upon shifting cultivation to meet their subsistence needs. In the foreseeable future, swiddening probably cannot be significantly reduced in scope, let alone eliminated. Yet most current swidden practices are clearly not sustainable.

Recent studies have convinced us that devising more sustainable methods of intensifying existing systems of shifting cultivation is the single, most important task that must be accomplished if any forest areas are to survive beyond the end of the century. We have initiated research aimed at developing and testing systems of upland resource management that will improve productivity in existing swidden areas, encourage and accelerate the regeneration of secondary forests as resources of economically valuable wild species, and reduce pressures to clear the remaining areas of primary forests.

BIBLIOGRAPHY

Central Census Steering Committee. 1991. *Vietnam population census,* Vol. 1. Hanoi: Authors.

Hirsch, P. 1992. *The social and environmental implications of resource development in Vietnam: The case of Hoa Binh reservoir.* RIAP Occasional Paper No. 17.

Ministry of Forestry. 1991. *Vietnam forestry sector review. Tropical forestry action plan.* Hanoi: Authors.

Nguyen Huy Khiem and Paul Van der Poel. 1994. Land use in the Da River watershed. In *Agriculture and forestry extension: An overview of institutions and policies with recommendations for Oxfam's program.* Hanoi: Oxfam (UK & Ireland).

United Nations Development Programme. 1991. *Vietnam national plan for the environment and sustainable development, 1991–2000.* Hanoi: Authors.

World Food Programme. June 1992. Project 3352 progress report.

CHAPTER 9

The Hmong and Dzao Peoples in Vietnam: Impact of Traditional Socioeconomic and Cultural Factors on the Protection and Development of Forest Resources

Nguyen Van Thang
Institute of Ethnology, Hanoi

INTRODUCTION

The population of Vietnam is composed of fifty-four ethnic groups. The Kinh, who are the ethnic majority, numbered 55,900,224 people, or 81.2 percent of the population in 1989. Ethnic minorities, on the other hand, numbered 8,475,538 people in 1989, making up only 17.9 percent of the total national population (Central Census Steering Committee 1991, 66).

Among the fifty-three ethnic minorities, fifty-one ethnic groups live in the highland areas, which make up two-thirds of the total national territory. Of them, forty-six ethnic groups depend on various forms of shifting cultivation for their livelihood (Institute of Ethnology 1979, 59–63). Although most of these cultivators are settled, some ethnic groups still practice a semi-migratory life (Dang et al. 1991). Whether settled or nomadic, highland ethnic minorities, such as the Hmong and Dzao, depend on the forest for their livelihood.

As we well know, the relationship between the ethnic minorities and the forests is interactive. The former are the authentic owners of the latter; the latter are the direct object of the former's exploitation. After living for many generations in the mountains, each ethnic group has accumulated its own base of knowledge and cultural practices regarding the natural environment. So, according to its level of socioeconomic and cultural development, each ethnic group has created its own way of life—modes of cultivation, technological traditions, social and cultural characteristics—adapted to the exploitation and use of forest resources (including land, water, animals, and plants) for subsistence. It could be said that the fate of forest resources partly depends on the way of living and mode of cultivation of the ethnic minorities.

Deforestation, through shifting cultivation and logging, threatens to reduce the total forested area dramatically during the coming decades. According to recent estimates, in Vietnam, approximately 200,000 hectares of forest are lost each year. About 75 percent of these are destroyed by people who moved from other regions to the highlands (ibid.) and 25 percent by indigenous people. Since the survival or degradation of forest resources impacts directly on the life of minority people, studies intended to preserve and develop forest resources cannot be separated from studying the socioeconomic and cultural characteristics of the ethnic groups subsisting on forest resources. But programs intended to preserve, restore, and develop forest resources have not always been sufficiently sensitive to the social and cultural situations of ethnic groups in highland locations. As a consequence, they rarely bring the economic or social benefits promised by their planners. Problems of preservation, restoration, and development of forest resources can only be addressed effectively on the basis of interdisciplinary research, dedicated to not only physical but also social contexts.

Since the 1960s, the traditional socioeconomic and cultural characteristics of the Hmong and Dzao peoples have been researched by ethnographers and concerned organizations. Their research results have been published in books and in journals, especially in the journal *Ethnographic Studies*. Some useful publications are available for reference.[1] I have participated in two relevant field research projects: *The Hmong People in Vietnam* and *Socio-economic Impacts of Swidden Agriculture in Northern Vietnam*. I have thus collected a great amount of valuable field material. However, there are still no publications specifically on the role of traditional, socioeconomic, and cultural factors on the protection and development of forest resources in regions inhabited by the Hmong and Dzao peoples. In this chapter, I would like to describe traditional land-use patterns and land-tenure systems, traditional social institutions and their role for community management, indigenous knowledge systems (mainly in the use of natural resources), and the traditional mechanisms for decision-making and allocation of resources (both inter-group and intra-group) among the Hmong and Dzao peoples.

POPULATION AND POPULATION DISTRIBUTION OF THE HMONG AND DZAO PEOPLES

During the colonial period, the people known today as the Hmong were called Meo, a term related to the Chinese Miao. The ethnonym Hmong, a term by which these people refer to themselves, has only gained general acceptance since the 1980s. The people now known as Dzao were called Man until the end of the colonial period. Since then, the ethnonym Dzao has become more commonly used in Vietnam. The Dzao people call themselves Dziu Mien, which means Mien people, though they are willing to accept being called Dzao today.

Both the Hmong and Dzao people migrated into Vietnam from southern China. Multistage migrations of Hmong people took place from the seventeenth century to the beginning of the twentieth century (Institute of Ethnology 1978, 295). Based on linguistic and cultural differences, the Hmong people in Vietnam are classified into four subgroups: Black, White, Flowered, and Green Hmong. But inter-group relationships have been close. Not only in Vietnam but also in other Southeast Asian countries, this ethnic community is known for its ability to conserve its distinct cultural identity.

The Dzao people's multistage migration took place from the thirteenth to the nineteenth centuries (ibid., 312). Based mainly on linguistic and cultural differences, the Dzao people are classified into at least seven subgroups: Dzao Trang (White Dzao), Dzao Quan Chet, Dzao Tien, Dzao Thanh Y, Dzao Do (Red Dzao), Dzao Lo Gang, Dzao Tien. Each Dzao local group also has other names (see Table 9.1). Because the Dzao local groups migrated into Vietnam in different stages and located separately from one another, intra-group and inter-group relationships are not as close as the Hmong people (ibid., 313).

Table 9.1 Classification of the Dzao groups (in Vietnamese)

Group by dialect	Large groups	Subgroups with their different names
Group I (Kiem Mien)	Dai Ban	a) Dai Ban, Dzao Do, Dzao Coc Ngang, Dzao Sung, Dzao Dzu Lay (Que Lam)
		b) Dzao Coc Mun, Dzao Lo Gang (O Gang, Lu Gang), Dzao Thanh Phan (Thanh Phan Lon, Thanh Phan Con)
		c) Dzao Quan Chet, Dzao Son Dau, Dzao Tam Dao, Dzao Nga Hoang, Dzao Ba Tieu
	Tieu Ban	Dzao Tien, Dzao Deo Tien
Group II (Kim Mien)	Quan Trang	a) Dzao Quan Trang
		b) Dzao Ho
	Lan Tien	a) Dzao Lan Tien (Lam Dinh), Dzao Thanh Y, Dzao Tuyen
		b) Dzao Ao Dzai, Dzao Binh Dau, Dzao Slan Chi

In 1979, there were over 300,000 Hmong and 200,000 Dzao living in Vietnam (ibid., 291 and 311). Ten years later, the 1989 population census recorded 558,043 Hmong and 473,945 Dzao, an increase of nearly 100 percent for both groups (see Table 9.2). Due to the need for labor, especially male labor for shifting agriculture,[2] the rate of natural population increase of both ethnic groups is very high, currently over 3 percent per year. Formerly, both Hmong and Dzao people led a subsistence life of migratory swidden cultivation. About 500,000 Hmong and 350,000 Dzao still live a semi-migratory life (Nguyen 1991, 1). Because of differences in modes of cultivation and land-use patterns, although both ethnic groups have a semi-migratory life, the Hmong people's movements are often separated by

Table 9.2 Distribution of Hmong and Dzao populations

Location/province	Hmong population	Dzao population
Cao Bang	38,433	60,333
Ha Tuyen[a]	152,452	130,497
Lang Son	1,068	21,629
Lai Chau	110,013	30,313
Hoang Lien Son[b]	144,510	108,519
Bac Thai	2,892	33,043
Son La	81,952	18,860
Vinh Phu	536	8,937
Ha Bac	53	5,333
Quang Ninh	8	36,177
Ha Son Binh[c]	2,970	10,406
Thanh Hoa	3,640	3,712
Nghe An	17,935	37

Source: Central Census Steering Committee (1989, 71–88).

a. Ha Tuyen has been divided into two provinces—Ha Giang and Tuyen Quang.

b. Hoang Lien Son has become Lao Cai and Yen Bai.

c. Ha Son Binh has become Ha Tay and Hoa Binh.

longer periods and over a wider territory than the Dzao (Nguyen 1989, 24). Their movements have taken them far from their old locations. For example, between 1974 and 1989, among 170 Hmong households living in Nam Mon and Lu Than communes (Bac Ha district), and Khau Mang commune (Mu Cang Chai district), 106 migrated to other places.

Within the uplands of northern Vietnam, the Hmong people tended to move northwestward out of the northeastern mountainous regions, from highlands to lowlands, around the base of mountains that were not occupied by other ethnic groups, practicing swidden agriculture in combination with dry rice and wet rice cultivation as available.[3] Recently, due to the Vietnamese government's policy banning opium poppy cultivation and reduction in the forest area available for making swiddens, Hmong people have begun moving into the remotest forests. Some Hmong villages and kin groups in Thanh Hoa and Nghe An provinces have migrated as far away as Laos. Others have moved in the opposite direction, to the lowlands (Nguyen Van Thang 1993, field notes). If any characteristic can be identified in these moves, the most general and obvious is that the Hmong population in Vietnam is very unstable in terms of the residence. For instance, in Ta Penh village, Moc Chau district, Son La province, out of forty-three Hmong households, ten households moved in May 1993.

Although some Dzao local groups have a semi-migratory life, they usually practice shifting agriculture within a fixed territory in a rotational system. Swidden fields are fallowed after a certain period and allowed to succeed back to forest. This eventually restores the land to a state in which it can be cultivated again. So, although the movement of their fields are more frequent (after about three years), the Dzao generally move within fairly limited bounds (Be 1993, 54). The Dzao population, in comparison to the Hmong, are thus quite stable in terms of their residence.

The Hmong are concentrated in the upland provinces adjoining the southern border of China and the eastern border of Laos where they dominate other ethnic groups in terms of population.[4] These concentrations of Hmong are separated from each other, however, by resident populations of other ethnic groups. In such regions, Hmong households belonging to the same kin group often reside in separate hamlets of a village or in separate villages.

Due to pressure on swidden land and frequent movement, the size of Hmong villages is often small, typically including about seven households. Their houses are separated by 1 to 3 kilometers. The Hmong house is constructed so that it can easily be disassembled and transported to a new location. Hmong furnishings are limited to things necessary to meet the pressing requirements of their daily life. Their choice of residence is characterized by weather and soil conditions appropriate to the cultivation of food crop swiddens and especially opium poppy swiddens. These often are dense forests on steep mountainous slopes or in small valley bottoms surrounded by rocky mountains that lie at altitudes of 800 to 1700 meters above sea level. Climatic conditions in these areas fall somewhere between wet and dry tropical and subtropical conditions. Rainfall, which averages between 2000 and 3000 mm per year, is erratic. Soils are shallow and often lateritic with bedrock emerging from the surface (Institute of Ethnology 1978, 291).

The Dzao extend over three regions, which correspond roughly to increasing altitude and rainfall: the lowlands (the lowest altitude area), the midlands (the middle area), and the highlands (the upper area). While they are mainly located in the midlands, the Dzao, in contrast to the Hmong, are not concentrated in particular areas. Rather, they mix with other ethnic groups such as the Kinh, Thai, Tay, and Nung. At such ethnically mixed locations, due to a requirement for ancestor worship in the male line (ibid., 311), Dzao households belonging to the same kin group usually live together in particular villages.

The Dzao Do, Dzao Ao Dai, Dzao Tien, and a part of the Dzao Tien live in highland areas of Cao Bang, Quang Ninh, Lang Son, Bac Thai, Tuyen Quang, Ha Giang, Lao Cai, and Yen Bai provinces. This terrain of karst mountains, at altitudes of 800 to 1000 meters above sea level, is full of obstacles and difficult to access. Land under forests is predominantly sandy loam. The climate is cool with high humidity. The Dzao living in this highland area have settled and practice fixed dry rice cultivation or rotational shifting cultivation.

Dzao Quan Chet, Dzao Lo Gang, Dzao Tien, and Dzao Thanh Y reside in the midlands. This region, an area of low hills and karst mountains, lies at altitudes of 400 to 600 meters above sea level and is rich in natural resources. The climate is tropical. Dzao groups in the midlands practice swidden agriculture.

Dzao groups practicing shifting cultivation in the midlands have small and dispersed villages. Each village includes only seven or eight households separated by 1 kilometer or so. The number of households in each village fluctuates because households must move after their swiddens are exhausted. The village is temporary to suit their frequent movements. Their houses are built with the front half raised above the ground on poles and the back half supported by the hillside. Due to frequent movements, their houses are also of a temporary character.

In the lowlands of Yen Bai, Tuyen Quang, Bac Thai, Phu Tho, and Ha Bac provinces, Dzao groups such as the Dzao Quan Trang, a part of Dzao Quan Chet, and Dzao Tien cultivate soil terraces situated at an altitude of 200 meters above sea level. These Dzao began moving to these lowland terraces from the uplands or midlands in the 1960s. They cultivate wet rice fields, terraced fields, and flat fields (Be et al. 1971, 12–14).

The villages of sedentary Dzao groups who practice wet rice agriculture or rotational swidden cultivation are usually larger and set on hillsides near water courses. Each village includes about thirty houses that are clustered in groups on the hillsides. This arrangement conserves rice land in valleys. These Dzao local groups build their houses on the ground or on stilts. Houses on stilts are found only among the Dzao groups practicing wet rice cultivation and living near the Thai, Tay, and Nung peoples (ibid., 125–44).

Average population density of provinces in which the Hmong and Dzao people live varies from 26 persons per square kilometer in Lai Chau to 135 persons per square kilometer in Quang Ninh (Institute of Ethnology 1987, 85).

LAND-USE PATTERNS AND LAND-TENURE SYSTEMS

The Hmong and Dzao ethnic minorities in Vietnam have three distinctive patterns of land use and cultivation, each of which is tied to a characteristic farming method. Each land use and cultivation pattern, in turn, is tied to a corresponding landownership system.

Open Cycle Swidden Cultivation

Open cycle shifting farming makes full use of all opportunities and means to exploit land and forest potential. This may be called the *pioneering* method of swidden agriculture for it requires a continuous supply of new territory. This is because forest land, once cleared for cultivation, is used until the soil is virtually exhausted and incapable of regenerating itself through forest fallowing. In many cases, the result of open cycle swiddening is a barren hill.

Open cycle swiddening is the typical pattern of cultivation employed by migratory Hmong, who, unlike the Dzao, use plows to turn over the soil. Because they cultivate their swiddens to near exhaustion, typically four to five years, and move on to open new areas, Hmong land tenure is temporary. In a traditional society, a Hmong household is a self-sufficient economic unit. Tenure is gained by clearing land and planting crops. When land is exhausted, it is transferred to the management of the rural community.

The Hmong in Vietnam are organized by exogamous patrilineal clans. In some villages, a clan is coextensive with the village, so that the clan chief is also the village headman. As the head of a clan, these village headmen play a decisive role in the affairs of the community. In particular, village headmen and heads of clans decide where the village or clan will migrate. Because of the observance of ancestor worship and marriage between clans, these moves involve whole clans or villages (Nguyen 1989, 22).

In the colonial period, when land and forest resources belonged to the State, both the feudal State and the French colonial rulers managed forest lands solely through taxes and tributes.[5] For all practical purposes, however, ownership of forests and forest land remained in the hands of the rural communities who controlled their use by customary law. Boundaries were elaborately defined by these communities, with some lands available for cultivation and others for preservation as forests. At the same time, outsiders were rarely permitted to exploit their forests and forest land resources. For this reason, despite the appearance of wide open frontiers, even the migratory Hmong were not able to settle anywhere they chose but had to find unclaimed lands, or, if there were claims on lands, negotiate use rights. Before 1950, when the Hmong population was small and widely scattered, and overall population density was much lower, the people could easily find new lands, and despite their practice of using lands until they were virtually exhausted, their impact on forest resources was negligible (Be 1993, 22–23). Nevertheless, population growth and the declining availability of open forests, combined with the particular characteristics of Hmong farming practices, have changed this situation.

Most Hmong swiddens, although on steep or rocky lands, are, in their later stages, plowed. As with other swiddening systems, Hmong swiddens are constructed through a process of (1) selecting land, (2) cutting large trees, (3) slashing the remaining brush, (4) burning fallen trees and bush when they have dried, (5) clearing the ground, and (6) sowing seeds.

What differs in the Hmong agricultural cycle is the introduction of plows during the second production cycle. Hmong plows, which can dig from 15 to 20 centimeters deep, are used to increase soil fertility (by turning up nutrients from below the soil surface) and reduce wild grasses. Land is generally first plowed in the dry season, prior to the Lunar New Year Festival. Plowing and harrowing is repeated before seeds are sown.

The main crops are rice and maize. Maize is sown in holes, whereas rice is either sown in holes with dibble stick or broadcast. Other crops, such as green or yellow beans, are interplanted in Hmong maize field. Vegetables or pumpkins are grown with rice. The choice of plants for intercropping is based on knowledge of which plants can co-exist and, in fact, support each other's development (Institute of Ethnology 1978, 295). After the summer-autumn harvest, the Hmong grow soya, green and yellow beans, and different food crops such as yam, taro, hemp, indigo, opium poppies, and various medicinal plants such as false ginseng, *ligusticum wallichii franchi* and *codomosis*. Hmong communities also reserve swiddens for manioc and fruit trees (apple, peach, pear, and plum) wherever land is not suitable for field crops.

Because rice and maize output on the swiddens is low (about 1.2 to 1.5 tons per hectare) (ibid.) and decreases after the first harvest, the Hmong, like the Dzao and other ethnic minority groups, are accustomed to exploiting other forest products to meet their needs. They exchange forest products at the market place for commodities they cannot produce. The principal forest products are vegetables, roots, honey and bee wax, fish, wild birds and animals, and medicinal plants. These products can be found under the forest canopy.

The Hmong, like most other shifting cultivators, never sold their produce, even when there were surpluses. Any food surplus was stored to meet frequent and unpredictable harvest shortfalls. Therefore, opium, along with various forest products, has served as the basic income source for the purchase of goods not available on the farm. By following a semi-migratory life, their living demands are, however, simple. Houses are made of small and light trees. Fuelwood is gathered from the trees and boughs of half-burned swiddens. When these run low, fuelwood can be acquired in the forest.

The Hmong, despite their habit of using swiddens until the land is nearly exhausted, also practice a form of land conservation. For example, swiddens are always situated on the lower half of hillsides. The forest portion above remains intact to lower the flow of rain water and to prevent soil erosion. The techniques of interplanting vegetables and beans on the rice and maize fields increase available nitrogen. The use of half-burned trees, boughs, and stones to build a swidden edge or the practice of growing a living hedgerow around swiddens is aimed at preventing erosion. When plowing fallow land, furrows are made horizontally to retain rain water and prevent erosion. The Hmong have selected many species of rice, maize, and other crops suitable to the soil and climate conditions of the uplands. They also have a method of classifying soils based on crop suitability.

Since the 1950s, a number of the Hmong households and villages have settled in the well-watered valleys of the Northwestern Highlands. This move has resulted in changes in their traditional farming systems and, as a result, the landscapes that their social systems develop. Swiddening initiates the process of transformation through clearing and initial crop cycles. But, due to the permanent nature of these settlements, landscape transformation must proceed beyond the typical pattern of exhaustion and abandonment. Land at the base of the valleys is converted into wet rice field, and land stretching along the foot of the mountain is made into terraced fields. Terraced fields that can be provided with water are put under wet rice cultivation and those that cannot are planted in maize, dry rice, and other food crops. Such communities of permanent Hmong settlement occur in Giang Ta Chai village, Ta Van commune, Sapa district, Lao Cai province, and a number of villages in Pha Long commune, Muong Khuong district, Lao Cai province (Thang 1993, field notes).

Along with this new way of life, the villages, the architecture of houses, and some other cultural characteristics have undergone changes, though these transformations exist within the framework of Hmong culture traditions. Landownership systems are also different. Fields and terraces reclaimed by households permanently belong to their ownership (ibid., 299).

Closed Cycle Swidden Cultivation

Closed cycle shifting cultivation follows a system of field rotation within a limited area. Although the area may be extensive, the amount of land in direct production may be limited. Other lands will be in different stages of fallow. Typical examples of this model of forest land exploitation can be found among Dzao groups living in the uplands and midlands. In their system of swidden farming, the Dzao use only rudimentary tools such as knives, axes, hoes, and dibble sticks to exploit the thin upper layer of the soil. They typically cultivate a site for three years, leaving it to fallow for ten to fifteen years before using it again. Unlike the Hmong system, this system allows the forest to fully regenerate itself. Particular households have use rights to both cultivated and fallowed land, though this land is shared within kin groups or villages. Land is not owned outright.

The Dzao people prepare their fields between January and April and their production cycle starts with the selection of a site. Dense old forests with big trees near water sources are considered the best sites for new swiddens. Site selection is followed by (1) the felling of big trees and brush, (2) drying, (3) burning, (4) field preparation, (5) planting, (7) fertilizing, (8) weeding, and (9) harvest. The main crops are rice and maize, intercropped with other vegetables. Rice and maize seeds are sown by broadcasting in the first crop and, in the following years, they are sown in holes. When swidden fields become exhausted, usually within three years, they are left to fallow. The household will move on to another place under the ownership of their village to start another cultivation cycle.

The Dzao people have exhibited in their traditional practices an awareness of the need to conserve and protect resources. For example, to prevent soil erosion, the Dzao interplant different crops on the same swidden field or overlap one crop with another and build hedges by planting trees or earthwork edges. The result is a multicanopy structure which, apart from its role in soil conservation, provides soil nutrients. The Dzao also cultivate large areas of tree crops like cinnamon cassia and tung (*Aleurites montana* wils), truc (bamboo-like *phyllostachys*), and vau (nodding bamboo). They also grow various tuber trees such as edible yam (*Dioscorea esculenta* Burkill), oppositifolius yam (*Dioscorea persimilis* Prain and Burkill), and yam bean (ibid., 216). These crops increase soil fertility by shedding their foliage, fruit, and dried boughs on the soil.

The output of rice, maize, and other crops in swiddens heavily depends on the amount of accumulated nutrients in the soil. With each successive crop, this fertility decreases. For instance, in the first year of production, the household of Mr. Trieu Tien Tai in Trung Son village, Yen Son district, Tuyen Quang province, grew some 2,400 kilograms of paddy per hectare on his 5 hectares of fields. In the second year, the household produced 1,800 kilograms per hectare, and the third year only 1,500 kilograms per hectare (Be et al. 1971, 82). Under ideal conditions (i.e., if population density is low and arable land is available) after the third year of production, the household would allow the land to fallow, moving on to a new farm plot within the community's territory. The application of this rotational field technique, under these conditions, is a sustainable means of providing for the material welfare of their communities while conserving and protecting natural resources.

Since the 1960s the Dzao population has increased considerably, complimented by increasing numbers of Kinh migrating from the lowlands. Under these conditions of reduced access to resources, the Dzao have turned to permanent settlement, relying on fixed swiddens, or moved to the lowlands to cultivate dry or wet rice fields. They make full use of farming available soil resources, such as mountain ravines or gently sloping hillsides, creating terraced fields where they use plows and harrows to practice intensive farming (Thang 1991, 1992, and 1993, field notes).

Intensive Paddy Agriculture

The Dzao and Hmong techniques for wet rice or rain fed paddy cultivation are very similar. Rice may be grown in valley bottoms or terraced hillsides. Plows and harrows with wooden or iron teeth, drawn by buffaloes or oxen, are used to prepare land for planting. Dams, water wheels, and bamboo gutters are used to supply water. The area of wet rice cultivated by the Hmong and the Dzao has been expanding. This has resulted in changes in land tenure. With wet rice cultivation, land has come under the permanent ownership of individual households and, as a consequence, has begun to be bought and sold (Be 1993, 22). The Hmong and Dzao also use nonirrigated fields to cultivate dry rice, maize, various kinds of fruit trees, industrial crops, and vegetables.

The Hmong and Dzao also engage in a number of subsidiary activities that provide additional income to households. Among these, the most common are raising buffaloes, oxen, horses, pigs, and poultry; fish farming in wet rice fields; iron work such as the casting of plowshares, hoe blades, and the forging of knives; making textiles and baskets; and the gathering of forest products.

Each of the three land-use patterns discussed earlier corresponds to a particular form of ownership. Open cycle swiddening involves temporary, communal landholding. Closed cycle swidden systems base land tenure on cultivation cycles. Permanent cultivation of wet rice follows a system of private landownership. The system of private landownership began appearing among the Hmong and Dzao before the 1960s. It involved not only agricultural land but also other natural resources such as bamboo, timber trees, trees with bee nests, plots of forest, *mu* oil tree forests, and cinnamon tree forests. Generally, with private ownership, the exploitation and use of land and forest resources always went alongside reforestation and forest protection.

SEDENTARIZATION

From the 1960s, with the policy of building agricultural cooperatives, many Hmong and Dzao villagers were moved from the uplands, where they practiced shifting cultivation, to the lowlands, where they were introduced to wet rice farming in large-scale agricultural cooperatives. Because this induced change in the mode of cultivation failed to consider the social and cultural characteristics of these two ethnic groups, the agricultural cooperatives dissolved and the Hmong and Dzao people returned to swidden farming in their old locations.

The process through which this return to swiddening occurred provides a clear example of the failure of earlier sedentarization programs. When the agricultural cooperatives were established, land and other natural resources were turned over to collective ownership. In spirit, this may have been consistent with earlier practices, but in reality, it brought with it changes in social institutions that had a deep impact on natural resources. This was because the establishment of agricultural cooperatives brought with them the destruction of customary law: the traditional and long effective forest land management mechanism. As a result, forests and forest land seemed to be ownerless. The cooperatives were only interested in managing irrigated and fixed swidden rice monocrop cultivation. Since the income from wet rice fields and dry rice monocropping on fixed swiddens was very low, households turned to shifting swiddens in the loosely managed forest lands for additional income. These areas provide a frontier, outside the management of cooperatives and no longer managed through customary law. As a result, the Hmong and Dzao exploited the forest indiscriminately.

At the same time, the policy of building New Economic Zones encouraged Kinh people to move from the densely settled lowlands to the highlands. This resulted not only in a demographic shift, but also increased competition for upland resources. For example, the population of Kinh in the uplands of northern Vietnam increased from 639,679 in 1960 to 2,142,646 in 1979, and to 2,556,630 in 1989 (Institute of Ethnology 1978, 299). As a corollary to this growth, large tracts of forest land were destroyed by State forest enterprises. Then, because of food shortages, the workers at the enterprises destroyed even more forest for farming land, dwellings, and commercial logging and for other consumption needs. In short, forests and forested land were exploited without restraint (Be 1993, 156). By the same token, deforestation due to shifting agriculture and logging increased dramatically when collective cooperatives were formed. With the building of State forestry farms and agroforestry farms and the rapid increase of the number of Kinh people in highland areas, many Hmong and Dzao were forced to move farther and farther into the remotest sections of forests to make their swiddens. Accordingly the forest cover at higher elevations also began to decrease. It is estimated that, in the areas where Hmong and Dzao live, only 7 percent of forest cover remains (ibid., 57). Forest productivity has been diminished; wild animals are becoming increasingly rare. The actual state of deforestation and the dramatic reduction of other forest resources in the Northern provinces were not recognized and considered until the late 1980s. Yet even then, Resolution No. 10 (1989), which introduced the production contract system, and the resolution of April 5, 1988, which allocated land, including forest land, to upland farmers, were implemented slowly. For the most part, tardiness in carrying out these resolutions have been due to perplexities involving the allocation of land in difficult terrain, the varying needs of a diversity of ethnic groups, imbalances between population and resources, forestry and agriculture, and reforestation and industrial tree production, technical questions, and, especially, shortage of investment capital.

While the policy of forest and land allocation has caused heated conflict about land-ownership and forest resource ownership in mountainous areas in general, it has posed particular problems in those areas inhabited by Hmong and Dzao (ibid., 154–58). For those Hmong and Dzao following a semi-migratory life, systems of private ownership were undeveloped, and conflict over land rarely took place. But for Hmong and Dzao who have engaged in wet rice fields and fixed swiddens, institution of the land allocation policy has resulted in intense conflicts. Most households formerly owned fields created or purchased by an earlier generation. With the introduction of the contract system, Hmong and Dzao households reclaimed their inherited fields from the agricultural cooperatives. The competition for land caused conflicts between minority inhabitants and Kinh people, as well as among the Hmong and Dzao, who had been persuaded to settle with the Tay, Nung, and Thai people, who shared their land with the Hmong and Dzao in order to build agricultural cooperatives. When agricultural cooperatives were dissolved and the Tay, Nung, and Thai people reclaimed their former land, the Hmong and Dzao had to return to their old way of life (ibid., 156). Conflict even arose among Dzao and Hmong people who had lived together in the same village for a long time. For example, Mr. Hoang Dinh Dinh, a cadre of the cultural section of Muong Khuong district, Lao Cai province, reclaimed all his own land (Thang 1993, field notes). This caused conflict between his family and other families who were forced to return land. The Hmong and Dzao people who ended up without land had to return to their old way of life, destroying the now limited forest area to make swiddens. The degree of deforestation was in direct ratio with the level of population increase in an area, and the needs for food and commercial logging of Hmong and Dzao households. The traditional pattern of land-use and land-tenure systems of Hmong and Dzao people had been completely destroyed. Techniques and cultivation habits that had combined land exploitation and use with protection of forests and forested land had been wiped out.

However, the policy of contract with farmers and the policy of assigning forest land to farmers, especially the recent Land Law, have had positive effects in reversing these trends. Here, it should be noted that solving the issues of nationalities essentially is solving issues of peasants, particularly the issues of mountainous peasants. Integrally tied to this are issues of forest land and forest resource ownership. The recent Land Law has given Hmong and Dzao households long-term ownership rights to plots of forest land.

With these resources in their possession, they have found ways to invest in planting rice and industrial trees, combining agriculture, livestock, and forestry, based on the potential of each plot and the potential exchange value of their products.

They have begun integrating production for use with production for the market. As a result, in Hmong and Dzao areas, there are now two production patterns, household and farm. With the household pattern, Hmong and Dzao households, typically including two or three generations, have a labor advantage in developing production for the market. The farm pattern involves the linkage of several households in the same kin group in order to invest in and develop production. For example, in the Hmong village of Ta Penh, Tan Lap commune, Mai Chau district, Son La province, Mr. Vang Lao Lu (village head) and Mr. Vang Ao Song, together with his relatives, contributed capital to buy a tractor and a truck in order to cultivate land and transport harvested agricultural products from their fields to their houses or to Moc Chau market for sale (Thang 1993, field notes). The traditions of intensive farming, intercropping and overlapping crops, crop rotation, multiplication of crops, or specializing in growing of some plants have been restored and redeveloped. Many households have borrowed capital, provided reciprocal labor, and introduced new plants and livestock with high exchange value. Forest gardens have been restored, creating sustainable development in place and restoring balance in the environment.

The economic life of the Hmong and Dzao people has been changed in many places, such as Hmong villages in Hua Tat village, Van Ho commune, Ta Penh village, Tan Lap commune, Moc Chau district, Son La province, and Dzao villages in Da Bac district, Hoa Binh province (Thang 1993, field notes).

TRADITIONAL SOCIAL ORGANIZATIONS AND THEIR ROLE IN COMMUNITY MANAGEMENT

Social Organization

In the colonial period, land and forest resources were the property of the State. Nevertheless, both the feudal State and the French colonial rulers administered forests and forest land solely through taxes and tributes. Real land management remained in the hands of the rural, territorial communities. The Hmong called this form of social organization *Giao*. Dzao names varied from group to group. For example, Dzao Tien called their community organizations *Tom doi chuong lang*. In either case, these social mechanisms controlled land and natural resources and organized economic, social, and cultural activities within the community through a system of customary law.

Space and Community Each community had its own sphere of territory, including land used as the place of residence and cultivation. Each rural community consisted of one village (*Giao* in Hmong) or some villages (*Drong* in Hmong) with a bounded territory. Each community had clearly defined borders often marked by natural demarcation lines (roads, streams, hills, mountains) and were recognized by common convention.

For example, Pha Too village, Nguyen Binh district, Cao Bang province, is a rural community with sixteen households. Dzao people have lived and worked in this place for eight generations. In the beginning, they followed a migratory life, cultivating swiddens far from their village. Later they settled down and engaged in the cultivation of fixed rocky fields. At that time, the territory of their rural community took its current shape. In front of their village were valleys where Tay people cultivated wet rice fields. A road served as the demarcation line between the Tay people cultivating wet rice below and the Dzao people cultivating rocky fields above. This demarcation line was defined in the following way. One person stood at the foot of a mountain and threw a rock up to the side of that mountain. Where the rock dropped was considered a demarcation landmark. Other points were established at the foot of steep mountainsides.

The total land area of the typical rural community was about 4 square kilometers. Apart from fixed rocky fields privately owned by individual households, the forest, mountains, streams, and rivers were the common property of the community. Within the sphere of territory embracing each community, the land and forest were clearly classified according to the traditional schema: forest and forest land used for cultivation, forests under exploitation, and forest and forest land forbidden for exploitation. The land was opened by individual households for farming, and this land was under their private ownership. That meant the farming land had owners. In fact the buying, selling, and transferring of farm land among individual households often occurred. In some areas, the Dzao people owned plots of cinnamon trees, tea, fruits, and bamboo. They also had ownership and transferability rights to some trees, such as precious woods, trees with bee nests, and herbs, growing naturally in forests. Customary law respected the labor value of people who found them. There were also prohibited forests such as ridge crests, ghost forests, and forests used for cemeteries. Nobody had the right to exploit or lay claim to land in such forests.

The community prohibited or limited the exploitation of land or forests within its territory by persons from the outside—especially the utilization of virgin land covered by primary forest. If a person from another rural community wanted to make a swidden or exploit forest products, he or she had to get permission and pay some money, meat, and rice to the community in order to worship the local spirit of the earth (Be et al. 1971, 189–90).

Community Organization Members of every community belonged to several kin groups, among which there was often one larger kin group. The latter was usually the first to break fresh ground and open new territory. Each community had common rituals involving agricultural activities, livestock breeding, and hunting. These rituals often were organized in the spring. On such occasions, members of a community assembled to discuss common issues involving production, livestock breeding, forest protection, and to express deep solidarity among all members of the community (ibid., 191).

Every rural community had a headman called by the Hmong people as *Lung Thau* or *Song Thau*, by Dzao Ao Dai and Dzao Quan Trang as *Xa Chau*, by Dzao Tien as *Chieu Con*. The headman of the community was selected by its members or chosen by rotation. He often was a head of the largest kin group. He was responsible for leading the members of the community in organizing production and doing public services. When Hmong or Dzao led a migratory life, the headman organized community members to seek new land for shifting cultivation. He also was responsible for mediating conflicts, maintaining customs and habits, consolidating community solidarity, and controlling security within the settlement (ibid., 194–99). It is clear that the headman of a community played an active role in the traditional societies of the Hmong and Dzao peoples. He was respected and believed by community members. In addition to the community headman, the oldest men of villages belonging to the same community also had an important role and helped the headman of the community organize and manage the community's affairs.

The spirit of common fortunes was expressed clearly in the productive activities and daily life of the community. This was intrinsically connected to the seasonal mode of agricultural cultivation, a pattern of cultivation in which available labor resources were under great pressure during the agricultural season and left idle during the off-season. There were various forms of mutual help among households within every community to deal with this periodicity of labor demand. Most common were patterns of reciprocal labor exchange in which several households cut and burned vegetation together and then divided the swidden area thus created among participating households. At other times, the commonly created swiddens were also cultivated jointly, with the harvest divided among participating households based on labor input. Men also hunted together, dividing their catch according to prescribed rules. Finally, households relied on mutual aid in constructing new houses, in conducting funerals, in planning weddings, and so on.

All economic and social activities within the community were governed by customary law. Public opinion and punitive methods were employed to keep order and enforce customary law in the community. Someone who violated customary law could be condemned or punished by a fine. One practice of the Hmong people worth noting was the oath which was called *Nao xong* by the Hmong (Loc and Nong 1975, 85). Essentially, it was established as a common convention of *Giao* or *Drong* in order to protect forests. For example, according to this convention, households only had the rights to clear forest for swiddens in defined zones. Some bamboo forests were owned by particular households, so other households could not clear them for swiddens. In prohibited forests such as the highest sections of forests or plots of forest for a cemetery, no one had the right to make swiddens. Violators would be punished by a fine. In order to ensure that the convention would be properly observed, each *Giao* nominated one or two *Song thau*, a *Giao* headman to enforce compliance and investigate violations.

In the traditional society of the Hmong and Dzao peoples, the rural community was the most important organization. Communities owned, managed, and assigned use rights to forest and forest land and protected forest and forest land by customary law. Use of land and forest resources was strictly controlled by customary law and was closely linked to its protection. The result was a form of sustainable development.

KINSHIP ORGANIZATION

The Hmong people have exogamous patrilineal clans, each of which has its own name. Among the largest are the Giang, Thao, Lu, Vu, Sung, Ma, Lung, Hau, Ly, Vang, Tan, Trang, Han, Then, and Cu. The Hmong consider each kin group to be descended in the male line from one common ancestor. The members of these clans are said to be brothers and sisters who have the same ancestor. They can give birth or die in any house within their patrilineal clan.

Patrilineal clan relationships are first based on the occupation of a common territory. This sharing of lifespace is the premise upon which the coalescence of socioeconomic relations among members of a patrilineal clan takes place. The origin of this pattern of co-residential clans lies in Hmong land settlement practices. Hmong communities were most frequently established by an original group of settlers, all from the same clan, who cleared the forest to build their villages and cultivate their fields. Once the site was established, families from other clans joined the original settlers. Although most Hmong villages thus contain more than one clan group, families belonging to the same clan usually live together in separate hamlets. Even now, this pattern of settlement is practiced by the Hmong in all regions. There are, however, many villages which still contain only one clan group.

The Hmong people have long depended for their livelihood on shifting cultivation, a mode of agricultural production that derives its social organization from the common clan origins. It created collective strength in order to help and protect one another in productive activities and in life's difficulties. Although farming land belonged to individual households, these rights being acquired by virtue of opening of primary forest, the community's activities were governed by the clan and in the clan's interest. For example, a family that held much land sometimes had to share it with relatives who had little or no land, or if a family moved out of a village forever or a couple died without children, the clan would share that land among households within their clan. If a household had to sell their farm land, they had to sell it to other members of the clan (ibid., 73).

The community characteristics of clan were expressed in religious rituals, marriage customs, and obligations to clan members. At the most fundamental level, this is based on the notion of being from "the same ghost" (*cung ma).* Being of the same ghost set Hmong clans apart from one another and is reflected in the distinctive funeral rituals, rituals for the veneration of ancestors, and obligations to help clan members. It is also evident in Hmong marriage customs. Each clan was, and is, strictly exogamous. Marriages are only allowed between men and women who share different family names, and hence different clan lines.

Socioeconomic and environmental pressures forced the Hmong people to live in dispersed, isolated settlements. In this context, the clan emerged as the most important social institution, the force behind customary law applied to the socioeconomic and cultural activities of its members.

Because clans were also patrilineal, males, especially male clan chiefs, held a high position in Hmong social life. Clan chiefs were the best informed and most prestigious members of the clan. They were, one might say, the very soul of the clan. As such, they held the title "holding ghosts, holding guests" *(cho dac nho kho)* and carried the responsibility for organizing and regulating the customary and religious rituals and festivals of their clans. Clan chiefs, however, not only had responsibility over the affairs of clan members, but they also represented their clans in dealing with other clans. Relations among kin groups in the *Giao* or *Drong* were very close.

The community characteristics of the clan were an important influence on the administrative organization of villages and regions. According to the ruling law, the chief of a large region *(thuong ly)* or a small region *(thuong quan)* was elected by the members of that region, but in fact he was always a representative of the most influential clan in the region.

Because the Hmong people assumed that their clans descended from a common ancestor, the Hmong clans have very high social solidarity. The Dzao people, on the other hand, do not ascribe the highest social values to common clan ancestry. Thus, although all Dzao kin groups recognized the Bun kin group as their origin, branch relationships hold greater significance. In the process of migration into Vietnam, each main kin group was separated into different lines. For example, the Trieu kin group was separated into several lines, such as the Red Trieu, Green Trieu, and Mold Trieu. Each line included many branches. The relationship among members in the same branch was closer than in the same line or in the same kin group. Each branch had its own middle names indicating the rank of men belonging to different generations in the same branch.

The common alter of the branch was placed in the house of the branch headman. His house was also a place to organize and carry out common ancestor worship, rituals for persons coming of age *(cap sac)*, and New Year's ceremonies. The headman was also the main person responsible for helping other families in his branch, organizing funerals, constructing houses, planning weddings, or dividing family properties.

Relationships among Dzao kin groups are much looser than among the Hmong (Be et al. 1971, 209). Because the Dzao people considered the branch a subsistence base, Dzao families with few relatives could organize a ritual called *quynh mien* in order to abandon their branch and join other larger branches. In doing so, relationships among members of the same branch could change.

In traditional Hmong and Dzao society, rural community organizations and kin groups have played a very important role in the management of land and forest resources. Under the control of rural communities and kin groups, little forest land was "ownerless." When the Hmong and Dzao people were induced to join cooperatives, the roles of the rural community organizations and kin groups in managing and controlling land and forest resources were abolished. All land and forest resources were managed by cooperatives. However, because of loose management by the cooperatives, in effect many land and forest resources became ownerless, a condition that has led to land and forest resource degradation and destruction.

Among the Hmong and Dzao people, village elders and clan chiefs have retained extremely important roles within the community. They themselves are persons who have sufficient prestige to manage productive, social, and cultural activities in the village. They summarize and transmit to succeeding generations a vast body of knowledge preserved in oral traditions, about nature, production practices, managing and protecting land and forest resources, and proper social behavior. These men creatively apply cultural traditions to new conditions. They are not conservative; they are quite willing to receive new things, but they do so carefully and at their own pace. They aspire to take advantage of new things while conserving their cultural identity. In this way, they instill self-confidence and pride in younger generations. The oldest persons in villages and the clan chiefs have the confidence of the community and the kin group. All socioeconomic development programs in the areas of the Hmong and Dzao people should be based on the advice, agreement, and active participation of these traditional leaders.

SUGGESTIONS

As mentioned, the Hmong and Dzao peoples live in three regions: highland, midland, and lowland. The natural geographical features of each region are distinctive. Each region has its own potentials. Even in traditional society, Hmong and Dzao peoples adapted their customs to the distinctive features of each region. They created a distinctive farming calendar appropriate to the conditions of climate and land of each region, selected various strains of crops and livestock, took advantage of terrain features in order to convert sloping land into terraced fields for growing both wet rice and dry rice, practiced intensive intercropping, overlapping crops, had technical measures for protecting land from erosion and for increasing soil fertility, and so on. They had their own traditional social institutions to manage forests, forest land, and forest resources. The Hmong and Dzao peoples have accumulated valuable experience and knowledge about the actual conditions of their localities. Forestry programs should be developed on the basis of this local knowledge in order to develop appropriate solutions for each region and each ethnic group. We should not hastily apply models developed in other regions that have different natural geographic and ethnic features. In other words, developmental patterns should be diversified, flexible, and participatory.

The Hmong and Dzao peoples often live in ethnically mixed locations. They thus constitute part of a larger social and economic system that should be understood as a complex whole. This whole not only includes ethnic minorities and majorities but also State enterprises. Forestry development programs should thus be interested in the histories and current experience of forest resources exploitation by State forestry enterprises, agroforestry farms, and other economic organizations in the regions in which Hmong and Dzao peoples live.

At present, many regions (such as Muong Khuong, Bao Ha, Bao Thang, and Sapa districts, Lao Cai province; Mai Son and Moc Chau districts, Son La province; Da Bac district, Hoa Binh province) are receiving sizable investments to settle the Hmong and Dzao peoples by planting industrial trees. But people have often been encouraged to plant crops they can neither eat nor sell. These investments must be scrutinized carefully.

Investment should go directly into villages. For example, in Pha Long community, Muong Khuong district, Lao Cai province, there has been a program of investment to grow and process hemp for the Hmong people. While 50 million Vietnam *dong* was allocated for construction of a workshop associated with this project, the Pha Long commune received only 12 million *dong* for construction.

In the process of implementing forestry projects, help of the village elders and the headmen of kin groups should be solicited. As mentioned, they are trusted by village members. They have the prestige and organizational capacities to mobilize, develop, and direct villagers' activities relating to forestry development projects in their localities. It should be noted that the customary law of traditional society is still a force that dominates all social and cultural relationships of the Hmong and Dzao peoples.

NOTES

1. *The ethnic minorities in Vietnam (in the Northern Vietnam)*, Social Sciences Publishing House, Hanoi, 1978; *Some problems of socio-economic development in the northern mountainous provinces*, Social Sciences Publishing House, Hanoi 1993; *Economic and cultural changes in the northern mountainous provinces*, Social Sciences Publishing House, Hanoi, 1993; Mr. Nguyen Anh Ngoc's articles on the various aspects of the swidden agriculture in the highlands, published in *Ethnographic Studies* and other works.
2. Male labor is used to clear forest and prepare fields.
3. For example, in Son La province, the Hmong population increased from 13,678 in 1960 to 51,809 in 1979 and to 81,952 in 1989. In Hoang Lien Son province, from the year 1981 to 1986, 7,954 Hmong moved from highland districts (Tram Tau, Bat Xat, Bac Ha, Sa Pa, Van Chan, Muong Khuong) to lowland districts (Van Yen, Van Ban Bao Yen); 1,782 Hmong moved to western provinces of Hoang Lien Son such as Son La, Lai Chau (Institute of Ethnology 1987, 85, and Central Census Steering Committee 1991, 79).
4. Dong Van; Hoang Su Phi-Bac Ha-Muong Khuong; Mu Cang Chai-Tram Tau-Bac Yen; Sa Pa-Phong Tho-Sin Ho-Tua Chua; Dien Bien and zones adjoining districts such as Thuan Chau and Tuan Giao; and Ky Son-Que Phong.
5. The Hmong had to pay various kinds of taxes such as poll taxes, market taxes, swidden taxes, and opium taxes. Also, every adult male Hmong had to contribute corvee labor two or three times each year from fifteen to twenty days at a time (Institute of Ethnology 1978, 299).

BIBLIOGRAPHY

Be Viet Dang, ed. 1993. *Nhung bien doi kinh te-van hoa o cac tinh mien nui phia Bac* [Economic-cultural changes in the northern mountainous provinces]. Hanoi: Social Sciences Publishing House.

Be Viet Dang, Nguyen Khac Tung, Nong Trung, and Nguyen Nam Tien. 1971. *Nguoi Dzao o Viet Nam*. Hanoi: Social Sciences Publishing House.

Be Viet Dang and Pham Quang Hoan. December 1991. *Rung, bao ve rung va truyen thong van hoa, phong tuc tap quan* [Forest, forest protection and cultural traditions]. Report at the conference on Culture and the Natural Environment, Institute of Ethnology, Hanoi.

Central Census Steering Committee. 1991. *Vietnam population census, 1989*. Vol. 1. Hanoi: Authors.

Institute of Ethnology. 1978. *Cac dan toc it nguoi o Viet Nam (cac tinh phia Bac)* [The ethnic minorities of Vietnam (in the northern provinces)]. Hanoi: Social Sciences Publishing House.

Institute of Ethnology. 1979. *Ethnographic Studies,* 1:59–63.

Institute of Ethnology. 1987. *Mot so van de ve kinh te-xa hoi o cac tinh mien nui phia Bac* [Some socio-economic problems of the northern mountainous provinces]. Hanoi: Social Sciences Publishing House.

Loc Binh Thuy and Nong Trung. 1975. *Tuc an uoc cua nguoi Meo o tinh Lao Cai* [The Nao Xong practice of the Meo people in Lao Cai province]. *Ethnographic Studies*, 3.

Nguyen Anh Ngoc. 1989. *Nhung van de ly luan va thuc tien cua cong tac dinh canh dinh cu* [Theoretical and practical problems of sedentarization]. *Ethnographic Studies*, 1–2.

Nguyen Van Huy. December 1991. *Dinh canh dinh cu va cac van de kinh te -xa hoi hien nay* [Sedentarization and the current socio-economic problems]. Report at the conference on Culture and the Natural Environment, Institute of Ethnology, Hanoi.

CHAPTER 10

Highland Development and Forest Resource Protection in Vietnam: Status and Research Priorities

Hoang Xuan Ty
Research Center for Forest Ecology and Environment, Hanoi

Government-initiated development programs in the highlands of Vietnam have focused on filling the social, economic, and educational gaps between the lowlands and the highlands. Forest resources, as providers of economic benefits and environmental services, play an important role in the modernization process. The long-term development of the highlands will require maintenance and enhancement of this resource base. How this can best be done remains a question requiring further research and assessment.

This chapter details some high priority research activities focused on the highlands of Vietnam. It includes discussion of forest resource protection, conservation, and use, as well as the role these policies continue to play in developing the highlands.

HIGHLAND ZONES

There are no commonly accepted geographic criteria used to identify the highland areas of Vietnam. Rather, the term "highland" is generally applied to any locality situated at elevations higher than sea level and frequently associated with an assumed set of environmental and socioeconomic conditions. In this chapter, the term "highlands" is used to specify all localities situated at elevations over 100–200 meters above sea level in which hills, mountains, and plateaus prevail, and in which the topography is generally rough and broken. Such definition, while useful, is very broad, applying to almost 75 percent of the territory of Vietnam. Given the rich social and ecological variation within the highlands, further distinctions can clearly be made. Based on topography, ecology, and socioeconomic conditions, seven ecological zones can be readily identified within the highlands. These are the Northern Mountains, the Northwestern Mountains, the Northern Midlands, the Central Midlands, the Central Mountains, the Central Plateau, and the Southeastern Midlands (Map 10.1). The main features of each zone are described on Table 10.1.

In a general sense, the seven ecological zones can be re-classified into three groups based on their physiographic characteristics. Mountainous areas occupy the north, northwest, and center of the country, encompassing all or part of Quang Ninh, Lang Son, Tuyen Quang, Ha Giang, Cao Bang, Lao Cai, Yen Bai, Lai Chau, Hoa Binh, and Son La provinces and all those districts bordering Laos. Mountain plateaus, situated in south-central Vietnam, are the primary topographical feature in Kon Tum, Gia Lai, and Lam Dong provinces. The midlands, areas of low hills and gentle slopes, run parallel to mountainous

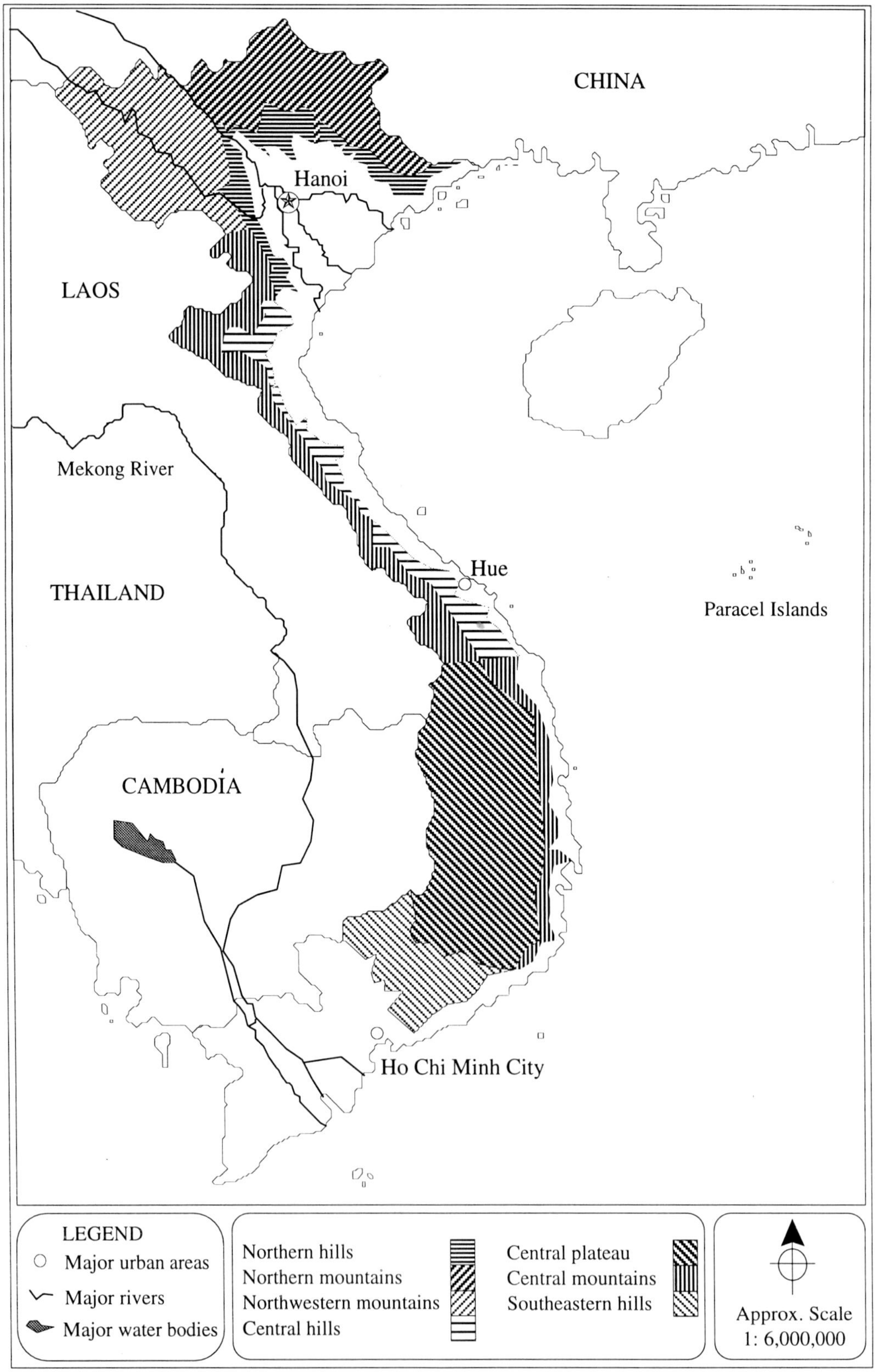

Map 10.1 Midland and mountain areas of Vietnam

Table 10.1 Characteristics of the midland and mountain areas of Vietnam

	Topography		Percent forest cover	Need for environmental protection	Infra-structure	Main products	Main ethnic groups	Standard of living
Area	Elevation (m)	Slopes						
Northwestern Mountains	Mountains 300–3000	Very steep	9–13	Very high	Very low	Tea Fruit	Thai Hmong Dzao Kinh	Very low
Northern Mountains	Mountains 300–1500	Very steep	11–35	High	Very low	Tea Fruit Wood	Tay Nung Muong Dzao Hmong	Very low
Northern Midlands	Hills 100–1000	Gentle and steep	14–24	Moderate	Low	Tea Fruit Wood Bamboo	Tay Nung Dzao Kinh	Low
Central Midlands	Hills 100–1000	Gentle and steep	25–30	High	Low	Wood Non-wood product	Mnong Van Kieu Katu Kinh	Low
Central Mountains	Mountains 300–2000	Very steep	30–34	Very high	Very low	Wood	Katu Coho Lao Jarai	Very low
Central Plateau	Plateau 300–1500	Gentle and steep	61	High	Low	Rubber Tea Coffee Wood	Jarai Ede Bana Kinh	Low
Southeastern Midlands	Midlands 100–500	Gentle	21	Moderate	Low		Kinh Stieng	Low

areas in the north, northwest, and center and form the southeastern flank of the Central Plateau. Midlands occupy parts of Quang Ninh, Ha Bac, Ha Tay, Hoa Binh, Song Be, Dong Nai, and Thuan Hai provinces, and run along the coast from Thanh Hoa to Quang Nam.

FOREST AND FOREST SOIL RESOURCES

Socioeconomic development in the highlands is organically linked to the protection and development of forest and forest soil resources. In 1993, out of a total area of 33 million hectares, Vietnam contained 8.6 million hectares of natural forest (26 percent of national territory), 0.5 million hectares of plantation forest (2 percent), and 12.5 million hectares of denuded hills and open wasteland (38 percent). Farmlands occupied 11.4 million hectares, or 34.5 percent of the national territory (GSO 1994).

Both wood and non-wood forest products are derived principally from natural forests, which account for 94 percent of the forested area. The standing stock in natural forests is 657 million cubic meters of timber. Plantation forests, which comprise only 6 percent of the total forested area, are still very young. The standing stock in established plantations, though not adequately inventoried, is estimated at 20 to 30 million cubic meters of small

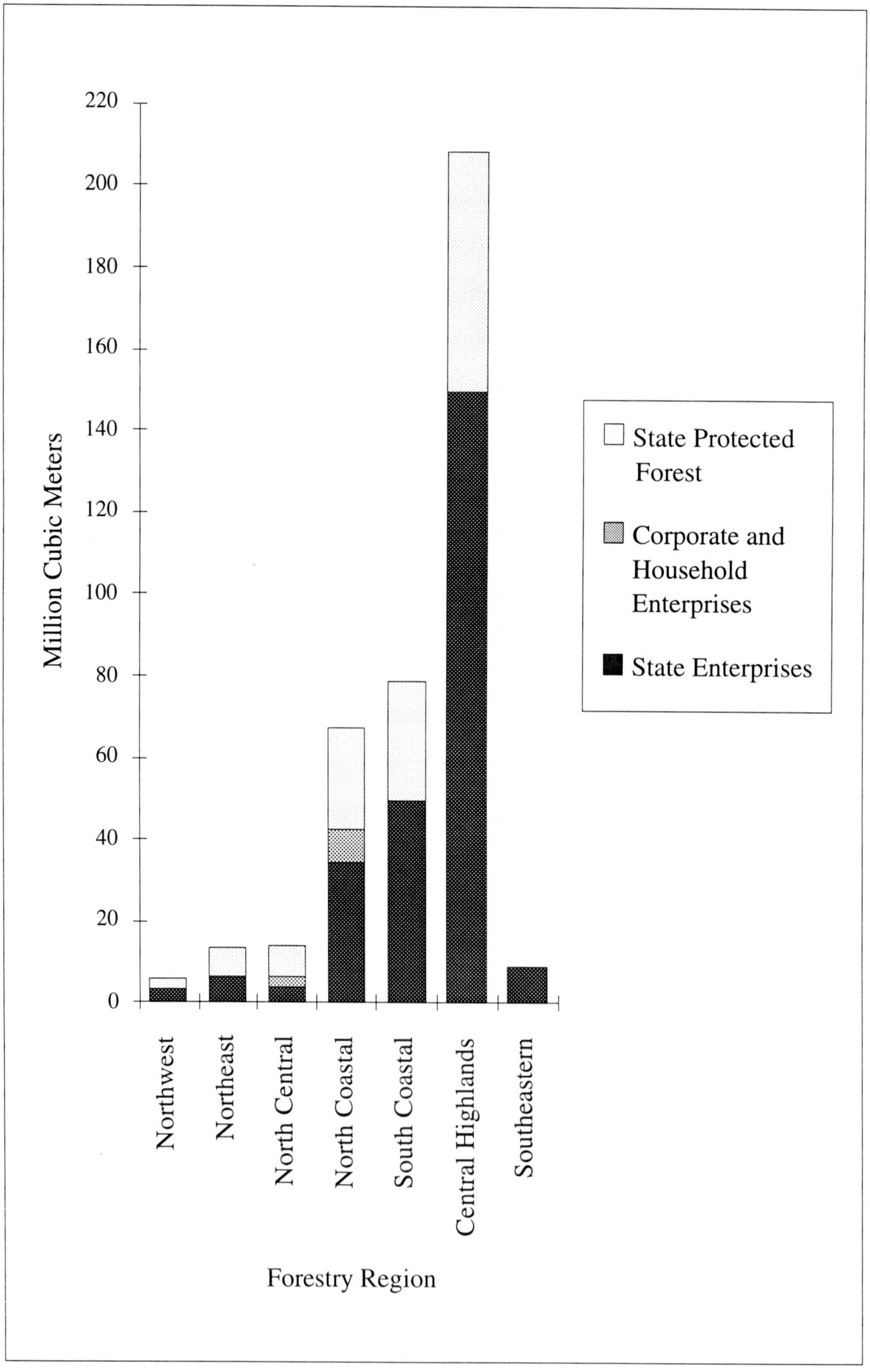

Figure 10.1 Total volume of wood and non-wood products by forest region and land ownership

diameter timber. Natural forests are not evenly distributed over the whole country (Figure 10.1). Approximately 44 percent are found in the Central Plateau and 38 percent in the Central Mountains zone (Map 10.1).

Forest soils in the highlands are of two main groups—yellow and red mountain ferrallitic soils and humic montane ferrallitic soils. In spite of their marginal fertility (acid soil reaction, deficiency in P, and high Al^{+++} content), high soil moisture contributes to rapid restoration of productivity and biodiversity in areas where natural forest has been cleared.

HIGHLAND DEVELOPMENT AND FOREST MANAGEMENT

Under the prevailing conditions of a tropical monsoonal climate—marked each year by many powerful storms with heavy rains—in this country, forest vegetation plays a very important protective role against widespread erosion and soil loss. It provides conditions not only for sustainable development in the highlands, but also for securing the living conditions of millions of people in the deltas.

Although most people recognize that the development of highland areas in Vietnam must proceed in such a way that environmental resources are protected, how this should be done remains highly contentious. The recent history of forest management and economic development offers some clues in this regard. Experience has shown that (1) autarky is a major contributor to deforestation, (2) market mechanisms are contributing to forest preservation, and (3) settling shifting cultivators will improve both their living standards and the condition of forests.

Economic Self-Sufficiency Inevitably Results in Deforestation

As in other Southeast Asian countries, overexploitation and the swidden practices of ethnic minorities have rapidly depleted Vietnam's forests. It has been estimated that 100,000 hectares of forest are being cleared annually by the roughly 2.87 million people (482,000 households) practicing shifting cultivation (Vo 1992). In the past, the detrimental effects of swidden were not very great due to the practice of fallowing for ten years or longer, a routine that allowed forests to rehabilitate. At present, population increase in the uplands has reduced per capita land availability and, as a consequence, the length of fallowing periods. Currently, fallow periods average three to five years. With shortened fallows, forests simply cannot recover. Since the fertility of mountain soils depends heavily on the condition of forest vegetation prior to swiddening, people from mountainous areas of the North have begun migrating to areas such as the Central Plateau and Southeastern Midlands where dense forests on fertile lands can still be found. From 1990 to 1993, 45,000 people emigrated from Cao Bang province and 5,500 from Lang Son province (Pham 1994). During the same period, 85,240 people emigrated to Dac Lac province, a forested province in the Central Plateau. A high proportion of these people were ethnic minorities in search of fertile forest lands for self-sufficient food production.

Market Economy Helps Reduce Deforestation in the Highland Regions

Uplanders clear forests mainly for food production. If food is transported from the plain to the uplands, it can be exchanged for forest products. Reliance on forest products for income, rather than the agricultural output of forest soils, creates an internal mechanism for preserving forests. Recent changes in the organization of lowland agriculture have served as a means of both creating a rice surplus and markets for its exchange. Upland peasants are now able to exchange forest products for rice produced in the lowlands. This exchange of surpluses has already resulted in convincing examples of market-oriented forest conservation.

Since 1982 Dzao people in Vien Son commune, Yen Bai province, have planted more than 606 hectares of *Cinnamomum cassia*, an average of 3 hectares per household. Many households have now begun exploiting their *C. cassia* plantations. Preliminary economic analyses have shown that 1 hectare of *C. cassia* on sloping land produces the equivalent income of 5 to 8 hectares of food crops on similar lands. The result, then, is an increase in the potential food supply through purchase. Furthermore, since less land is required for production of *C. cassia* as compared to upland food crops, and since *C. cassia* is a perennial tree crop, the clearing of forests for shifting cultivation in the Vien Son commune has ended.

Another example of market-oriented forest conservation can be found in Quan Hoa district, a mountainous area along the border between Vietnam and Laos. In the past, almost all the families in this district cleared forests for subsistence production. With the opening of a market for *Dendrocalamus membranaceus*, a large, straight bamboo used in house construction, a number of communes have almost abandoned subsistence food production on widely scattered and ephemeral swidden fields in exchange for the cultivation of *D. membranaceus* on permanent plots that collectively occupy much less space. Many families have become comparatively rich through the sale of this bamboo, and consequently the clearing of forests for shifting cultivation has almost ceased. There are currently 12,000 hectares of this bamboo species being farmed in the district, an average of 1 hectare per household. Five years after planting, each hectare of this bamboo allows the annual selective cutting of 800 to 1,000 clumps. The income from the sale of each clump of *D. membranaceus* at the point of production is equivalent to the cost of 1,200 to 1,500 kilograms of rice, an amount sufficient for a family of five in a year.

As the circulation of food into the highlands from lowland points of production has improved, farmers have begun cultivating a wider range of fruit crops for sale. For example, the cultivation of the *Tam Hoa* prune has been fully established in Moc Chau and Bac Ha districts (Northwestern Mountains area), and in Yen Bai province (Northern Mountains area). Some households have been able to earn annual incomes of tens of millions of *dong* from only 1.1 to 1.5 hectares of well-tended orchards.

The linkages between forest protection and the development of the highland economy are organic. Their interrelatedness is such that the condition of one is an indicator of the condition of the other. The destruction of forests under conditions of subsistence-based swidden agriculture, on the other hand, has had detrimental effects on both the varied ecosystems and diverse cultures of the highlands. Production of higher value agricultural and forest products for sale offers a means of both reducing pressure on forests and increasing incomes and living standards. The development of markets for highland products will no doubt increase the range of goods available in the highlands and, depending on the potential of each locality, the range of commodities available for export outside the highlands. Only by doing this can highland cultivators be weaned from shifting cultivation to more sedentary land-farming systems and better protection of forest resources.

Settling Shifting Cultivators Promotes Their Interests and Fosters Forest Protection

If the opening of markets for highland products has provided cases of improved living and environmental conditions, there are equally many examples of poverty, environmental degradation, and food shortages among upland peasants due to reliance on shifting cultivation for food production.

Results of a survey of the Dzao and Tay ethnic minority households in a mountainous region in Cho Don district, Bac Thai province, show that the total income of rich households was six to eight times that of poor households (Hoang 1991). Only 8 percent of the income of rich households was derived from shifting agriculture while poor households earned 75 percent of their income this way. At the most basic level, this indicates that the economic efficiency of swidden agriculture is much lower than other forms of income earning like livestock rearing, market gardening, and handicraft production.

In an effort to raise living standards, the government has made sustained efforts to gradually limit shifting cultivation and to sedentarize swidden farmers. More than 2.88 million people from over forty-eight ethnic groups have participated in this program. After twenty-two years of sustained effort, 66 percent of the original shifting farmers registered in the program (about 1.9 million persons) have been induced to settle and practice fixed cultivation. However, the number and percentages of swidden agriculturalists involved in the program vary by ethnic group and region. Roughly 80 percent of eight ethnic minority groups, including the Jarai, Muong, and Tay, are involved in the program. However, only 30 percent of six other ethnic groups, including the Kho Mu, Churu, and Pu Peo, have been induced to join the program.

This differentiation may, in part, be explained by access and customary agricultural practices. For example, each of the six ethnic minority groups with low levels of enrollment in the resettlement program lives in isolated highland settlements far from access roads. Land availability may also play a role. Finally, the emphasis of the program (wet rice cultivation) may appeal more to those ethnic minorities who have experience in wet rice cultivation.

Thus, one can say that in an area where lands cannot be developed for wet rice cultivation and access roads have not been constructed, self-sufficient swidden cultivation will remain a necessity. In these areas, the main emphasis should be to improve methods of swidden farming on sloping lands with an aim toward reducing soil erosion and forest destruction. Improved seed varieties should be supplied at no cost and farmers should be helped in the construction of terraces so that they can sustainably produce larger quantities of food on less land.

PRIORITIES FOR RESEARCH AND ACTION

A wide range of research programs and interventions will be required to carry out the related tasks of raising standards of living and protecting the environment in the highlands. In general, comprehensive strategies for highland development, and identifying economic, social, and cultural objectives and related activities need to be formulated. At the same time, linkages between agencies and sectors should be developed for the execution of these strategies. These documents and the institutional relationships they foster will constitute the base upon which all highland development projects should be referred.

In a similar vein—though there are now many projects funded by the government, various NGOs, and other international aid agencies dealing with highland development—these projects have been operating independent of each other. As a result, their projects in health care, education, forestry, agriculture, and children's welfare have not been very effective. In order to improve the effectiveness of these projects, closer relationships between the government, interested NGOs, and aid agencies should be established through the creation of integrated projects.

Within these integrated projects, priorities should be given to research activities and the transfer of appropriate technology that support economic and social development in the highlands. It is essential to develop facilities to introduce appropriate technology to individual households, to help them obtain improved seeds, high-yielding cultivars, fertilizers, and new techniques. At the same time, the training of technicians for technological development in the highlands should be promoted. Technicians working in the highlands should definitely receive better pay.

Market studies for and research designed to improve the processing of high-valued commodities such as cinnamon bark, pine resin, tung oil seed, prune, apricot, and traditional handicrafts should also be initiated.

An interdisciplinary working group of competent scientists for highland development in Vietnam must be created and facilities provided for them to efficiently conduct research. They should then recommend various policies that are most suitable for development in the mountain areas, and at the same time act as focal points for the transfer of knowledge and technology.

BIBLIOGRAPHY

Agucta, M. 1991. *Socio-economic attributes of trees and tree planting practices.* Rome: FAO.

Anonymous. 1990. Final report on the 22-year campaign for fixed cultivation and sedentarization. *Forestry Review.* Hanoi.

Be Viet Dang. 1990. On the economic and cultural development of the highlands and the movement of fixed cultivation and sedentarization. *Forestry Review.*

Chambers, R. 1983. *Rural development: Putting the last first.* London: Longman.

Do Dinh Sam. August 1992. National background paper on shifting agriculture in Vietnam. Paper presented at workshop on Shifting Agriculture in Thailand, Laos, and Vietnam: Its Social, Economic, and Environmental Values Relative to Alternative Land Uses, Chiang Mai, Thailand.

General Statistical Office. 1994. *Statistical data for agriculture, forestry and fisheries.* Hanoi: Statistical Publishing House.

Government decree on forest and forest land allocation. 11/1993.

Hoang Xuan Ty. 1991. *Evaluation of production potentiality of forest land in Vietnam through application of a geographic information system.* Final report of the project. Forest Science Institute.

Le Trong Cuc, K. Gillogly, and A. T. Rambo. 1990. *Agroecosystems of the midlands of northern Vietnam.* East-West Center Occasional Paper No. 12. Honolulu: East-West Center.

Ministry of Forestry. 1992. *Tropical forest action plan.* Hanoi: The Authors.

Nguyen Dinh Khoa. 1983. *Cac dan toc o Viet Nam* [Ethnic groups in Vietnam]. Hanoi: Social Science Publishing house.

Pham Do Nhat Tan. 1994. *Illegal migration and measures for stopping it.* Final report of the state project. Hanoi: Research Center for Population and Labor Force Resources.

Resolution of the Communist Party's Central Executive Committee on Rural Socio-Economic Development in Vietnam. June 1993.

State Committee for Sciences. 1990. *National plan for environment and sustainable development, 1991–2000.* Hanoi: UNDP.

Vo Quy. 1992. Environment and development in Vietnam. In *The challenges of Vietnam's reconstruction,* ed. Neil Jamieson, Nguyen Manh Hung, and A Terry Rambo. Fairfax, Virginia: The Indochina Institute, George Mason University.

CHAPTER 11

Community-Based Natural Resources Management in Lam Dong Province in the Highlands of Southern Vietnam

Bui Cach Tuyen
Environmental Protection Research Center, University of Agriculture and Forestry at Ho Chi Minh City

INTRODUCTION

Lam Dong is one of four highland provinces (Lam Dong, Dac Lac, Gia Lai, and Kon Tum) in the western High Plateau of south-central Vietnam. Lam Dong, like the other three provinces, is the home of many aboriginal people such as the Lach, Chil, K'ho, Churu, Mnong, and Chau Ma, who in the past formed the majority population. Since the end of the nineteenth century, however, the percentage of Kinh people, who first migrated to Lam Dong province following the French, has been increasing.

Most inhabitants, both ethnic minorities and Kinh, live by agriculture. Depending on their means of cultivation (i.e., whether it is settled or shifting) each group has exploited natural resources at different levels of intensity. Regardless of the intensity of their appropriation of resources, the activities of the highland people of Lam Dong have led to many adverse ecological consequences such as forest destruction, soil erosion, problems in watershed management, dam siltation, and agrochemical pollution. In addition, there exist other difficulties such as lack of credit for production, unstable market outlets, weak infrastructure, and inadequate information on production techniques.

The definition and prioritization of challenges in the development process of highland areas are essential, especially in terms of the formulation of pertinent policies, regulations, and projects at the central and provincial levels. Through projects such as KX-08, SALT 1, SALT 2, SALT 3, and IDRC-funded efforts, the University of Agriculture and Forestry of Ho Chi Minh city has been engaged in a number of development schemes in Lam Dong province. This chapter reviews some essential aspects of these development projects.

GENERAL CONDITIONS OF LAM DONG PROVINCE

Lam Dong province contains 122 villages occupied by 735,000 people, 141,179 of whom are ethnic minorities. A total of 23,888 minority households live in 70 villages forming 273 *buon* (or minority village). Twenty-four *buon*, mostly in remote mountain areas, are inhabited entirely by minority people. The average population density in Lam Dong is 72.3 persons per square kilometer, though this number ranges from 9 to 300 persons per square kilometer in minority and Kinh communities, respectively.

Predictably agricultural and forestry production are the most important sectors of the provincial economy. More than 70 percent of Lam Dong province's total area of 1,017,260 hectares is either forested or designated forest land. Cultivated land covers only 86,000 hectares, or 8.45 percent of the total provincial area.

Agricultural Production

The aboriginal people of Lam Dong province have practiced shifting cultivation for centuries. Only a few groups, such as the Churu, grow wet rice in small valleys. Kinh people mainly cultivate wet rice, vegetables, fruit trees, and mulberry for silk production. During the colonial period, the French, using Kinh and minority labor, established coffee, tea, and chincona plantations over large fertile areas. Vietnamese people also set up their own small-scale orchards, planting tea, coffee, prunes, apples, persimmons, and peaches, among others. Additionally they produce temperate vegetables, flowers, and livestock, including buffalo, pigs, cows, goats, and poultry.

After 1975, the Government of the Socialist Republic of Vietnam launched the New Economic Zone (NEZ) program in order to redistribute people from cities, towns, and other densely populated areas. As in other highland provinces, emigrants under the NEZ program were settled on unoccupied lands in Lam Dong, where they cleared the forest and started cultivating crops and raising livestock. Recently, to meet market demand, wherever the conditions are appropriate, farmers have begun growing cashew nuts in their orchards.

Annual food production in recent years varies from 110,000 to 125,000 tons. Areas grown to upland rice increased from 3,600 hectares (1988) to 8,406 hectares (1992). Various upland rice and corn varieties were introduced through extension programs and proved to be appropriate.

Forestry Production

Pine trees (*Pinus* spp.), which supply wood and resin, are one of the main forest products in the higher elevations of Lam Dong, especially in the areas around Dalat. The exploitation of pine wood began in 1927. From that time on, the natural pine forest areas have gradually shrunk. In the 1980s, when the Government of Vietnam promoted a regional reforestation movement, areas grown to pine trees began to increase. Recently, the government promulgated a new policy on landownership, which allows farmers to receive forest land to grow long-term tree crops. This policy has helped to increase forested areas.

Forests in the areas at lower altitudes are mixed. Continuous raw material demand by the paper industry has led to massive cutting of bamboo. Rattan has already been harvested to exhaustion to meet the overseas market. Big timber trees such as those in the family Dipterocarpaceae and others are cut by state-owned companies for export to overseas markets. Access roads to these cutting sites in the deep forest are usually built by these companies to help local people, who generally respond by intensifying their forest exploitation. Besides wood resources, people hunt various kinds of wild animals and gather medicinal plants and orchids.

Lam Dong contains 571,995 hectares of natural forest and reforestation areas. The potential productivity of these areas is 48,971,821 m^3 of wood and 410,491 m^3 of bamboo. According to various sources of information, the rate of forest loss is between 6,000 and 10,000 hectares annually. The rate of reforestation is 1,800 hectares per year, though only 65 percent of the yearly total grows to maturity. In light of this reality, local authorities have given first priority to the protection of reforested areas and second priority to the expansion of new reforestation areas. Due to a lack of finances, protection activities have been limited in some areas.

According to local authorities, in recent years, more than 80,000 people in some 20,000 families emigrated to Lam Dong from northern provinces without government permission. Their practice of clearing forest for cultivation has contributed greatly to the forest depletion rate.

With the recently promulgated Decree No. 327, forest exploitation has been restricted and minority shifting cultivators have been encouraged to reside in fixed locations and practice settled agriculture as the Kinh people do. In addition, 3,823 hectares of forest have been allocated to ethnic minority people to preserve and protect these areas from fire and illegal cutting. This has created income-earning jobs for 7,000 people.

In the province as a whole, a total of 92,242 ethnic minority people have been settled so far (65 percent of the total) and practice some form of permanent agriculture. Another 38,541 highlanders are effectively settled, but still engage in supplementary swidden farming. The remaining 10,396 minority people retain their traditional life as nomadic shifting cultivators.

IDENTIFICATION OF HIGHLAND PROBLEMS

Researchers from the University of Agriculture and Forestry, Ho Chi Minh city, have found a general coincidence of problems identified through the use of Participatory Rural Appraisal and data from provincial reports. These prioritized problems are analyzed in the next section.

Credits for Production

The vicious circle of poverty is a constant threat to rural farmers, especially those who belong to highland minority groups. Tables 11.1 and 11.2 illustrate the existing living conditions of ethnic minority people in the province.

Lack of credit for production is a major factor hindering the improvement of minority people's living standards. Even though high-interest private loans are locally available at any time, farmers hesitate to borrow money because the possibility of paying back the loan is small.

Theoretically, with the policy of "Famine Eradication and Poverty Alleviation" launched by the Government of Vietnam a few years ago, farmers can take out loans from the state bank for production. But in reality, this policy has faced two constraints. Bankers have the tendency to only give loans to middle-income farmers who have collateral for mortgages.

Table 11.1 Living standards of ethnic families in Lam Dong province

Category[a]	Families surveyed (no.)	Percentage
Very rich	7	0.1
Rich	375	5.6
Middle income	2,671	39.9
Poor	3,634	54.4

Source: Committee for Public Propaganda (June 10, 1994).

a. This classification is based on the minority people's viewpoint. For example, families with good housing, TVs, VCRs, radios, motorcycles, and means of production (e.g., small tractors, trucks, or milling machines) are considered very rich in the community. In contrast, families without the above, who suffer from constant food shortages, are considered very poor.

Table 11.2 Housing conditions of ethnic people in Lam Dong province

Type of house (material)	Families surveyed (no.)	Percentage
Brick	14	0.2
Wood	1,821	28.4
Bamboo and grass	4,591	71.4

Source: Committee for Public Propaganda (June 10, 1994).

Second, due to the lack of knowledge of production techniques and pest damage or market failure, farmers may not be able to pay back their loans. The State Bank for Agricultural Development of Lam Dong province offered credits to farmers totaling 1.5 billion *dong* (US$135,000) between the years 1992 and 1993. This amount of money is rather small compared to the demand throughout the province.

Irrigation System

In the dry season, sloping lands at high altitude cannot be used for agricultural purposes. In some areas where water is available, the lack of adequate irrigation systems hinders the production of various crops. In order to increase the water supply, help from the government is vital. Effective water management activities will help increase the yield and improve the living standards of people.

Agricultural Inputs

Plant Varieties and Animal Breeds Provincial authorities have introduced new high-yield varieties of corn, wet and upland rice, vegetables, beans, coffee, and tea, as well as pigs, cows, chickens, and silkworms in order to improve local production. These new plant varieties and animal breeds, however, are being used mainly within Kinh communities. Most ethnic minority people stick to traditional varieties and breeds. This is due to two factors: (1) new plant varieties or animal breeds require intensive inputs (fertilizers, feed, veterinary medicines), which are difficult for minority people to obtain, and (2) inadequate production techniques.

Agrochemicals There are two differences in the use of agrochemicals (inorganic fertilizers, pesticides, growth regulators) between Kinh people and various ethnic minorities. Among the Kinh, the use of agrochemicals is widespread, leading to both higher production and the steady accumulation of chemical residues in food and the environment. Among ethnic minority communities, the use of agrochemicals is less frequent due to financial constraints and lack of knowledge. This situation results in low crop yields.

Land Degradation and the Need for Fertilizers After clearing the forest and cultivating crops, yields decrease gradually due to the loss of soil fertility. After four or five years, ethnic minority farmers shift to other forests and repeat the cycle. With the policy of settled agriculture, it is necessary to instruct people to use inorganic and organic fertilizers and intercrop with nitrogen-fixing plants, so that soil fertility can be maintained.

Infrastructure

Roads and Bridges Access roads to highland minority communities are inadequate or incomplete, even though the Government of Vietnam has invested a huge amount of money for improving the road system. In many ethnic villages, the lack of bridges over swift streams makes travel during the rainy season quite dangerous or difficult at best.

Electricity Due to many constraints, electric power is rarely available in remote villages of minority peoples of the mountain realm. Only in areas along the main road system do villagers enjoy ready access to electricity. This lack of electricity retards the dissemination of information, knowledge of science, and technology.

Education The government has invested 4.9 billion *dong* in education for the children of people settled in the highlands. At least 1.4 billion of this total was reserved for the establishment of schools for ethnic minority students. Presently there are 19,000 pupils receiving instruction in village primary schools. Four hundred minority teachers have also been trained.

The literacy rate of the ethnic minorities is quite low. This may be due to the remoteness of their houses, poverty, and somewhat weak motivation on the part of elders for the provision of education to young generations. Table 11.3 shows the status of education among minority people.

Health and Sanitation

Authorities have invested several billion Vietnamese *dong* in order to improve the existing health-care delivery systems in the Southern Highlands, especially in the communities of ethnic minorities. In 1992 alone, the central government allocated 1,158 billion *dong* for the prevention of malaria and goiter.

Table 11.3 Educational status of ethnic minority people in Lam Dong province

Educational status	People surveyed (no.)	Percentage
Illiterate	23,802	57.5
Primary school graduate	9,215	22.2
Junior high school graduate	1,578	3.8
Senior high school graduate	137	0.3
University graduate	38	0.09

Source: Committee for Public Propaganda (June 10, 1994).

Even though the Government of Vietnam has been trying to improve the health-care system, the existing situation among ethnic communities needs improvement. Tables 11.4 and 11.5 provide some general information on the health status and the occurrence of diseases within minority communities.

In some ethnic minority communities, particularly the Stieng community living in Song Be province, people think that diseases are the result of spirit possession. Spirits infect certain people, who then spread diseases throughout the community. When diseases reach epidemic proportions, witch doctors are called to identify these disease carriers and secretly kill them. Fortunately, in Lam Dong province, there are no such cases of killing persons accused of being spirits by witch doctors.

Market Outlet Difficulties

Agricultural production in Lam Dong province is strongly affected by market mechanisms. There have been many cases in which farmers have been forced to destroy crops instead of harvesting them because the cost of hired labor was higher than the revenue from products (e.g., the harvesting cost of sugarcane). Or they have been compelled to cut down one type of tree in order to grow other tree species that produce more marketable products. Small-scale post-harvest technologies are badly needed to generate surplus agricultural products. It is necessary to have a forecasting entity within the Ministry of Agriculture and Food Industries to identify trends in production and market prices of some essential agricultural products, so that farmers can regulate their production to avoid surpluses. Cotton production, for example, faced many difficulties due to widespread infestations of pests and low market prices. Additionally some textile companies were importing essential raw materials from other countries. Naturally this has led to many difficulties in the local production of cotton.

In the highlands, the main products are temperate vegetables and flowers. These products face stiff competition from similar products produced in expanding green belts around big

Table 11.4 Health classification of ethnic minority people in Lam Dong province

Health condition	People surveyed (no.)	Percentage
Good	8,121	19.6
Medium	22,037	53.0
Weak	7,082	17.0

Source: Committee for Public Propaganda (June 10, 1994).

Table 11.5 Diseases among ethnic minority people in Lam Dong province

Type of disease	People surveyed (no.)	Percentage
Malaria	4,438	10.70
Goiter	120	0.12
Leprosy	52	0.10

Source: Committee for Public Propaganda (June 10, 1994).

cities and towns. Most ethnic minority people are at a distinct disadvantage in this competitive struggle because their orchards and fields are located in remote areas, inaccessible to mechanized transportation. It is very difficult to bring their products out of the production site, let alone to sell these products.

IMPLEMENTATION OF GOVERNMENTAL POLICIES FOR AGRICULTURAL AND SOCIAL DEVELOPMENT IN LAM DONG PROVINCE

The developmental problems of Lam Dong especially impact indigenous people who live in the province. Because they remain economically weak, and their production techniques and living standards are low, without the help of the Government of Vietnam, it is very difficult for them to improve their existing situation.

Resolution No. 22 NQ/TW, introduced in November 1989 by the Politburo of the Communist Party of Vietnam, stipulates some essential directions and policies for highland socioeconomic development. This Resolution emphasized the importance of highlands, which account for three-fourths of the country's territory. In addition to past achievements, the Resolution recognized weaknesses in the development of mountainous areas such as (1) low rate of economic development, (2) fledgling market-oriented production, (3) prevalence of shifting cultivation, (4) low living standards, (5) threats of famine, (6) poor social and cultural activities, (7) high illiteracy rates, (8) prevalence of diseases, and (9) the unsuccessful activities of cooperatives. The Resolution also noted causes of the aforementioned weaknesses and proposed essential directions and policies for future development of highlands. On March 13, 1990, the Council of Ministers promulgated Decree No. 72-HDBT, which consists of five parts and thirty-eight articles. The five parts are (1) Innovation in the Economic Structure and Organization of Production in Mountainous Areas, (2) The Social Relations of Production, (3) Culture and Society, (4) Cadre Organization, and (5) Implementation.

Two years later, the Chairman of the Council of Ministers issued Decree No. 327-CT dated September 15, 1992, stipulating directions and policies on the use of unoccupied lands, barren hills, forests, coastal alluvial dunes, and water bodies. After its promulgation, the Committee for Ethnic Minorities and Mountainous Areas delivered Communication No. 818/UB-TT, which contained guidelines for implementing the Decree. On June 6, 1990, the Lam Dong Provincial Committee of the Communist Party of Vietnam issued Resolution No. 22/NQ/TU (see Fifth Convention [1990]).

The provincial party and the government also issued several documents relating to ethnic minorities and mountainous areas development:

- Science and Technology Report of the Department of Science, Technology and Environment of Lam Dong Province, Dalat, April 1994.
- Science and Technology Report No. 316/BC-NLT, Department of Agriculture, Forestry and Water Management, Dalat, April 1994.
- Department of Communication and Transportation Report, Communication and Transportation Infrastructure of Lam Dong Province, Dalat, April 1994.

- People's Committee of Lam Dong Province, Report No. 08/BC-UB, The Progress of Implementing Socioeconomic Plans in the First and Second Trimester of 1994, Dalat, April 19, 1994.

PROJECTS IMPLEMENTED BY UAF IN THE SOUTHEASTERN PART OF SOUTH VIETNAM

IDRC-Funded Project for Highland Natural Resources Management in Lam Dong Province

With financial and technical support from the International Development Research Center (IDRC), Canada, the University of Agriculture and Forestry implemented a project entitled "Community-Based Conservation Farming in Upland Fragile Resource Zone of Lam Dong Province." The Project is aimed at (1) investigating constraints and introducing institutional and technological changes and opportunities in order to improve upland farmers' livelihood without further degrading the natural resources and the environment, and (2) improving the capacity of university staff to do participatory research and development in local resource management.

Specifically, the secondary objectives of the project include (1) achieving a comprehensive understanding of agro-ecological, socioeconomic, formal and informal community rules and conditions determining land and other resource use and management patterns in small watershed areas; (2) developing capacity at the community level for making gender-sensitive village resource management plans aimed at enhancing farmers' livelihoods and sustainability; (3) identifying constraints and potentials to the adoption and adaptation of opportunities and interventions regarding farming enterprises and other livelihood projects that lead to sustainable, improved farmers' income and welfare; (4) monitoring and evaluating changes associated with practices and activities that are adopted or adapted by the community or individual farmers; and (5) building the participatory research capacity of university staff in the area of local resource management.

The project began with a two-week training course on the methodology of Participatory Rural Appraisal (PRA), which was organized at the University of Agriculture and Forestry (UAF). The first part of the training course was conducted at UAF and the second part at Kado village. It included field practice using PRA methodology. Participants were selected from the Don Duong district authority, the Kado village, and the Don Duong State-owned Forest Plantation. Some staff of UAF also attended the training course.

Data were collected following eight steps in PRA methodology—site selection, preliminary visits, data collection, data synthesis and analysis, ranking problems, ranking opportunities, adopting a village resource management plan, and implementation.

With the participation of local people, problematic fields existing in the community were prioritized as follows: (1) credits for production, (2) irrigation system, (3) plant varieties, animal breeds, soil fertility, and information on production techniques, (4) clean well water, (5) school, (6) health-care system, (7) electricity, (8) transportation, and (9) orchard development.

After the problem identification step, UAF staff cooperated with local people to formulate the Community Action Plan, including two kinds of activity:

1. Short-term activities to help improve social conditions of the community by providing funds to:

- supply books and stationery for school pupils,
- establish one sluice at the muddy part of the main road to improve village transportation of agricultural products, and
- construct several wells in the village for clean water.

2. Long-term activities for multipurpose development include:

- introducing new upland rice and other varieties,
- providing contractual cow, goat, and other livestock production,
- disseminating agricultural production technologies and low-cost biogas digesters using nylon bags through extension works,
- collaborating in government forest orchard projects to settle shifting cultivators,
- preventing soil erosion by introducing nitrogen-fixation plants growing on contour lines, and
- supplying some credit for farmers through local branches of the State Bank for Agricultural Development.

One engineer was hired to work permanently at the site. Six students are doing their theses relating to all aspects of the project.

The KX-08 Project in Dinh Quan District, Dong Nai Province

KX-08 is a national project funded by the Government of the Socialist Republic of Vietnam. This project aims at improving socioeconomic conditions of people in rural areas, especially those of ethnic minorities. UAF joined the project as implementor of its activities in Dinh Quan district, Dong Nai province. This district is located 110 km east of Ho Chi Minh city. There are about 160,000 inhabitants and 33,000 hectares of cultivated land. The primary crops in the district are rubber, sugarcane, soybeans, corn, and upland rice.

In this district, Kinh are in the majority (125,000 inhabitants) and are followed by Chinese (29,000 people). The remainder includes sixteen minorities with a total population of 6,000. Living standards of the Kinh and Chinese are rather high compared to that of the minorities, who live mainly in isolated areas of La Nga valley. Dinh Quan used to be a sparse forest, but about 70–80 percent of forest was destroyed due to war and human activities.

The goal of this regional project up to the year 2000 is to settle the minorities in this area, help them adopt a sedentary way of life, and improve their living standards. The main components of the project are to (1) establish schools, clinics, water supplies, small electricity-generating facilities, (2) develop agriculture and social forestry, and (3) improve per capita net income.

From September 1992 to July 1993, the University of Agriculture and Forestry (UAF) helped develop these villages. Although many aspects of the project have been implemented, the results have been limited due to financial constraints. UAF tried to contact NGOs to seek their support. The American Veterans' Association, for example, gave some funds for village infrastructure development. UAF also collaborated with the Vietnamese Ministry of Health to help develop villages.

SALT 1, SALT 2, and SALT 3 Projects in Lam Dong and Dong Nai Provinces

In Lam Dong province, Lan Tranh forest plantation manages 2,000 hectares. In 1992 alone, 1,000 hectares were destroyed. The adverse consequences of forest destruction are realized everywhere. The causes of existing deforestation are wood cutting for export, shifting cultivation, and exploiting for fuelwood. In order to reduce the intensity of deforestation, besides improved management, it is essential to help inhabitants improve production on their own lands and increase their living standards.

From experience obtained in the Philippines by the Asian Rural Life Development Foundation and with financial support from Cooperative Services International, staff members of UAF collaborated with farmers to establish demonstration sites using three SALT technologies.

- SALT 1 is an agroforestry model with agricultural and forestry crops at a percentage ratio of 25:75. Experience shows that among its various benefits, this model can help reduce soil erosion and increase crop yields, and farmers' income.

  The main activities of this model are to determine contour lines on sloping lands using a simple A frame and to grow leguminous plants along these contour lines to prevent soil erosion, preserve soil fertility, and supply nitrogen through the nitrogen-fixation process and green manure.

  Plants grown on contour lines are *dau cham* (*Indigofera teysmanii*), *do mai* or *anh dao* (*Gliricidia sepium*), *keo dau* or *binh linh* (*Leucena leucocephala*), *Flemingia congesta*, and *Desmodium renzonii*. The last two species were imported from the Philippines and proved to be promising in the project areas.

- SALT 2 is a goat-based agroforestry system with a land use of 40 percent for agriculture, 20 percent for forestry, and 40 percent for livestock. The output of this system is the same as SALT 1 with the exception of additional livestock production.

- SALT 3 combines small-scale reforestation projects with food production. Some 40 percent and 60 percent of the land are used for agriculture and forestry, respectively. Intercropping supplies abundant food and generates income for highland farmers.

Training courses for each SALT system were organized at UAF for officers of provincial Departments of Agriculture, Forestry and Water Management, Extension Services, provincial leaders, Agricultural Research Institutes, State-owned Forest Plantations, the Union of Sericulture Enterprises, and farmers.

UAF is currently negotiating with Lam Dong authorities and the Union of Sericulture Enterprises of Vietnam to establish an Upland Rural Life Development Center at Bao Loc district. This project will be supported by the Asian Rural Life Development Foundation and will transfer sloping agricultural land technology to upland farmers. Besides these schemes, an FAO-funded project, coordinated by UAF, is being implemented in Vietnam, China, Laos, Cambodia, and in several other countries on the use of low-cost agricultural by-products for livestock production. Uplanders of Lam Dong province will be among the beneficiaries of this project's activities.

CONCLUSION

Lam Dong province, and the High Plateau in general, with its diversified natural characteristics, is a land of great productivity in both agriculture and forestry while also possessing considerable tourism potential. Nevertheless, in order to achieve an increasingly bright future, there are several constraints to be overcome.

An overall sustainable development plan is the prerequisite for rapid progression of this region. A process of mobilizing all sides to stop seemingly irreversible environmental change is crucial. This plan requires appropriate policies, regulations, and projects at the central and provincial levels, as well as support from international communities.

BIBLIOGRAPHY

Committee for Ethnic Minorities and Mountainous Areas. December 4, 1993. Guides for the Implementation of Direction No. 525TTg, November 2, 1993, of the office of the Prime Minister on Directions, Methods for the Continuation of Socioeconomic Development of Mountainous Areas. Communication No. 818/UB-TT. Hanoi: The Authors.

Committee for Public Propaganda. June 10, 1994. Preliminary Results of the Survey on Socioeconomic Conditions of 25 Ethnic Villages. Dalat: The Authors.

Council of Ministers. March 13, 1990. Some Practical Directions and Policies on Socioeconomic Development of Mountainous Areas. Decree No. 72. Hanoi: The Authors.

Council of Ministers. September 15, 1992. Some Directions and Policies on the Use of Unoccupied Lands, Barren Hills, Forests, Coastal Alluvial Dunes and Water Bodies. Decree No. 327-CT. Hanoi: The Authors.

Department of Agriculture, Forestry and Water Management. April 1994. Plan for the Implementation of Direction No. 525/TTg of the Prime Minister. Dalat: The Authors.

Department of Health. April 1994. Draft Plan for the Implementation of Direction No. 525/TTg on Health Activities in Lam Dong Province. Dalat: The Authors.

Department of Science, Technology and Environment of Lam Dong. December 1993. The Establishment of Natural Reserve Area of Da Tan La. Dalat: The Authors.

Fifth Convention of the Provincial Committee of the Communist Party of Vietnam. Dalat, June 6, 1990. Directions and Methods for Socioeconomic Development of Ethnic People's Living Areas. Resolution No. 22/NQ/TU.

IDRC. 1994. Results of a Field Survey at Kado Village Using Participatory Rural Appraisal. Highland Project Document. Ho Chi Minh city: The Authors.

People's Committee of Dalat City (1993). *Dalat, a City in the High Plateau*. Dalat: The Authors.

Politburo of the Communist Party of Vietnam. November 27, 1989. Some Essential Directions and Policies on the Socioeconomic Development of Mountainous Areas. Resolution No. 22 NQ/TW. Hanoi: The Authors.

University of Agriculture and Forestry. 1993. Documents of Projects SALT 1, SALT 2, and SALT 3. Ho Chi Minh city: The Authors.

University of Agriculture and Forestry. 1993. Report on the Implementation of Project KX-08 in Dinh Quan District, Dong Nai Province. Ho Chi Minh city: The Authors.

CHAPTER 12

Decree 327 and the Restoration of Barren Land in the Vietnamese Highlands

Thomas Sikor
University of California, Berkeley

INTRODUCTION

The Government of Vietnam has recently initiated a nationwide program of barren land development that has strong implications for the highlands. In Decree 327, issued by the Council of Ministers on September 15, 1992, the government announced an ambitious public investment program that aims at improving the productivity of barren land. The decree provides for programs that increase agricultural and forestry outputs and afforestation activities. The allocation to the program of US$68 million in 1993, which is a large share of central government transfers to provinces, underlines the importance attributed to barren land development by the government.

Attempts to exploit the highlands' natural resources and utilize them for national development have been undertaken by the government for decades. Rural development programs in the Vietnamese highlands have primarily followed two strategies. Since 1961, the government has resettled millions of lowland farmers into highland regions. These resettlement programs had the primary goals of ameliorating population pressure in the densely populated lowland regions of the country and intensifying resource use in the highlands (Vu 1992; Feeney and Xenos 1992). Since 1968, the government has organized programs to settle itinerant highland cultivators. Sedentarization was an essential element in an effort that was supposed to bring economic and cultural development to the ethnic minorities and improve national security in border areas (Do 1992). Both programs have been plagued by poor results and frequent failures (Do 1992; Hyles 1993; Witter 1993; Sargent 1990; Hill 1984).

The question of which strategy to pursue for most successful highland development has not been resolved. Decree 327 appears to provide for three different target groups and development strategies for barren land development in the highlands. Barren land could be developed through (1) colonization by lowland farmers, (2) resettlement of itinerant highland cultivators, or (3) agricultural intensification in sedentary highland communities.

This chapter discusses the relative prospects of each of these strategies for successful barren land development in the Vietnamese highlands. The first part introduces the provisions of Decree 327 and reviews the occurrence of barren land in Vietnam. In the second section, the several strategies for barren land development will be analyzed with regard to their relative potential for barren land and highland development. Seven differentiating conditions in the highlands that shape the expected outcomes of each strategy will be identified and their effect on each strategy analyzed. The chapter concludes with a summary interpretation of the Decree 327 program as a rural development policy.

DECREE 327: BARREN LAND FOR NATIONAL DEVELOPMENT

Decree 327 puts barren land at the center of rural development efforts by the government. Barren land—or land that had so far been marginal to the national economy—is to be integrated into national development. In the preamble, the decree states as the goal of the public investment program to "utilize unoccupied land, 'barren' hilly areas, forests, denuded beaches, and waterfront."[1] Decree 327 is expected to lay "the groundwork to restore denuded or 'barren' hills and mountains, to protect the environment and forests, and to exploit the potential of unoccupied land . . . in order to increase the production of raw materials and commodities for industries."

The Provisions of Decree 327: A Summary

Decree 327 provides a mix of technical guidelines, financial incentives and subsidies, and legal provisions that apply to barren land development projects.

Households and government agencies assume complementary roles in the implementation of barren land development programs. Households are considered the basic production unit (Article 3). Land is allocated to them on a long-term basis, encouraging private investments such as measures to conserve soil fertility and replant forests (Article 2).[2] Government investment into infrastructure (roads, water supply systems, social services), "start-up" packages for new settlers during the initial months after colonization, and interest-free credits support agricultural development and settlement. In total, 40 percent of Decree 327 financing is earmarked to provide interest-free loans to households (Article 10). The remaining 60 percent is used by the government for the construction of infrastructure, scientific and technical facilities, public welfare services, afforestation, and initial support to settlers. Further financial instruments considered by Decree 327 to support households are tax cuts and exemptions, which are to be included in the new version of Agricultural Tax Law (Article 13).

The conditioning of land use, based on detailed land-use planning, guarantees its appropriate use for forestry or agricultural production. Decree 327 explicitly mentions three specific production models for barren land development in the highlands: forest plantations (Article 6), industrial crop plantations (Article 7), and livestock breeding projects (Article 8).[3] In addition to market-oriented production, all production models incorporate food security aspects by allocating land for food production. Applied research and extension services, which improve their performance through incentive systems and bonus payments to staff, deliver technical advice to households (Article 14).

Decree 327 emphasizes the necessity to integrate production aspects with other components of rural development. The areas targeted by public investment are expected to be eventually transformed into integrated agribusiness zones that combine the production of agricultural commodities with industries supplying necessary inputs and processing agricultural outputs (Article 2). Agricultural development is seen as interconnected with rural development in general, including broader goals such as social welfare, national security, and environmental protection (Articles 3, 5). In addition, the non-state sector, including joint ventures between Vietnamese companies and foreign investors, is expected to be successfully tapped for economic development (Article 11).

Investment projects under Decree 327 financing are planned and executed in a process that involves the State Planning Committee, several central government ministries, and provincial and local governments. The State Planning Committee determines the overall investment amount and has a supervisory role in the approval of investment projects and design of policies (Articles 12, 18). The Ministry of Agriculture and Food Industries (MAFI) and Ministry of Forestry, along with provincial authorities, translate general policies into a master plan up to the year 2000, assist provincial and district administrations in the development of pilot projects, and select the project managerial staff (Articles 15, 16, 20). Depending on the size of the project, supervision and evaluation are done by the Council of Ministers (large-scale projects covering several provinces), central government ministries and provincial authorities (projects in areas of over 700 hectares), and provincial agencies (small projects) (Article 17). The Ministry of Science, Technology, and Environment and two national science centers inspect the scientific components of the projects (Article 17).[4]

The provisions of Decree 327 thus attempt to lay out a strategy for barren land development. This strategy recognizes the central role of individual households in barren land development, as most strikingly expressed by the designation of a large share of the funds for credit to households. Government entities are confined to services that complement and support household activities, though land allocation is conditioned upon prescribed land use. In addition to productive components in agriculture and forestry, Decree 327 emphasizes the integrated character of rural development.

The Occurrence of Barren Land in the Vietnamese Highlands

Barren land has been used as a land-use category by various governments in Vietnam. As far back as 1943, 3 million hectares of land was classified as barren land (CRUNREP 1985). In 1960, the Food and Agriculture Organization of the United Nations identified 9.3 million hectares of "other" land in Vietnam, land that was not classified as either agricultural or forestry land nor used for urban development. In 1975, barren land was reported to have grown to 10.5 million hectares (CRUNREP 1985).

According to statistics by the current government, barren land can today be found in all eight major agroecological regions of Vietnam (see Table 12.1). In 1993, between 35 percent and 42 percent of the potential agricultural or forest land within the country, which corresponds to about 12 to 13 million hectares, were classified as barren land. Land classified as barren land thus exceeded agricultural and forestry lands.

Barren areas are much more frequent in highland areas than in the two deltas and lowlands.[5] The occurrence of barren areas is especially drastic in the Northern Mountains (60 to 65 percent). In the Central Highlands, barren land amounts to one-fourth to one-third

Table 12.1 Forest cover and barren lands

Region	Area (1,000 ha) 1991	Forest cover (% of area) 1943	1991	Barren land (% of area) 1993
Total	33,104	67	29	35–42
Northern Mountains	7,645	95	17	60–65
Northern Midlands	3,982	55	29	27–33
Red River Delta	1,030	3	3	5–14
North Central Coast	4,002	66	35	40–44
South Central Coast	4,582	62	32	42–49
Central Highlands	5,557	93	60	25–32
North East Mekong	2,348	54	24	23–34
Mekong Delta	3,957	23	9	12–21

Source: World Bank (1994).

Note: The estimates of barren land in 1993 include only the following areas that could potentially be developed for agriculture or forestry:

Northern Mountains = Lang Son, Cao Bang, Ha Giang, Tuyen Quang, Lao Cai, Yen Bai, Lai Chau, and Son La

Northern Midlands = Quang Ninh, Ha Bac, Bac Thai, Vihn Phu, Hoa Binh, and Thanh Hoa

Red River Delta = Hai Hung, Thai Binh, Nam Ha, Ninh, Ha Tay, Ha Noi, and Hai Phong

North Central Coast = Nghe An, Ha Tinh, Quang Binh, Quang Tri, and Thua Thien-Hue

South Central Coast = Quang Nam-Da Nang, Quang Nai, Bind Dinh, Phu Yen, Khanh Hoa, Ninh Thuan, and Bihn Thuan

Central Highlands = Kon Tum, Gia Lai, Dac Lac, and Lam Dong

North East Mekong = Tay Ninh, Song Be, Dong Nai, Ba Ria-Vung Tau, and Ho Chi Minh city

Mekong Delta = Long An, Tien Giang, Dong Thap, An Giang, Ben Tre, Vinh Long, Tra Vinh, Can Tho, Soc Trang, Ken Giang, and Minh Hai

of the land. In the North and South Central Coast, between 40 and 50 percent of the land is classified as barren, mostly in hilly and mountainous areas (Hyles 1993).

Barren areas in highland regions have very diverse origins and are ecologically heterogeneous. According to MAFI, barren land includes (1) steep mountain slopes that have been degraded by human interference, such as shifting cultivation and logging, (2) hilly regions with bush and scrub vegetation, pasture, and high grass, and (3) rocky mountains. The sizes of the barren plots show considerable variation, ranging from plots of less than 1,000 hectares to areas of more than 10,000 hectares (MAFI 1993). The occurrence of barren land has often been viewed as directly connected to the deforestation process. As Table 12.1 indicates, regions with a high incidence of barren land show relatively high rates and amounts of forest loss (World Bank 1994).

Barren land cannot be understood as a classification merely describing the physical characteristics of land. Nor is land classified as barren simply "empty land" that is currently not used. Political and economic criteria influence land classification as much as ecological aspects. In Vietnam, land is classified according to its intended use, and land classification is tightly connected to the jurisdictional authority of the different line ministries of agriculture, forestry, etc. (Sargent 1991). For example, during the mid-1980s the government redefined natural forest from areas with over 30 percent crown cover to areas with over 10 percent crown cover. The re-classification of land had the purpose of designating additional land as forest land to protect it from encroachment. Correspondingly barren land, as classified by the government, diminished since more land was put to forestry purposes (Table 12.1). In short, land is classified as barren if its actual land use does not coincide with its designated use, hence does not meet its function in national development planning. The occurrence of barren land should thus better be understood as an indicator of differences between the government's perception of appropriate land use and actual land-use patterns.

ALTERNATIVE BARREN LAND DEVELOPMENT STRATEGIES

As the preceding discussion suggests, the current state and use of barren land in Vietnam do not coincide with the government's perception of appropriate land use. The Decree 327 program is intended as a mechanism to integrate barren land into national development. Decree 327 lays out a strategy and provides policy instruments for the rehabilitation and intensification of land use. The decree, however, does not explicitly define the target groups at which it is aimed, nor does it specify a strategy for barren land development that pays attention to the interplay between policy instruments and local conditions.

Vietnamese policy-makers need to identify the target groups for government intervention and designate rural development strategies to assist them. Target groups and strategies have to be defined to facilitate understanding of the social dynamics that determine resource use. Once rural development strategies and local socioeconomic, cultural, and agroecological factors have been clarified, the expected outcomes of their interplay can be predicted. The implications of local conditions in the highlands for each strategy can be determined. Comparative assessment of the different strategies will then allow for analyzing the conditions under which each strategy will be most conducive to achieving the goals of Decree 327.

Three Target Groups and Strategies

Analysis of the provisions of Decree 327 suggests that the decree contains three scenarios of barren land use and development. These scenarios differ in the population targeted and the strategy proposed for developing more productive uses of barren land. Target groups and strategies can be briefly described in the following way:

- The *"resettlement strategy"*: Poor farmers from the lowlands resettle in the Vietnamese highlands to utilize the highlands' untapped resources.
- The *"sedentarization strategy"*: Migratory shifting cultivators move to permanent settlements and adopt fixed cultivation practices on previously unused land.
- The *"community development strategy"*: Sedentary highland cultivators, both Kinh and ethnic minorities, intensify agricultural production.

There are several indicators that the government has given priority to the resettlement and sedentarization strategies. In the first year of implementation (1993), resettlement and sedentarization projects received funding priority. In the forestry sector, a total of 430 projects were directed to resettlement (Hyles 1993). The Committee for Fixed Cultivation and Sedentarization was allocated US$10 million to support its plans of eventually settling 80,000 families (Smith 1993). A proposal by MAFI for central government and donor contributions to Decree 327 financing indicates a strong emphasis on resettlement. More than half of the targeted beneficiaries of barren land development projects come from regions outside the province in which the project is located (MAFI 1993).

The emphasis on resettlement and sedentarization projects under Decree 327 financing coincides with the government's renewed commitment to the sedentarization of shifting cultivators and resettlement of lowland farmers. The Ministry of Labor, War Invalids, and Social Affairs continues with resettlement activities at a rate of moving about 250,000 people each year (Witter 1993). The Master Plan 69 for Highland Development, issued in March 1992, emphasized the goal of assisting 3 million shifting cultivators in developing sedentary cultivation practices (Hyles 1993; Ohlsson 1990).

Differentiating Conditions in the Highlands and Their Relative Effects on the Strategies

Any development strategy generates a diversity of outcomes shaped by the interplay between the elements of overall strategy and highly localized conditions. The strategy will fail in certain localities, partially succeed in some, and meet its objectives in other places. Particularly in the Vietnamese highlands, which are culturally and ecologically very diverse, each of the three strategies described previously will result in a broad range of outcomes.

As an approximation, seven variables can be identified that help characterize the conditions in the Vietnamese highlands: land quality, wood balance, population density, land-use regime, food security, access to markets and support services, and government outreach. Each of these variables assumes different expressions in different localities, with different implications for each barren land development strategy. The combination of those expressions determines local conditions and thus the relative prospects of each strategy.

Land Quality Barren land occurs in all agroecological zones of Vietnam and, depending on the location, has very different agro-climatic characteristics. For example, estimates of slope, geology, soils, rainfall intensity, and seismic activity reveal that land in the highlands shows different degrees of susceptibility to degradation (Aldrick 1993). Agricultural and forestry activities may be rendered unsuccessful when developed on inappropriate sites.

Good land quality is an important factor of success in all three strategies. Yet a suitable land capability survey is lacking (Gray 1991). It is therefore probable that land of low quality, which does not allow economically viable production, will be identified for development. The risk of allocating low-quality land to beneficiaries in barren land development programs speaks for the community development strategy. When low-quality land is assigned to highland cultivators, they can often rely on traditional or already established systems of subsistence. This is not the case for those who have just moved into a new area and have no alternative sources of livelihood. In addition, local people can be expected to be more knowledgeable about land quality than outsiders and therefore make better informed land-use decisions.

Wood Surplus Expected future shortfalls in wood supply have motivated a strong forestry component in Decree 327. Regional fuelwood balances in the highlands, however, indicate that the sustainable supply of fuelwood, the main component of wood products, still far exceeds demand in the Northern Mountains and Central Highlands (UNDP/World Bank 1993). Although some highland areas may suffer from fuelwood shortage due to high local population density or favorable access to lowland markets, wood products are generally not scarce.

The prospects of fuelwood plantations are further constrained by the fact that the current distribution of rights to forest access does not favor conservation nor afforestation. As most forests are managed by the state, fuelwood collectors generally have few problems in exploiting the forests. The labor costs of fuelwood collection are low, putting downward pressure on the price of fuelwood. Local people thus lack incentives to invest into forest plantations and manage forests in a sustainable way.[6] In addition, many existing forests are on low quality and poorly stocked land, thus rendering forest plantations unprofitable (MFPD 1993; Smith 1993).

In the prevailing situation of de facto open access to forests and low price for fuelwood, any of the three strategies for barren land development will therefore face massive problems to encourage forest plantations.[7] Yet highland cultivators may be more inclined to plant trees since trees have been an essential part of most highland cultivation systems. Although tree planting is not likely to take the form of forest plantations, the widespread occurrence of scattered tree plantings indicates the viability of a strategy that aims at integrating trees into existing farming systems (UNDP/World Bank 1993). In addition, local people already practice subsistence-oriented cultivation, which can support them in the years before the long-term investment into trees bears fruit.

Population Density Population density and its implications for resource use show considerable variations among regions.[8] In 1989, while highland population densities were as low as around 30 persons/km^2 in Lai Chau and Gia Lai-Kon Tum provinces, population densities in Lang Son and Ha Tuyen provinces were more than double that figure (World Bank 1992; Hyles 1993). High population growth rates among the ethnic minorities and in-migration have led to increasing localized population pressure on resources. For example, the average per capita area of hillside plots in Lai Chau and Son La provinces decreased by about one-fourth between 1965 and 1985 (Do 1992).

Highland cultivators have responded to population pressure on their resource use strategies in various ways. Population pressure has led to agricultural intensification in some areas. For example, in Son La province, a trend toward more stable cultivation systems can be observed (Hyles 1993). On the other hand, some minority groups have responded to increasing population pressure and land scarcity by expanding into new areas or migrating to new areas in the Central Highlands and the cities (Witter 1993). Some Hmong are reported to go as far as 50 to 70 km to find suitable land for swidden plots (Do 1992).

The relative potential of the different strategies varies between regions with relatively low and high population densities. In highland areas with medium or high population densities, in-migration by new settlers will increase population pressure on the natural resource base and lead to increased out-migration and displacement of the original population. Supporting highland cultivators, sedentary and migratory, in their efforts to adapt their farming systems to increasing population pressure will strengthen the process of intensifying and stabilizing agriculture begun by many highland cultivators. In regions with low population densities, attempts to sedentarize migratory shifting cultivators will be prone to failure since shifting cultivation practices often present the economically most viable production system under these conditions (Smith 1993; Sargent 1991). In these regions, land colonization schemes may be the most effective strategy to intensify their agricultural productivity.

Land-Use Regime Barren land can neither be exclusively characterized as degraded land due to human overexploitation nor pristine land of low agricultural productivity that has not yet been touched by civilization. Barren land is subject to different land-use regimes. Barren mountain slopes may function as secondary land for rice farmers in valleys, providing grazing land and fuelwood. Barren slopes may also be fallow land in rotational cultivation systems and be claimed by ethnic minority groups through elaborate individual and common property regimes (Pham undated). Or they may also be pristine grasslands or land that has been abandoned by settlers from the Vietnamese lowlands after they had exhausted soil fertility due to inappropriate agricultural techniques (World Bank 1994).

In most locations, barren land cannot be presumed to be "empty land" that can be reclaimed without interfering with other people's resource use strategies. Moving lowland settlers into the highlands or highland cultivators to new areas in the highlands may thus generate and aggravate land-use conflicts between original inhabitants and settlers. Experience from resettlement efforts has shown the detrimental consequences of land-use conflicts for people's livelihood and resource base.

Lack of Food Security Many highland cultivators have not achieved food security. Nutritional surveys among ethnic minorities indicate that food availabilities are generally low and range from 100 to 300 kg paddy equivalent per person per year (Witter 1993). For example, the Thai and Ha Nhi are said to have an average 335 kg per person per year, while the Hmong and La Hu have 180 to 250 kg per person per year. Further, over the past decades, differences in food availability have widened. For example, the slight gap in annual per capita food production between Lai Chau and Son La provinces in 1965 has almost doubled between 1965 and 1985 (Do 1992).

It is not unlikely that land development that does not emphasize food security might actually promote food shortages and worsen the nutritional situation in already food-deficient areas. Lack of food security and severe poverty will lead to increasing pressure on resources and unsustainable resource use. Moving new settlers into already food-deficient districts will aggravate food deficiencies for the original population as well as prevent new settlers from achieving food security. The general lack of food security in the highlands therefore attests to the need for first stabilizing highland livelihood strategies and intensifying their agricultural production before moving more people into such areas.

Access to Markets and Support Services Integration into the national economy and the effectiveness of the administrative system vary among highland regions and villages. Poor transportation and communication systems curtail access to markets in many regions (Hyles 1993). Government services are generally scarce in highland areas, and the mass organizations are weak among ethnic minorities (Witter 1993). The effectiveness of extension is limited since extension activities concentrate on technical components of rural development, mainly forestry.[9] Provincial extension systems often lack the staff capacity to assist a bigger number of farmers in improving their livelihood strategies. State enterprises have been the main organizational units in many regions, often being more powerful than district- and commune-level administrative units (Ohlsson 1990).

Access to markets and the existence of effective government services are crucial for the effectiveness of barren land development programs.[10] Yet access to markets depends on costly investment in infrastructure, and government agencies do not build capacity to support highland cultivators overnight. Barren land development programs can therefore be expected to be more successful in areas that already have some basic infrastructure and government administrative capacity. Opening new areas for resettlement and sedentarization will be very expensive and require longer-term commitment. In addition, developing infrastructure into new areas is very likely to increase deforestation rates.

Government Outreach Government officials and extension agents, of whom most are Kinh, can rely on a common cultural framework and shared language when in contact with resettled Kinh cultivators in the highlands (Witter 1993). Communication with the ethnic minorities, however, is seriously constrained by language barriers and the extremely high illiteracy rates among them. Total enrollment for primary and secondary school is only 16 percent among ethnic minorities, with some groups, including the Tay, Thai, Muong, and Nung, above 20 percent and others, such as the Hmong, at about 5 percent (Witter 1993). Among the twelve largest ethnic groups, literacy rates vary between 83 percent (Tay) and 10 percent (Hmong), and in many villages, only few villagers are able to communicate in Vietnamese (Witter 1993). Development programs that target ethnic minority groups thus face more difficulties in the interactions between program staff and beneficiaries than programs that work with Kinh people.

The Relative Potential of the Strategies

After analyzing the effects of each variable on the three strategies, it remains to assess the three strategies from a comparative view. This section identifies the conditions under which each strategy can be expected to meet the objectives of Decree 327 and evaluates the likelihood of each strategy's success. Table 12.2 presents summary assessments.

The resettlement strategy can be expected to succeed on fertile barren land in regions with relatively low population densities. Those areas should currently not be used, and it should not be too costly to link them to surrounding infrastructure, markets, and support services. Ethnic affinity makes communication between settlers and officials easier. The resettlement strategy will therefore be most successful in regions where in-migration meets favorable conditions and does not cause negative impacts on the livelihood of original inhabitants.

Table 12.2 Differentiating conditions and their relative effects on the strategies

		Impact on strategy		
Variable	Condition	Resettlement	Sedentarization	Community development
Land quality	Uncertain	Negative	Negative	Positive
Wood balance	Surplus	Negative	Positive	Positive
Population density	High/medium	Negative	Positive	Positive
	Low	Positive	Negative	Negative
Food security	Lacking	Negative	Negative	Positive
Land-use regime	Currently used	Negative	Negative	Positive
Access to markets and government services	Limited	Negative	Negative	Positive
Government outreach	Favorable to Kinh	Positive	Negative	Neg./pos.[a]

a. The prospects of the community development strategy are better for Kinh villages than for villages with ethnic minority populations.

The sedentarization strategy will be successful in areas where migratory cultivators face increasing pressure on their livelihood and food security due to limited access to land and rapid population growth. The rapidity of deterioration, combined with lack of infrastructure and assistance from outside, has so far prevented such cultivators from significantly adjusting their livelihood strategies. Land quality has to be adequate to allow agricultural intensification, and physical and economic infrastructure, as well as government support services, should not be too costly to establish.

The community development strategy is likely to succeed in areas with relatively high population density where most of the land is currently used in intensive or extensive ways. Some basic infrastructure and limited access to markets may be available, but infrastructure and government assistance to the cultivators, who may live in precarious conditions, are lacking. Food security has barely or not yet been achieved, but land is fertile enough for agricultural intensification. Cultural affinity makes it easier for government agents to deal with Kinh villages than with members of ethnic minority groups.

The conditions for successful resettlement are rarely in place. Accessible land that is currently not cultivated or used in any form has become rare in the Vietnamese highlands. Resettlement programs in areas that are claimed by original inhabitants cause or increase land-use conflicts. Since food security has not been achieved in most highland regions, increasing pressure on the resource base would have detrimental impacts on the livelihood of settlers and the original inhabitants. Out-migration has been a frequent consequence of those conflicts in past resettlement programs (Do 1992; Nguyen 1992). Truly unexploited land is located in remote areas. Opening these areas for in-migration would require costly infrastructure investment and development of support services. In addition, colonization programs that open those regions for new settlers are likely to increase deforestation around new settlements.

The risk of allocating low-quality land to new settlers is significant, and its potential consequences on livelihood and resource use dramatic. In the past, Kinh settlers in the highlands have often been directly responsible for environmental degradation. Due to low-quality land and the lack of adequate farming techniques, lowland farmers have depleted highland colonization areas rapidly and often responded to declining yields by expanding the areas cultivated (Nguyen 1992).

Out-migration by ethnic minorities from densely populated areas indicates that some highland cultivators face increasing problems to meet subsistence demands on their original land (Witter 1993). The possibility of clearing new land in remote areas and the lack of infrastructure and outside support have so far prevented agricultural intensification. Yet, out-migration does not appear to be widespread, and, as experience has shown, the reasons underlying shifting cultivation practices are complex. Difficult access to markets, together with lack of infrastructure, experience with sedentary farming systems and sufficient land, can render rotational practices more profitable than fixed cultivation. In addition, there are only about one million migratory shifting cultivators (Ohlsson 1990), a small number in comparison with the total population of approximately seven million in the Northern Mountains and Central Highlands (World Bank 1992). Migratory swidden cultivation also contributes only a small portion to overall deforestation (World Bank 1994). Policies directed toward supplemental shifting cultivation, practiced on a secondary basis by about three million sedentary highland cultivators for reasons mostly related to poverty, present greater potential for successful development interventions (Ohlsson 1990).

Most highland cultivators live in established settlements and have developed land-use practices that utilize most of the accessible land in intensive or extensive ways. They have generally not achieved food security nor produced market-oriented crops giving them significant cash incomes. Yet some of them have proven the capacity to diversify their subsistence-oriented production and integrate cash crops in response to increasing access to markets and economic liberalization.[11] The community development strategy would build upon these responses to new economic opportunities. Assistance to highland communities would support agricultural intensification by improving infrastructure and social services, providing agricultural services and credit, and facilitating technical advice. Government assistance would facilitate them in achieving food security and integrating market-oriented products into their cultivation systems. After these communities have been stabilized and land-use intensified, land would have been freed up for lowland settlers. Secure livelihood and clear distribution of land rights would prevent land-use conflicts caused by in-migration or sedentarization programs.

DECREE 327 AS RURAL DEVELOPMENT POLICY: SUMMARY CONCLUSIONS

Decree 327 presents a programmatic statement by the government about national development policy. Poised for rapid economic development, the government attempts to tap all resources that are apparently not used for national development. Barren land, which covers between 35 and 42 percent of Vietnam and exceeds agricultural and forestry lands, is a prime target in these efforts. The term "barren land" itself alludes to government's dissatisfaction with the actual use and state of areas classified as barren. The designation of a large share of central government transfers to provincial and district authorities underlines the importance attributed to the integration of barren land into national development.

The goals of the Decree 327 program are enormous. The program expects to lift the production of industrial crops, replant forests on a large scale, and protect critical watersheds by improved vegetation cover. In a preliminary evaluation of 1,800 projects approved in 1993, the State Planning Committee estimated that the investment program will facilitate restoring agricultural production on 900,000 hectares and planting forest on 2,000,000 hectares by the year 2000.[12] Probably 500 of these projects fall into the agricultural sector; another 900 are in the realm of forestry; and about 300 are best classified in "other" sectors (Hyles 1993).

The highlands have played an increasingly important role in Vietnam's economic development strategy. Efforts to expand agricultural production have shifted to the highlands. The siltation of the Hoa Binh reservoir has brought watershed protection to the forefront of Vietnamese policy-makers' concerns. Drastic rates of forest loss have caused worry about future shortfalls in wood supplies. Correspondingly, the Committee for Ethnic Minorities and Mountainous Areas, established first in 1990, was upgraded to the status of a ministry in 1993 (Witter 1993).

Previous policies aimed at integrating Vietnam's highlands into national development have mostly taken the form of strategies that transform traditional highland livelihood adaptations and ecosystems. Entire villages of lowland farmers have been resettled to upland regions. Millions of hill and mountain cultivators have been moved and encouraged to abandon their traditional livelihood. The development of hydropower dams has displaced numerous villages and drastically changed highland landscapes. The establishment of plantations has attempted to rationalize resource use and modernize the upland economy.

Decree 327 appears to adhere to the approach taken in the past. Resettlement and sedentarization projects have received funding priority in the first year of the Decree's implementation. Comparative analysis of different rural development strategies has, however, revealed strong reasons speaking for concentrating barren land development efforts on programs targeted at existing highland communities. Supporting existing communities, as compared to sedentarization and resettlement programs, will be quite conducive for achieving the goals of Decree 327. Under diverse conditions, community development programs will be most likely to succeed in intensifying highland agriculture and stabilizing highland livelihood.

NOTES

1. An English translation of Decree 327 can be found in Appendix 1 of Smith (1993).
2. The provisions of Decree 327 on land allocation have been superseded by the new land law, passed by the National Assembly in July 1993. According to the new land law, households will be given twenty-year renewable tenure rights on land growing annual crops and fifty years for long-term crops (*Far Eastern Economic Review*, July 29, 1993). This summary assumes these new regulations as the relevant ones for the implementation of Decree 327.

3. The model that is often used to demonstrate the goals and instruments of Decree 327 is one of stratified forestry and agricultural production down the hillside (Smith 1993).

4. Le Trong Cuc notes in his chapter (this volume) that, in 1993, guidelines for the implementation of Decree 327 programs have been issued by the Ministry of Finance, General Department of Land Management, and Ministry of Forestry.

5. For the purpose of this chapter, the Vietnamese uplands are defined as the Northern Mountains, Central Highlands, and parts of the North and South Central Coast.

6. Officials in Son La province estimate that more than 90 percent of timber logged and wood cut each year in the province is "illegal" (Hyles 1993).

7. Various sources report experience from forest allocation programs that, despite input subsidies, financial incentives, and technical support, farmers did not want to take up land that requires afforestation (Sargent 1991; Bergman 1990; Hyles 1993; Gayfer and Shanks 1992; Smith 1993).

8. Population density is used here as a variable approximating the average area of farmed land per capita, a better measure for population pressure on resources.

9. For example, in Dac Lac province, 10 agriculturists, 2 livestock professionals, and 7 foresters on the provincial level and a total of 15 agricultural, 15 livestock, and 45 forestry professional staff at the district level served a population of about one million (Smith 1993).

10. According to Do (1992), regions with access to markets have seen the introduction of marketable cash crops (cinnamon, coffee, fruit trees, etc.) into highland cultivation systems in recent years.

11. Reports of successful farmer adaptation to changing conditions can be found in Hyles (1993), Eriksson (1993), Do (1992), Nguyen (1992), Ohlsson (1990), and Witter (1993).

12. These numbers refer to barren land development programs in all regions of Vietnam, not only the highlands.

BIBLIOGRAPHY

Aldrick, J. M. 1993. Annex 2: Land use assessments. Unpublished consultant's report. The World Bank.

Bergman, Axel. 1990. Report on forest plantations (fuelwood, agroforestry and industry). Field Document No. 4. *Forestry sector review: Tropical forestry action plan, Vietnam.* Hanoi: Ministry of Forestry, United Nations Development Programme, Food and Agriculture Organization of the United Nations.

CRUNREP (Committee for Rational Utilization of Natural Resources and Environmental Protection). 1985. National conservation strategy (draft). Delhi: Environmental Services Group.

Do Dinh Sam. August 1992. National background paper on shifting agriculture in Vietnam. Paper presented at workshop on Shifting Agriculture in Thailand, Laos, and Vietnam: Its Social, Economic, and Environmental Values Relative to Alternative Land Uses. Chiang Mai, Thailand.

Eriksson, Arne. 1993. Vietnam environmental policy and program priorities for an economy in transition. Unpublished consultant's report. The World Bank.

Far Eastern Economic Review, July 29, 1993.

Feeney, Griffith, and Peter Xenos. 1992. The demographic situation in Vietnam: Past, present, prospect. In *The challenges of Vietnam's reconstruction*, ed. Neil L. Jamieson, Nguyen Manh Hung, and A. Terry Rambo. Fairfax, VA: Indochina Institute, George Mason University.

Gayfer, Julian, and Edwin Shanks. 1991. *Northern Vietnam: Farmers, collectives, and the rehabilitation of recently reallocated hill land.* Social Forestry Network Paper 12a.

Gray, K. M. 1991. Fuelwood supply analysis. Technical Report No. 9. *Forestry sector review: Tropical forestry action plan, Vietnam.* Hanoi: Ministry of Forestry, United Nations Development Programme, Food and Agriculture Organization of the United Nations.

Hill, R. D. 1984. Aspects of land development in Vietnam. *Contemporary Southeast Asia* 5(4): 389–402.

Hyles, G. W. 1993. Environmental policy and program priorities for an economy in transition. Unpublished consultant's report. The World Bank.

MAFI (Ministry of Agriculture and Food Industries). 1993. *Bare lands in Vietnam: The existing situation, improvement, and use orientations up to the year 2000.* Hanoi: The Authors.

MFPD (Ministry of Forestry, Planning Department). 1993. *Economic realities to consider in developing strategies for forest land use.* Hanoi: The Authors.

Nguyen Manh Tuan. 1992. Real conditions of cultivation on high lands in four communes of two districts: Cho Don and Vo Nhai Bac Thai provinces. Unpublished project document. CIDSE.

Ohlsson, Bo. 1990. Forestry and rural development. Technical Report No. 2. *Forestry sector review: Tropical forestry action plan, Vietnam.* Hanoi: Ministry of Forestry, United Nations Development Programme, Food and Agriculture Organization of the United Nations.

Payne, Lina, and Georgina Houghton. 1993. Visit report: Mai Son district. Unpublished consultant's report. Action Aid.

Pham Quang Hoan. Undated. Common property in the high plateaus of Central Vietnam.

Sargent, Caroline. 1991. Land use issues. Technical Report No. 1. *Forestry sector review: Tropical forestry action plan, Vietnam.* Hanoi: Ministry of Forestry, United Nations Development Programme, Food and Agriculture Organization of the United Nations.

Smith, G. A. 1993. Livestock and barren land development. Working Paper No. 1, Vietnam Environment Program and Policy Priorities. Consultant's report. The World Bank.

UNDP (United Nations Development Program) and the World Bank. 1993. Vietnam: Rural and household energy issues and options. Energy Sector Management Assistance Programme (ESMAP). Consultant's report. The World Bank.

Vu Quy Nhan. 1992. Population policies and development in Vietnam. In *The challenges of Vietnam's reconstruction,* ed. Neil L. Jamieson, Nguyen Manh Hung, and A. Terry Rambo. Fairfax, VA: Indochina Institute, George Mason University.

Witter, Sophie. 1993. *Working with ethnic minorities in Vietnam: An introduction to the issues.* Program document, Save the Children Fund (UK).

World Bank. 1992. *Vietnam: Population, health and nutrition sector review.* Country sector report. Washington, D.C.: The World Bank.

World Bank. 1994. *Environmental program and policy priorities for an economy in transition.* Washington, D.C.: The World Bank.

PART FIVE

Comparative Analyses

CHAPTER 13

Functions of the Forest for Laotian Households: Supermarket, Gold Mine, and Welfare Subsidy

Carol Ireson
Willamette University, Oregon

INTRODUCTION

In highland Vietnam and rural Laos most residents farm for a living, but their agricultural livelihoods are enhanced and supplemented by nearby forests. This study of forest use in rural Laos suggests that the forests of the Vietnamese highlands may also be central to the rural economies of those regions.

The forest has a number of functions for the rural Laotian household, providing a variety of products necessary for survival of household members. Many rural residents regularly use the forest like a supermarket, to obtain food and medicine for their own use. Other rural residents use the forest like a gold mine, to obtain a cash income. Nearly all rural residents use the forest like a welfare subsidy during difficult crop years when drought, insects, or flooding destroy crops; the forest provides a "safety net," providing food and income in a time of economic insecurity.

Even in good cropping years, though, the forest is one of three major "pillars" of the rural economy in Laos. The other two pillars are rice agriculture and animal husbandry. The importance of these three "pillars" varies from village to village and from year to year. This study describes the importance of the forest as a pillar of the rural household economy in three different kinds of rural households: farming households with access to old-growth forest, farming households with access only to degraded forest or brush fallows, and households with at least one salaried employee.

LITERATURE REVIEW

Forest foraging is sometimes a principal source of subsistence for rural villagers throughout Southeast Asia as among the Mnong Gar peoples of Vietnam's Central Highlands (studied by Georges Condominas before their village was destroyed by war in 1962). Among this group, wild foods, "especially bamboo shoots, were eaten in the greatest numbers when the rice was growing but not yet harvested" (1977, 120). Long fallow shifting rice cultivation was the main source of subsistence among this group.

Filipino villagers of Leyte depend on the forest for staple food and income products during drought years when their agricultural crops wither and their surpluses are depleted. Leyte villagers who lost their upland crop to drought visited the nearby forest more frequently, gathering rattan, cutting lumber, trapping game, collecting shrimp and fish in the streams, and foraging for edible plants. While the village standard of living declined during the drought, the maintenance of their irrigated paddy crops and their increased forest activities enabled the village households to weather the drought year without suffering nutritional or economic hardship (Belsky and Siebert 1983).

During the rainy season in northeast Thailand, natural food gathered from paddies, ponds, and forests may account for up to half of the total food consumption of some rural villagers. Although such food is usually less available during cold and hot seasons, it is still "extremely important" (Somnasang, Rathakette, and Ratanapanya 1988, 78). Natural food provides essential calories and protein, as well as vitamins and minerals that would otherwise be lacking in village diets. Market-oriented irrigated paddy rice farmers also supplement their diets and incomes with wild foods. In fact the modern irrigation scheme near Kalasin (northeast Thailand) ensures the year-round availability and abundance of many wild foods (Leimar and Price 1987). These foods flourish near irrigation ditches, in areas of irrigation water seepage, around trees growing along paddy dikes, and near wells.

Both upland and paddy-farming Laotians depend on forest products for subsistence and sometimes for income like the farmers of Vietnam, the Philippines, and Thailand. Most of the chroniclers of rural life in Laos mention the subsistence forest activities of Lao villagers as a minor source of income (Kaufman 1956; Wulff 1972), as a dietary supplement or a food source during a lean year (Halpern 1964; Orr 1966), as a regular part of the household economy (Condominas 1970; Branfman 1978; Maynard and Kraiboon 1969), or as "hunting or gathering . . . . and [other] forms of disguised pleasures" (Taillard 1971; translation by Barber 1979, 85). Forest processes are essential for the continued fertility of Khmu and Lamet (two midland ethnic groups) rotational swidden-farming systems, while forest products are a central element of both midland and upland household economies (Izikowitz 1951; Tayanin and Lindell 1991; Lemoine 1972). A brief study of four villages (three midland and one lowland Lao village) in Savannakhet province reported the use of forest products for food (four villages), construction materials (three villages), staple food (two villages), and medicine and income (one village each) (SUAN 1991). Little detail is available, however, which describes village forestry activities in the context of the household and village economy.

VILLAGE FORESTRY STUDY IN BOLIKHAMXAY PROVINCE, LAO PDR

The present study focuses on rural households in Bolikhamxay, a province located in the narrow central part of the Lao Peoples' Democratic Republic (PDR), which has a variety of forest types and three active timber/forestry enterprises. It includes respondents from 200 rural households randomly selected from village lists of eight pre-selected villages and two enterprise centers. Nearly all respondents are ethnic Lao, though a minority are from midland groups. Three types of rural households are represented in the sample: eighty households with at least one salaried employee of a forestry enterprise, fifty-four households in villages with access to old-growth forest, and sixty-six households in villages with access only to forests with small trees and brush and without access to old-growth forest. Women were selected to represent the household during the interview since they are more commonly forest foragers than men. Respondents range in ages from twenty to fifty-five.

Forest Foraging

Forest activities and products are an integral part of the household economy in Bolikhamxay. Nearly all village households depend, to some extent, on forest gathering for food, medicine, income, or construction and craft materials. Most village households gather forest products at least four to five times per week; 45 percent of these women consider forest gathering a "vocation" (n = 120). Forty percent of all rural families studied ate a forest food the day before we visited them, and a similar proportion (38 percent) sold forest products recently (n = 200). Respondents report a total of 141 different products gathered by household members: 37 types of food items, 68 types of medicinal products, 18 types of products for use, and 18 types of animals. Even richer households or households of richer villages engage in regular forest collection. On the average, members of each household studied gather eight different kinds of items from the forest. Most families gather only one kind of medicinal plant, sarsaparilla, which is used to make tea or to flavor rice whiskey. Male and female herbalists collect a greater variety of forest products. The most common items gathered or hunted (reported by at least thirty households) are listed in Table 13.1.

Composite village lists combining all forest products gathered or hunted by respondents' families in each village reveal that each village gathers at least twenty-eight forest products, with the longest listing fifty-three items. The number of items collected in each village does not seem to be related to the apparent poverty or wealth of a village, since one of the better-off villages gathers the same number of different products as the poorest

Table 13.1 Items gathered or hunted by household members in Bolikhamxay province

Product	Gatherers (no.)
Food plants	
Bamboo shoots (*Noh Mai*)	165
Mushrooms (*Het*)	142
Calamus shoots (*Noh Boun*)	64
Rattan shoots (*Noh Wai*)	56
Medicinal plants	
Sarsaparilla (*Ya Hua*)	57
Uravia micrantha (*Kamlang Seuakhong*)	37
Use products	
Rattan (*Wai*)	55
Elephant grass (*Nya Kha*)	43
Thitga resin (*Khi Si*)	40
Bamboo for weaving (*Mai Hi*)	37
Forest animals	
Fish/freshwater shrimp (*Pa/Kung*)	61
Mouse/rat	56
Birds	50
Squirrel	34

village. Members of 38 percent of the 200 households supplement their own household production by selling or bartering the following types of forest products: food items, 74 households; use items, 73 households; animals or animal products, 53 households; and medicinal items, 11 households.

Households most commonly sell mushrooms, bamboo shoots, resin, rattan, cardamom, freshwater shrimp, and small animals. Other than sarsaparilla, the gathering of medicinal plants appears quite specialized and is usually done by an older man or woman in the village. Only one of our respondents gathers medicinal plants regularly and sells nine different varieties.

Household Economy

Members of the "average" study household cultivate paddy rice and maintain a highland field where they also grow rice and a few vegetable or fruit crops (based on the full sample of 200). They clear a "new" upland field every one or two years, returning to the old field after four years. Members of the average household consume all of their paddy rice and highland field production and grow a small "kitchen garden" also. The average family experienced at least one natural disaster within the previous five years, which destroyed its rice crop so family members did not have enough rice to last through the year. They have three buffalo they use for paddy production, and also raise two pigs and a dozen chickens.

This "average" picture, though accurate, masks some striking differences: differences between village and rural enterprise households, and differences between villages with and without access to old-growth forests. The following discussion of forest use and the household economy first compares forest use in rural village households with forest use in rural enterprise households. Second, it compares forest use in rural village households that have access to old-growth forest to forest use in rural village households that do not have such access.

Forest Use: Village vs. Enterprise Households

Enterprise households utilize the forest less than village households; however, their living conditions are generally better. Furthermore, the two types of household economies derive their livelihoods from different sources.

Forest Activities Village households clearly gather from the forest and brush land around their village more frequently than do enterprise households ($t = 3.76$; $p < .001$). Members of considerably less than one-half of enterprise households had visited the forest in the week preceding the study, while members of almost three-quarters of village households had gathered in the forest (41 percent vs. 72 percent). Village families are much more likely than enterprise families to have included forest products in their meals the day before their interview ($X^2 = 29.11$, $p < .001$). Village families are much more likely than enterprise families to acknowledge that gathering is a "vocation" for at least one of its members. Finally, village households gather more forest products and more different types of products than enterprise families ($t = 6.03$, $p < .001$; $t = 5.27$, $p < .001$, respectively).

Household Economy and Living Conditions Economic levels of enterprise and village households appear similar, though sources of household support are different. However, enterprise living conditions are better than those of villagers on almost every measure.

Village and enterprise respondents report similar levels on most family economy indicators measured in the interview study. The average amounts of rice available, and crops and forest products sold are similar (Table 13.2). Two of the three indicators of family wealth are also similar: condition of the family house and larger household goods owned. However, over one-quarter of enterprise families do not own their own house. In addition, villagers own twice as many larger animals (buffalo, cattle, pigs) as enterprise households. Enterprise cash income reported, though, is more than double the income reported by villagers, thus offsetting other enterprise economic disadvantages.

The selling of forest products provides a secondary source of income in some village and enterprise households (14 percent vs. 10 percent). Enterprise respondents report two other main income sources for their households: income from the enterprise and the sale of animals or crops. A minority of enterprise households trade or sell processed food or drink. Village households rely even more heavily than enterprise households on agricultural produce for their cash income. They commonly sell an animal or crop if cash is needed. Village families produce most of their own subsistence, while three-quarters of enterprise households supplement their cash incomes with swidden rice cultivation as insurance against family emergency or government insolvency. Half of all villagers (49 percent) depend on a combination of shifting agriculture and paddy cultivation, 29 percent grow only paddy rice, and 22 percent cultivate only swidden fields.

The living conditions of enterprise households are better than those of village households on almost every measure. Enterprise households surpass village households in child survival, mothers' educational and literacy levels, boiling drinking water, eating protein food, and births assisted by a trained birth attendant. Women in enterprise households also have a less burdensome workload, since enterprises provide convenient drinking water and rice milling (see Table 13.3).

Table 13.2 Household economy—T-tests of differences between enterprise and village

	Mean			
Variable name	Enterprise	Village	T-test	
Rice available	1283	1220	– n.s.	
Crops sold	1.76	1.58	– n.s.	
Forest products sold	1.21	.79	1.62	n.s.
Cash available	4404	2012	– 4.18	***
Housing quality	1.73	1.64	– 1.44	n.s
Animals	2.53	5.07	3.58	***
Households goods	5.68	5.50	– n.s.	
Wealth	– .15	.09	– n.s	

*** = $p < .001$

n.s. = Not statistically significant

Table 13.3 Living conditions—T-tests of differences between enterprise and village

Variable name	Mean: Enterprise	Mean: Village	T-test
Child survival	.79	.70	– 2.25 *
Boil water	2.95	2.45	– 7.00 ***
Birth conditions	4.13	2.47	– 6.61 ***
Educational level	3.62	2.08	– 5.36 ***
Literacy	2.56	1.68	– 4.04 ***
Diet quality	2.84	2.43	– 4.35 ***
Children in school	.96	.92	– 1.42 n.s.
Overall workload	12.98	17.91	6.01 ***

* = $p < .05$
*** = $p < .001$
n.s. = Not statistically significant

In sum, economic levels seem to be similar, with the cash income of enterprise households approximately matching the animal wealth of villagers. The type of economy is different though: a cash economy vs. subsistence economy. Enterprise families report more diverse sources of income, but villagers report a greater variety of food sources. Enterprise households enjoy somewhat better living conditions than villagers.

Relationship Between Forest Use and Household Economy Rural villagers seem to use the forest like we use an urban supermarket. They go "shopping" almost daily in their forest supermarket for household food and other items they need. A larger proportion of enterprise forest users utilize the forest like a gold mine, "mining" its products for the income they provide. Some villagers also use the forest in this way.

Households with Access to Old-Growth Forest Versus Those Without Villagers from all eight study villages forage in forests with small trees or brush land, swamps and waterways, and the margins of fields, while villagers from four villages are also able to forage in old-growth forest. Households in these two types of villages use the forest somewhat differently. Villagers with access to old-growth forest gather daily while households without such access gather less often but sell some of what they gather. The economic conditions of households in both types of villages appear similar, though households with access to old growth have a somewhat higher quality of life.

Households with access to old-growth forest visit the forest somewhat more frequently than those without such access. That is, households with access to old growth are more likely to visit the forest "every day" (41 percent vs. 15 percent) while households without such access are more likely to report that it has been more than two weeks since they last visited the forest (27 percent vs. 16 percent). Perhaps as a result, respondents from old-growth households tend to more frequently identify their forest work as "a vocation" ($X^2 = 3.7$, $p < .10$). Villagers with no access to old growth report selling more types of forest products ($t = -1.98$, $p < .05$).

There are a few differences between the two types of households on economic indicators. Villagers without access to old growth sell more varieties of forest products. These same villagers tend to report less rice available for their families, are more dependent on swidden cultivation alone, and have a greater variety of income sources than old-growth households. Over half of the households without access to old growth sell animals or produce, while a number of these families sell forest products, run shops, sell prepared food or drink, or engage in casual wage labor (see Table 13.4). These are all income opportunities created by or available to women, with the exception of casual wage labor, which can be done by either sex. Old-growth households rely almost entirely on sales of animals or agricultural produce for cash income, though a few sell forest products.

Old-growth villagers have a somewhat better quality of life than villagers without access to old-growth forest. Respondents in old-growth households are more likely to report that they gave birth most recently with the assistance of an experienced attendant or in a hospital, and that they ate a protein food in their meals the previous day. Educational and literacy levels of mothers are higher in old-growth households than in those of the other households, though still quite low. Old-growth foragers report a greater variety of subsistence work tasks, however, reflecting their more diverse subsistence base.

Although the differences between these two types of households are not dramatic, old-growth households have a more diverse subsistence base, while households without access to old growth are somewhat more oriented to market activities.

Forest and the Household Economy While nearly all villagers use the forest as a supermarket, villagers without access to old-growth forest are more likely to "mine" the forest for its income potential. This is consistent with other aspects of their economy. Somewhat rice-short due to dependence on less productive swidden cultivation, villagers without access to old growth exploit several cash-earning opportunities, including the sale of forest products.

Forest as a Welfare Subsidy The forest has, for generations, been the source of food, shelter, and safe haven for needy Lao. With Laos' historically low population density and low forest resource exploitation, the mixed rural economy of paddy, swidden, gardening, forest gathering and hunting, and animal raising has been an adaptive one. In this village economy, the forest provides regular sustenance and also becomes the welfare system for years of crop shortage, while animals provide cash in cases of emergency. The wealth of the Lao is in their rice fields and animals, but the welfare system of the Lao is in their forests.

Table 13.4 Income sources—Cross-tabulated with type of village: With or without access to old-growth forest

	With access		Without access		
Income source	No.	(%)	No.	(%)	
Sell animals, crops	29	(88)	20	(54)	
Sell forest products	3	(9)	7	(19)	$x^2 = 31.95$
Sell cooked food, whiskey; shopkeeping	0	(–)	4	(11)	$p < .001$
Craftwork, sewing, hairdressing	1	(3)	2	(5)	
Clear forest, plant trees	0	(–)	4	(11)	
Total	33	(100)	37	(100)	

This study was not done at a time of rice shortage or government insolvency. It was carried out within two or three months of the rice harvest and at a time when enterprise workers had been paid regularly (in rice and cash) for several months. Therefore, few of the households were economically stressed. Most village households, though, reported rice shortfalls every year of two to three months with a major loss of their rice crop at least once in the last five years. Periodically, also, units of government like the enterprises are unable to pay their workers. During a time of shortage, all rural people rely on the bounty of the forest for their survival. One group of villagers showed us their dietary staple during these rice-short months, digging up a bulbous tuber in a wooded area near their village. Conveniently, they said, these tubers are at their biggest in April, just when rice shortages usually begin. I doubt, though, that the growing cycle of these tubers is so sensitive to cycles of government insolvency! Unfortunately, the forest welfare system will be available to a smaller and smaller proportion of Laotians as the population density increases and as the remaining forest is commercially exploited.

IMPACT OF COMMERCIAL LOGGING ON RURAL FOREST USE

Gathering forests of Laos today are informally held as "commons" by villages and are protected by government policy against the clearing of large trees for swidden cultivation. These forests, though, are not currently protected against commercial logging. Government policies of economic liberalization (the New Economic Mechanism), a strong world market in tropical hardwoods, and the construction of better roads and bridges have led to a dramatic increase in logging since the mid-1980s. Logging rates are estimated at far above sustainable levels designated by even industry spokesmen. As a result, more forest-dependent households are being affected every year by commercial logging, often carried out by companies backed by Japanese, Thai, and Taiwanese capital or supported by Swedish foreign aid.

This study not only demonstrates the integral part played by gatherers and by forest products and activities in the economies of rural households, but also suggests the direction of change likely with the deterioration of forest resources. Three of the villages without access to old-growth forests seem to be adjusting to the depreciated economic value of their forests. Respondents in these three villages report a more diverse set of income sources than villagers with access to old-growth forests, though economic levels of both types of villagers are similar.

The fourth study village without access to old-growth forest was actually in the process of losing its old-growth forest to logging during the time of fieldwork. This village was not the poorest village among our eight villages; yet, it was still quite forest dependent. Resentment toward logging activities was palpable in this village. These villagers reported that logging activities included killing or scaring away all forest animals, killing all the fish, and destroying other forest foods. Even the ancient large water animals, which may have spiritual powers, had been destroyed. These villagers expected drier streams in the dry season and more flooding in the rainy season because logging roads have filled in the stream beds. During the logging period, animals fled from the forest area, fish in ponds and streams were harvested by grenade, and downed timber made it difficult to negotiate forest paths.

Households in this fourth village have not yet developed other income or livelihood-producing activities, like the aforementioned three villages, to replace products and income from the forest. Further research might follow economic changes in this village as villagers struggle to adjust to their diminished resource base. In conclusion, an adequate gathering forest is an important pillar of the Lao village economy, important to more villagers for its subsistence functions as a supermarket and welfare subsidy than for its income function as a gold mine. A loss of gathering forests requires more or different village production, an increase in cash to purchase items that can no longer be manufactured from gathered forest products, and a different kind of welfare system.

Forests are likely to be just as important to the rural economy in highland Vietnam as they are in rural Laos. Forest resources in both countries undoubtedly are used similarly for household subsistence, income, and welfare. Protecting gathering forests and creating rural economic opportunities in both rural Laos and highland Vietnam, then, will maintain the rural household subsistence base while enabling household members, both women and men, to expand their sources of income. It is hoped that the price of integration into the world economy is not the unemployment of forest gatherers and the destabilization of rural household economies in both Laos and Vietnam.

BIBLIOGRAPHY

Barber, Martin John Philip. 1979. Migrants and modernization: A study of change in Lao society. Ph.D. dissertation, University of Hull.

Belsky, Jill, and Steve Siebert. 1983. Household responses to drought in two subsistence Leyte villages. *Philippine Quarterly of Culture and Society* 11:237–56.

Branfman, Fred. 1978. The village of deep pond: Ban Xa Phang Meuk. Occasional Papers Series No. 3, Asian Studies Committee. Amherst: University of Massachusetts.

Condominas, Georges. 1970. The Lao. In *Laos: War and revolution*, ed. Nina Adams and Alfred McCoy, 9–28. New York: Harper and Row.

Condominas, Georges. 1977. *We have eaten the forest.* New York: Hill and Wang.

Halpern, Joel. 1964. Economy and society of Laos: A brief survey. New Haven: Southeast Asia Studies Monograph 5. Yale University.

Ireson, Carol. 1989a. The role of women in forestry in the Lao PDR Vientiane. Swedish International Development Authority (unpublished report).

Ireson, Carol. 1989b. The friendly forest: Forest gathering and the subsistence food system of rural Lao families. Paper presented at the Annual Meetings of the Rural Sociological Society, Seattle, August.

Ireson, Carol. 1991. Women's forest work in Laos. *Sociology and Natural Resources* 4:23–36.

Izikowitz, Karl Gustav. 1951. Lamet: Hill peasants in French Indochina. Etnologiska Studier No 17. Goteborg, Sweden: Etnografiska Museet.

Kaufman, Howard. 1956. Village life in Vientiane province. Vientiane: USAID Mission to Laos (unpublished report).

Lemoine, Jacques. 1972. *Un Village Hmong Vert du Haut Laos.* Paris: Centre National de la Recherche Scientifique.

Liemar, Lisa, and Michael Price. 1987. Wild foods and women farmers: A time allocation study in northeast Thailand. Paper presented at Association for Women in Development Conference, Washington, D.C.

Maynard, Paul, and Polachart Kraiboon. 1969. Evaluation study of the Muong Phieng cluster area. Stanford Research Institute, Menlo Park, California (unpublished report prepared for the USAID Mission to Laos).

Orr, Kenneth. 1966. Behavioral research project for the Sedone Valley program: Southern Laos—Preliminary presentation of interviews and questionnaire data from Lao officials and villagers. Vientiane: USAID Mission to Laos (unpublished report).

Somnasang, Praphimporn, Pagarat Rathakette, and Sumalee Ratanapany. 1988. The role of natural foods in northeast Thailand. In *Rapid rural appraisal in northeast Thailand: Case studies*, ed. George Lovelace, Sukaesinee Subhadhira, and Suchint Simaraks, 78–104. Khon Kaen, Thailand: KKU-Ford Rural Systems Research Project, Khon Kaen University.

SUAN (Southeast Asian Universities Agroecosystem Network). 1991. Swidden agroecosystems in Sepone District, Savannakhet province, Lao PDR. Khon Kaen, Thailand: SUAN Regional Secretariat, Khon Kaen University.

Tayanin, Damrong, and Kristina Lindell. 1991. *Hunting and fishing in a Kammu village.* Malmo and London: Curzon Press.

Wulff, Robert. 1972. A comparative study of refugee and nonrefugee villages. Part 1: A survey of long-established villages of the Vientiane Plain. Vientiane: USAID Mission to Laos (unpublished report).

CHAPTER 14

Coffee and Culture: Smallholders, Minorities, and Plantations in Highland Southeast Asia

Eric Crystal
University of California, Berkeley

SOUTHEAST ASIAN COFFEE IN HISTORIC PERSPECTIVE

According to an ancient legend, the discovery of coffee is traced to Khaldi, an Abyssinian goat herder who often spent long weeks with his animals in remote rural areas. Normally the goats would sleep calmly throughout the night, allowing Khaldi also to enjoy a good sleep. One night, however, the goats continued to play and frolic all evening, never showing the slightest indication of fatigue. The next day a tired Khaldi noted that the animals had been feeding on a strange hard red berry appearing under the glistening leaves of a low bush. Intrigued, Khaldi tossed some of these unknown berries into water and drank the steaming hot brew. From such experiments with wild plants ultimately emerged what today is a universal passion for brewed coffee.

Wild coffee trees are known to have originated in the mountain and hill environments of lands around the horn of Africa. Local and subsequent international trade in coffee was initially managed by Arab traders from the port of Mocha in what is today Yemen on the southern tip of the Arabian peninsula. By the thirteenth century, the port of Mocha flourished as a vital entrepot. European cargo ships sailed north to coffee houses in Venice, Vienna, and Amsterdam while maritime and overland traders brought cargoes of dried coffee beans to much of the Arab world. The exclusive shipping and cultivation monopoly of the merchants of Mocha was finally threatened in the latter decades of the fifteenth century as the port began to silt up.

Interruptions in the European coffee trade were especially felt by the dominant seafaring nation of the era: Holland. The Dutch by this time had established a far-flung mercantile empire that ranged from the Caribbean and north Atlantic seaboard of America to South Africa, Ceylon, and the vast tropical Asian archipelago of the Netherlands East Indies. Looking to the future, the Dutch succeeded in stealing a number of young coffee plants for trials on the island of Java. Predictably coffee flourished there at higher altitudes, nourished by especially rich and well-drained volcanic soils. Before long Java had surpassed the horn of Africa as the world's major coffee-producing area. By 1724, a total of 800,000 pounds of coffee were purchased in Batavia for export (Wrigley 1988, 40). From Java, coffee cultivation was spread both by colonial policy and by indigenous trading networks to Sumatra, Sulawesi, and even as far afield as Timor and Papua New Guinea. By the mid-nineteenth century, Southeast Asia had become the prime producer of quality coffees in the world. Indeed, even to this day in the United States a synonym for a cup of coffee is a "cup of Java."

Although South America currently produces the world's largest volume of coffee, many of the finest quality coffees are grown in Southeast Asia. In Indonesia, the most valuable of coffees is found on the island of Sulawesi northeast of Java in the mountains of the Quarles Range. Here reside a highland minority people known as the Toraja who have cultivated coffee for the last 150 years. In former times, this coffee was traded to lowland middlemen at the market town of Kalosi. Even today coffee continues to be termed "Kalosi Sulawesi" in the retail trade. Coffee cultivation in the Toraja culture area long preceded the arrival of Dutch colonial forces.

Indeed, thirty years before the establishment of Western colonial administration in 1905, lowland Muslim warlords conducted vicious wars with their upland tribal allies for control of the valuable coffee trade. By the time the Dutch colonial administration began to sink roots, coffee cultivation was established over much of Tana (Land of the) Toraja (Bigalke 1981, 32). Dutch plantations were ultimately established in Tana Toraja, but they never exceeded the smallholder output in the region either in the area of plantings or the volume of coffee production.

In sum, coffee was distributed by means of indigenous market networks throughout the Indonesian archipelago. A combination of cool climate, limestone soil, and assiduous techniques of cultivation conspired to render the crop of the Toraja highlanders one of the most valued of coffees in the world. Meanwhile coffee came to be planted elsewhere in Southeast Asia: in the Luzon highlands of the Hispanic Philippines, on the Shan Plateau of Burma, and in hill and mountain areas of the Indochinese peninsula where France maintained a colonial presence. In highland areas of Laos (Pakse) and in the southern highlands of Vietnam (Ban Ma Thuot), coffee was extensively planted, largely in estates managed by expatriate personnel.

Coffee consumption is rising worldwide with especially high consumption curves in countries such as China and Japan, which traditionally have preferred tea to coffee. For countries such as Brazil and Colombia, coffee has for decades been a major source of foreign exchange. Because coffee is so important as a cash crop, government policies aimed at enhancing production levels, promoting exports, and maintaining prices are often crucial in determining household returns, plantation profits, and national foreign exchange earnings. Coffee production in Southeast Asia is uniquely confined to higher altitude farming areas. The most valuable coffee throughout this region—Arabica—normally can be grown successfully only at altitudes exceeding 1,000 meters above sea level. However, Arabica is often susceptible to disease and for that reason plantings remain limited. Robusta varieties are grown at lower altitudes, but the quality of these beans is generally considered inferior.

In Southeast Asia, the higher one ascends in altitude the more distant one moves from centers of political administration, urban culture, and national politics. Traditionally, upland areas have been inhabited by ethnic minorities, tribal peoples whose languages, ceremonial and religious systems, and worldviews differ significantly from dominant lowland peoples. Oftentimes there is a striking difference in technological sophistication, population density, and physical appearance between the residents of the distant mountains and the tillers of wet rice in the lowlands. Throughout Southeast Asia, it is the highlanders who remain the growers of coffee.

COFFEE IN UPLAND EASTERN INDONESIA

This chapter focuses on issues in Southeast Asian highland coffee production that have emerged during ongoing studies on the Toraja region of eastern Indonesia. It will highlight the prospects for economic development, stabilization of settlement, assurance of equity in development, and maintenance of minority cultural rights in upland Vietnam.

Indonesia, with a population of 190 million dispersed over more than 5,000 inhabited islands in the largest archipelago in the world, is an extraordinarily diverse nation. Here ethnic distinction is not only a function of the highland-lowland bifurcation, but also of a broad marine dispersal of Austronesian-speaking peoples in late Neolithic times. Prime coffee-producing areas today are found in the Batak-populated Mandheling mountains of Sumatra, the Toraja highlands of Sulawesi, and the upland areas of Indonesian New Guinea (Irian Jaya). In the Toraja culture area, a fairly densely populated region of 50,000 highlanders were able to keep Dutch colonial forces out of their homeland until the dawn of the twentieth century. Although notions of imperial expansion rather than motivations of pecuniary greed motivated the final Dutch assault on the region in 1905, by the time the Toraja highlands had fallen under the control of Holland a valuable coffee crop was already firmly established.

Artisanal (folk, peasant, and household) coffee production has thus been the norm in this part of Southeast Asia. The management unit here is the ambilineal extended family; plantings are limited by the availability of garden land, altitude, and the supply of family labor. Dutch plantations were established in the Toraja highlands during the relatively brief (1905–1942) interregnum of colonial rule. Nevertheless, most coffee in this region in the present as in the past has been planted by smallholders. The economic consequences of this indigenous planting regime have been significant. Coffee has long served as the single, most important source of cash for local villagers. The Toraja highlands, even with extensive terracing and some high valley fields, have always been less than self-sufficient in rice. Cash crops (traditionally coffee, and more recently, cloves, garlic, and cabbage) have facilitated a vigorous trade in lowland rice, precious metals, and manufactured clothing for over a century.

During the last decade a significant change has been under way in Toraja coffee cultivation. A major Japanese company, P.T. Toarco Jaya, and several highly capitalized Indonesian firms have established new coffee plantations. The Japanese corporation negotiated with the national government to manage coffee-producing lands formerly under private Dutch plantation management. Indigenous Indonesian companies within the last five years have aggressively moved to take over lands formerly planted to coffee by local villagers. Central government concern with expanding export crop earnings, private business interest in profiting from the international coffee trade, and local government acquiescence to national policy has led to significant tension over land-use issues.

In Indonesia, the government maintains ultimate control over "forested" lands. Tenure certificates are granted only for irrigated rice lands, not for hill tracts that might be suitable for coffee. Under these circumstances, interested private concerns negotiated plantation management rights directly with the Ministry of Agriculture. When companies arrived in the Toraja region in 1990, they were supported by administrative decrees and the force of law in evicting farmers from their upland coffee lands. Several mass demonstrations and instances of passive resistance (lying in the path of a bulldozer) reflected peasant displeasure at the confiscation of coffee gardens by outside companies. Many displaced smallholders have filed claims in the local court to try to regain control of their land and coffee harvests. Others have become resigned to the situation and are now residing in company-built housing, working as wage laborers on land that they formerly considered their own. The private firms that have entered the area have confiscated coffee trees previously planted and tended by the villagers. Homes have also been confiscated if they were situated within the boundaries assigned to the new estate.

At Aouan village, local residents in 1992 vociferously proclaimed their outrage at having lost their land and livelihood. Village officials professed ignorance of negotiations leading to the award of plantation rights and suggested that they had no alternative but to enforce the national law. Local farmers also noted that the estate cultivation techniques were bound to degrade the land, threaten the stability of the soil, and shorten the life of the coffee trees. Great amounts of fertilizer and pesticide were applied, new plantings were judged to be much too close together (threatening landslides), and hybrid varieties of beans were said to be not of the same quality of those planted previously.

UPLAND DEVELOPMENT ISSUES IN VIETNAM

Unlike the relatively densely populated upland Toraja region of Sulawesi Indonesia, most highland areas of Vietnam have been quite lightly populated. Extensive rather than intensive agricultural production techniques have been the norm. Most particularly, swidden agricultural practices have facilitated the migration of minority populations across mountain ranges and high valleys in search of new trees to fell, fields to till, and crops to harvest. In previous times, population densities and growth rates were low enough to facilitate stable systems of shifting cultivation. After two decades or more, farmers could return to an original farming plot, now covered with secondary forest growth, and fell the trees again. Currently, however, population densities are rising, forest cover is rapidly diminishing (due to more commercial logging than to swidden), and environmental stability is rapidly waning. Over the past thirty years Vietnam has lost more than 50 percent of its forests (Witter 1993, 17). Intensive warfare, the application of massive amounts of herbicides by the U.S. Air Force, clear cutting by commercial timber exploiters, and intensified upland cultivation by both traditional minority farmers and lowland migrants have taken a severe toll on the upland forest resource.

Throughout much of Vietnam, shifting cultivation has become untenable. Population pressures emanating from the lowlands expressed through programs of mandatory resettlement or voluntary colonization have greatly increased the pressure on fragile highland soils. Commercial logging has destroyed much watershed, and reforestation programs have not yet been initiated in much of highland Vietnam. Political events have necessarily impacted the Vietnamese highlands, especially on the southern plateau where much of the most intense combat of the American war took place. Here defoliants were applied, bombing was incessantly carried out over extensive "free fire zones," and mass migrations of local populations (planned and unplanned) destroyed traditional settlement patterns over a fifteen-year period. According to anthropologist Gerald C. Hickey (1993), over 80 percent of the southern highland villages were displaced as a result of the conflict.

Stabilization of settlement clearly remains an important issue with respect to the highlands of Vietnam. In both the northern and in the southern part of the country today, swidden systems rarely can be described as environmentally sound. On the other hand, irrigation facilities, access to agricultural extension assistance, improved seed stocks, and affordable fertilizers are seldom available to highland populations. Land tenure issues continue to be matters of contention when the traditional law of highland minorities reflects a substantially different view of land rights than do statutes of the nation-state. Most shifting cultivators believe that tribal land encompasses all territory within the normal swidden cycle, a cycle that over many decades may encompass hundreds of hectares of land for individual families. Government tends to view all land covered in forest as the domain of the state, to be exploited, assigned, and utilized in accordance with national needs and policies.

Settlement issues are becoming more complex over time in Vietnam. Because Vietnam is poorly endowed with irrigated rice lands, expansion of agricultural activities most probably will continue to take place in midland and highland areas. The settlement of lowland populations on territories considered at least in theory to be the traditional domain of highland swidden cultivators has several possible consequences. First, the land may, in rare cases, be brought into intensive irrigated rice production. If water, soil, and topographical circumstances facilitate such a positive outcome, then very high yields may be expected from lands that formerly were minimally productive. Most often, however, upland conditions are not conducive to irrigated rice agriculture. In this case lowland colonists may be forced to open swidden fields themselves, either to provide subsistence foodstuffs or to cultivate cash crops such as peanuts, soybeans, or pepper. Such fields may not reflect the typical mixed-cropping complex refined by shifting cultivators throughout the highlands of Southeast Asia over many generations. Mono-cropping such swidden fields may result in more rapid soil degradation and thus to the opening of yet additional fallowed forest land for short-term gain.

Stability of settlement is in the end probably more determined by tenure considerations than any other factor. According to anthropologist Neil Jamieson, shortly after reunification in 1975, government officials enacted policies following "a master blueprint prepared in Hanoi that envisioned relocating ten million people within twenty years" (1993, 365). Jamieson further notes that a quarter million highland people were relocated by 1978. The highlanders would, it was hoped, become more "civilized" (i.e., more like the Vietnamese). They were also to make room for an influx of industrious lowland Vietnamese, who were expected to exploit more effectively the upland ecosystems that seemed to lowland bureaucrats to be "empty" and "underutilized" (Jamieson 1993, 365). In the case of officially sponsored colonists, for instance war veterans to whom land was consigned after 1975, there is some assurance of land security. In such a case the planting of tree crops such as rambutan, longan, jack fruit, durian, and coffee might be well advised. On the other hand, highland indigenous populations, even though they may have been living in a particular region for generations, normally have no assurance of tenure. Tree crops such as coffee and durian take several years to yield first fruit, sometimes coming to maturity only a decade after planting. No one will invest the time and effort in shading newly planted trees, watering and fertilizing young trees, and pruning and harvesting mature trees under threat of confiscation by local or state authorities.

In the recent past, much of rural Vietnamese agriculture was organized according to socialist tenets. Currently land tenure certificates are being issued as state farms and cooperatives are replaced by smallholder production. In the case of upland populations, traditional concepts of use and ownership rights were formerly displaced by state control of resources. Now the question arises, will highland minority populations be able to secure land rights to upland tracts sufficient to promote stable agriculture, enhanced family income, and cultural continuity?

The per capita income of Vietnam residents was reported by the World Bank to be only $220 per year in 1991. The income of highland residents, especially tribal peoples, is certainly far below this figure. Inadequate transportation for produce, difficulties in road and river communications, and general lack of a highland development plan all conspire to depress economic activity in highland villages. There are many potential paths, some direct, some indirect, to enhancing highland incomes. First, by establishing some type of land security (perhaps by means of distributing Land Tenure Certificates), villagers will be more confident in stabilizing their agricultural production techniques. Here, coffee emerges as an interesting option. Smallholder production can be facilitated by agricultural extension work with the distribution of enhanced seedling stock, training in cultivation and pruning, and assurance of a fair farm gate price. In the longer run, access to education (which is by no means universal at this stage, especially in indigenous minority villages) is crucial to assuring an economic, political, and cultural future for upland minorities.

Education facilitates the capabilities of minorities to advance their representatives through the government bureaucratic structure within which they can act as effective advocates for their people. Second, education, especially through high school and beyond, always affords new employment opportunities. Traditional agricultural production techniques in the highlands are already constrained, if not legally forbidden. New avenues for employment will have to be explored in terms of commercial agriculture, small-scale entrepreneurial activity, tourist enterprise, and an expanded role in the government bureaucracy. Highland minority populations will have to adapt to survive. Government and international donors must recognize, assess, and meet the needs of these populations as their natural resource base rapidly recedes and as their participation in the national economy and political process inevitably deepens.

COFFEE AND THE CENTRAL HIGHLANDS

Coffee can have a role in linked processes of agricultural development, social security, and preservation of indigenous cultures. As perhaps the most valuable tropical tree crop, and one that is uniquely suited to upland locales, expanded smallholder coffee production can offer some relief to villagers concerned about land rights, to government concerned about stabilization of settlement, and to minority rights advocates concerned about the future of isolated tribal peoples. Coffee is not a panacea; it is not suited to many soils and upland environments. It is simply one of many options that might fruitfully be explored in this time of change and policy reformulation in Vietnam.[1]

At the beginning of this essay, reference was made to coffee cultivation in upland eastern Indonesia. There are many differences and contrasts between the highlands of Toraja and those of the southern plateau of Vietnam. Coffee was introduced through indigenous market channels in eastern Indonesia. Plantation agriculture was until recently only a small factor in local production. Coffee returns have greatly enhanced the ability of Indonesian highland villagers to pay for the education of their children, to erect great traditional houses, and to display status and wealth by the slaughter of water buffalo on ceremonial occasions. In the Toraja highlands, coffee production, integrated into a diverse agricultural system, has until recently been controlled by market forces and climatic conditions. Toraja coffee is today sold in generic coffee shops throughout the United States where it currently commands a premium price of more than $10 per pound for roasted beans.

On the southern highland plateau of Vietnam, coffee was first planted in the early twentieth century by French entrepreneurs. Initially, then, plantation enterprise carried coffee to the highlands of Vietnam. Nevertheless, smallholder production by minority Ede highlanders began to evolve in the 1960s. Thus Hickey reports that "In 1965 Y Yong Nie Ktuol of Buon Drie Hling cleared a half-hectare plot for 300 coffee seedlings obtained from a nearby estate, and by 1970 his yield was 450 kilos. . . . At Buon Ea Khit, Y Ngung Knuol had a coffee estate of four hectares with 4,000 trees, and because of the wartime price rise his profits increased tenfold between 1969 and 1970" (1993, 44). Presumably large plantations were nationalized to become state enterprises between 1975 and 1985. What became of indigenous smallholder production is unclear, but it would be fair to assume that such private holdings were either abandoned or co-operatized.

Western markets for coffee from the southern highlands of Vietnam were largely supplanted by consumers in the Eastern Bloc after reunification in 1975. Trade between Vietnam and the Soviet Union rose dramatically in the decade following the end of the war. Between 1976 and 1986, bilateral trade between Vietnam and the Soviet Union rose from 35 percent to 71 percent of the national total. According to Gareth Porter, Vietnam developed economic cooperation with the Soviet Union and other COMECON countries through contracts and joint ventures between sectoral and local production and trade organs of the two states. These agreements initially centered on oil exploration and export crops such as rubber, coffee, tea, coconuts, and tropical fruits (1993, 221).

In 1993 Vietnam produced 125,000 tons of coffee, with 72,000 tons of the total originating in the southern Central Highlands. In 1994 Vietnam projected a harvest of 150,000 tons with an expected 80,000 tons originating in Dac Lac province alone. By August 1994 global coffee prices had reached a ten-year high, averaging $3,500 per ton. According to Mr. Hoang Anh, Director of Cafe Controle (a state-run agency that monitors coffee quality), "Vietnam is among the world's top ten robusta exporters, but aims to capture fifth place by the year 2000" (*Vietnam Economic Times*, August 1994, 5). In 1993, according to the same *Vietnam Economic Times* article, coffee earned Vietnam US$105 million in foreign exchange.

In late September 1994, the first trade fair of Vietnamese products to be staged recently in the United States—"Viet Expo '94"—was held at Fort Mason in San Francisco by the San Francisco–Vietnam Foundation in conjunction with the city's Office of the Mayor. Two enterprises representing coffee exporters were present at this historic event, which was both endorsed and organized by the Socialist Government of Vietnam. Vinacafe, the state trading company that controls most Vietnamese coffee exports, dispatched three senior managers to San Francisco. Inexim-Dak Lak (the Dak Lak Investment Export-Import Corporation) also sent several representatives. Notable among the representatives was the chairman of the provincial Peoples Committee, a member of the Ede ethnic minority which, with several other highland peoples, is said to now constitute 30 percent of the province's total population. This organization not only brought samples of locally grown robusta, but also prepared a shopping list of prospective investments in the coffee industry including proposals for new plantations, intensive cultivation, and export processing near the provincial capital of Ban Ma Thuot.

Currently, Inexim-Dak Lak is apparently conducting US$20 million worth of business each year. Ninety percent of this sum is garnered from the coffee trade. According to Inexim-Dak Lak planning documents, the province currently has over 60,000 hectares planted in coffee, resulting in a yield of 100,000 metric tons of coffee beans per year. Although almost all of this production now consists of robusta, Inexim-Dak Lak representatives reported that Arabica trials are now under way. Also, the privatization of coffee production is in progress throughout the province. Local smallholders in 1994 are reported by these officials to be receiving up to US$1.50 per kilogram for dried coffee beans under open marketing arrangements. As late as 1992 local state farms were remunerating smallholders with the *dong* equivalent of US$.30 per pound. Within two years, remuneration rates have increased 500 percent, largely due to the restructuring of economic relations within Vietnam. Coffee prices have also doubled on international markets during this period. Field research to verify these developments is clearly needed. For the present, suffice it to say that the privatization of landholdings in upland areas such as Dac Lac would seem to bear the potential for significant family income enhancement in the immediate future.

The shared concern of all participants in this conference on the highlands of Vietnam is the preservation of its unique environment, the future of indigenous minority populations, and the measured exploitation of the diverse resources of upland Vietnam. Although traditionally peopled by ethnic minorities, the mountains and hills are now being settled also by increasing numbers of migrants from the lowlands. No consideration of the development of this region can proceed without concern for the complexity of human settlement patterns, land rights, inter-ethnic relations, modes of subsistence, and cash economic systems. Because the southern highlands have only recently been opened to foreign business analysts and academics, much research remains to be undertaken to assess the fundamental human needs of local populations, the extent of commercial enterprise currently under way, and the appropriate opportunities for the investment of government and international agency resources.

In the Toraja highlands of Indonesia and in the southern highlands of Vietnam, the production of coffee as a cash crop has resulted in fundamental changes in local agriculture. In Indonesia, the success of smallholder production has stimulated the recent appropriation of farmers' land by major Jakarta-based corporations. The unrestricted appearance of capital-intensive plantation enterprises in the Toraja highlands has led to the displacement of farmers and the confiscation of their coffee gardens. In Vietnam, private plantations have in the recent past been transformed into state-owned corporations. Smallholdings have been merged into local producer cooperatives. More recently, most cooperative agriculture in Vietnam has once again reverted to small-scale household production.

CONCLUSION

It is hoped that the indigenous peoples such as the Da and Am in the southern highlands will be encouraged in the present political environment to expand private development of coffee production. World markets and national development priorities both suggest that the expansion of coffee production will provide additional income for farmers in remote and relatively impoverished highland Vietnamese villages. Whether minority highlander can be assured equity in the context of expanded markets will depend upon the commitment and resources of local, provincial, and national government agencies.

Unlike past years, the Vietnamese highlands are now free of warfare, aerial bombardment, and herbicide attack. The uplands are also free from rigid economic control. Mountain areas are now also increasingly of concern to international humanitarian non-governmental organizations, resource developers, and energy producers. The time to assure the future of the residents of the highlands is now, before additional damage is visited upon fragile ecosystems and before new economic and demographic trends make the alteration of prior adverse economic and social conditions difficult to accomplish. Within the next quarter century the highlands are destined to become a major tourist destination, a key source of mineral and gems, the locus of additional hydroelectric projects, and a continuing if diminishing source of commercial timber. Collaborative research between academics of Vietnam and friendly countries, such as the United States, will allow policy-makers to formulate development plans based on precise and accurate information. Ongoing investigations will also be invaluable to the Government of Vietnam as multilateral donors and bilateral aid agencies increasingly focus their interest on the highlands of Vietnam. Such research, it is hoped, can mitigate the least desirable consequences of development and at the same time recommend appropriate projects for investment.

NOTE

1. My own observations in highland Vietnam began in 1966 when for three months I was a student intern for USAID in what is now Lam Dong province in the southern highlands. I have since visited Dzao and Muong villages in Hoa Binh and Bac Thai provinces north of Hanoi and have visited a Maa village and a Ra'glai village in Lam Dong province. I have been encouraged by my observations in the north, perplexed by what I have seen in the south. In Bac Thai I found Dzao villages permanently settled, some with active tea and herb garden industries. I noted that local religious traditions were respected and maintained by those who wished to do so. In visits to six Dzao villages I found varying degrees of acculturation—based on the wishes and inclinations of the villagers themselves. My observations in the south have been all too brief. In the two villages that I visited, no school was available to highland children, even though Kinh children in settlement villages nearby were attending school. At the Maa settlement, villagers were actively engaged in trading bamboo with roadside merchants. In this locale a vast forest remained, as did a clear running stream. Resettled Vietnamese villagers here noted that ethnic Vietnamese residents were oriented toward the roadway and actively engaged in commerce and trade with Bao Loc, Dalat, and Ho Chi Minh city. By contrast, the highlanders were said to be oriented toward the mountains and the streams, toward farming on hillsides and exploiting the riches of the forest.

BIBLIOGRAPHY

Bigalke, T. A. 1981. *Social history of Tana Toraja, 1870–1965.* Unpublished Ph.D. dissertation, University of Wisconsin, Madison. University Microfilms, Ann Arbor.

Hickey, G. C. 1993. *Shattered worlds: Adaptation and survival among Vietnam's highland peoples during the Vietnam war.* Philadelphia: University of Pennsylvania Press.

Jamieson, N. 1993. *Understanding Vietnam.* Berkeley: University of California Press.

Porter, G. 1993. *Vietnam: The politics of bureaucratic socialism.* Ithaca: Cornell University Press.

Witter, S. 1993. *Working with ethnic minorities in Vietnam: An introduction to the issues.* Consulting Report. Save the Children Inc., U.K.

Wrigley , G. 1988. *Coffee.* London: Longman Publishers.

CHAPTER 15

Tropical Upland Development Policy: China and Vietnam

R. D. Hill
University of Hong Kong

The tropical lands of China and Vietnam share many characteristics—monsoonal climates that impose significant limitations on cropping cycles; mainly leached sedentary soils in the uplands contrasting with fairly rich transported soils in the lowlands; dense agricultural populations in those lowlands, combined with rapidly growing cities both in population and areal extent; and lowland agricultural frontiers that have long been closed. Such features, combined with continued population growth, especially in Vietnam, together with limited prospects for increasing agricultural production in the lowlands, have resulted in substantial pressures being placed upon the environmentally fragile uplands.

These pressures arise from many sources. They are the result of rising populations in the uplands themselves, in turn a consequence of "death control," usually unaccompanied by effective birth control. They arise from planned and unplanned colonization of uplands by lowlanders, many of whom are unwilling or unable to attune lowland agricultural practices to the limitations of fragile upland environments. Pressures also arise from the lack of simple and profitable tree-crop agricultural systems such as those based on rubber, coconut, and oil palm that characterize the humid equatorial parts of the region. Pressure arises, too, from the relatively slow though recently quickened pace of structural change in national economies in which, despite decades of development, there are still roughly 50 percent more farmers than there were twenty years ago.

While in both countries the progressive dismantling of communal and cooperative forms of social and economic organization has led to substantial increases in rural production, that organizational change has by no means been an unmixed blessing, especially with respect to the development and management of the uplands. The question of what policies and structures are appropriate, especially to "open-access" common lands, remains open. For China at least, there is no overall coherent policy, let alone one that is fully supported and enforced. That there are likely to be substantial but as yet undefined diseconomies in the present largely uncontrolled situation is unquestionable.

The communal structures, authoritarian though they were, offered a means of rationally managing the uplands (though the actuality was sometimes seriously damaging). For example, under the commune system in China, it was customary to close sections of upland areas used for the collection of wood fuels in order that they might be allowed to regenerate to the point at which further collection might be permitted. This rational form of management can no longer be enforced, and it is clear that the cutting of grass and scrub for fuel is seriously suboptimal as the collection frequency has been allowed to increase, probably, at least in part, in response to the partial commercialization of fuel collection and the development of trade in such fuels (Chen 1993). Similarly in areas where animal husbandry is of some importance, for example Yunnan and western Guizhou, a problem of controlling the increase in stock numbers has emerged. Whereas under the commune system it was possible, at least in principle, to ensure that there was a reasonable match between the amount of fodder produced on the hillsides and the animals that consumed it, that situation has changed. Farmers are now able to herd as many animals as they wish. Indeed they may, as in western Guizhou, be actively encouraged to increase numbers by receiving government loans to enable them to do this. But since administrative control over the areas where the fodder (mainly low-producing native grasses) grows is now very limited or nonexistent, overgrazing and the general deterioration accompanying it is inevitable.

UPLAND DEVELOPMENT POLICY

Although for lack of materials in English it is difficult to be sure, it seems that China has no specific upland development policy, and, like Vietnam, certainly has no single government agency charged with the task of upland development. Rather, in China upland development is subsumed within the general rubric of ameliorating land degradation. For example, in a recent statement by Madame Deng Nan, one of Deng Xiaoping's daughters, there was no mention, beyond "soil erosion and desertification," of specific problems and policies relating to upland regions. Most of her discussion referred to arid and semi-arid regions in the north-west, north, and north-east of the country (Deng 1993).

By contrast, in Vietnam official statements on overall policy in upland development have been numerous and frequent. Additionally they have occasioned considerable debate and consequently upland issues are well to the forefront in public awareness. For example, an important statement was made by the Communist Party's Central Committee on 29 January 1985, published in *Nhan Dan* on 4 February (in Vietnamese), translated, and published in English on 4 April (JPRS-SEA-85-057). Within a year further important policy statements and reports appeared (e.g., JPRS-SEA-85-062; 85-093; 86-015).

More recently the Vietnamese government has directed specific attention to upland areas, especially through Decree 327 issued by the Council of Ministers on 15 September 1992. While this Decree somewhat perversely refers to lands not used for either forestry or agriculture as "barren," it nevertheless sets out the basic objective of improving the productivity of such lands that cover some 12–13 million ha, or 35–45 percent of the nation's area (see Sikor, this volume, for details). Similarly, the highlands form a major part of Vietnam's Integrated Rural Development Programme, which began in July 1992 (Socialist Republic of Vietnam, n.d.). Other Vietnamese organizations with upland interests include the Committee for Ethnic Minorities and Mountainous Areas and academic institutions such as the Forest Science Institute, the Agricultural Universities, the University of Hanoi (Center for Natural Resources and Environmental Studies), and sections of the Vietnam National Center for Natural Science and Technology.

For China a major journal, *Chinese Sociology and Anthropology,* which carries English translations of scholarly articles published in China, has not carried a single paper on upland development in the two decades it has existed. Other outlets such as *Beijing Review* very rarely contain information on the subject. Consequently it is necessary to infer from general statements and from practice what Chinese policy may be. Thus broad agricultural and forestry policies are examined since they form the matrix in which hill farmers, foresters, and development agencies in China must work.

NATIONAL DEVELOPMENT POLICIES IN AGRICULTURE

Since the late 1970s and early 1980s, there was a general and dramatic surge in agricultural production in China.[1] As a consequence of the spread of the now nearly universal household responsibility system that replaced the managerially unwieldy communes, people generally ate better, were able to invest in new housing and some basic durable consumer goods, though significant pockets of severe poverty remain, especially in the uplands of the southwestern provinces—Sichuan, Yunnan, Guizhou, Guangxi. What seems likely is that reported improvements in Chinese living standards were largely confined to the towns, where average incomes are reported to be about two-and-a-half times greater than the rural average, and to most lowland areas, especially those with easy access to urban markets. By contrast at least some upland areas have remained seriously disadvantaged. For example, as Hill (1993a) has noted, the poor mainly limestone upland province of Guizhou in the southwest is failing to keep pace with coastal provinces. As recently as 1983 the "grain" ration in some counties was only 147 kg/person (Wang and Bai 1991, 16), though a later survey of three such counties indicated that mean daily food intakes per person were in the range of 2,400–2,620 Kcal with barely adequate levels of fat and protein intake (Chen et al. 1990). With a mean per person annual income of less than US$35 in thirty-one of the province's eighty-two counties, Guizhou certainly is a nation-sized pocket of upland poverty (Hill 1993a). The number of counties in that province below the poverty line has now increased (to forty-three counties) since the mid-1980s.

Efforts to deal with basic problems arguably may be hindered by the failure to admit to basic reasons for those problems. Thus Madame Deng refers to "lack of knowledge of protection of natural resources" and to "improper production practices" (Deng 1993, 16); yet she fails to recognize poverty as the fundamental issue, as the root cause of land degradation. Hill (1993b, 1994) has argued that the search for a single widely applicable "solution" has also hindered the emergence of a range of locally appropriate development interventions. He has suggested further that such appropriate interventions as developed have mostly not yet been subjected to the acid test of economics as distinct from technical feasibility (Hill 1994).

At the national level it seems clear that there are some important contradictions. One is between the ideologically and politically based desire to improve "backward" regions and the pragmatic need to invest capital in rapidly and highly productive spheres, such as providing physical infrastructure in coastal provinces where growth rates are reported to be 15–20 percent annually. In earlier times, investing in the interior was sound in terms of Marxist-Leninist doctrine, which aimed not only to reduce and destroy interclass socioeconomic differences but also to reduce regional disparities, especially rural/urban ones. This was reinforced by the strategically driven need to develop industry in the interior. That development had important local multiplier effects for agriculture while also creating such problems as shortages of irrigation water and localized industrial pollution. Both doctrinal and strategic imperatives have disappeared, leaving the interior provinces, many of which contain major uplands, starved for investment funds from the center.

A further central-government policy that is contradictory is the recent Party Plenum decision that the provinces shall, by the year 2000, become self-sufficient in basic foodstuffs. The contradiction, of course, is with the whole thrust of market socialism that assumes that ultimately all prices shall be determined by supply and demand, that China shall become a single, unified market, and that in it comparative advantage shall have free play as a means of maximizing economic growth. In the interim, food-surplus regions such as Guangdong will be required to continue to export their surplus to other regions in the land, a policy with which that province has no difficulty in complying. It merely imports foreign rice to meet its quota and gets on with producing higher-value commodities. The "owners" of many of its farms move to higher-paying industrial employment and (illegally?) engage impoverished farmers from elsewhere to work the land in what is basically a landlord-tenant arrangement. That option is simply not open in the poorer, mainly upland provinces, though if current restrictions on labor mobility are relaxed or simply ignored, they may to some degree benefit from the remittances from migrant workers thus generated in the developing lowland regions upon which they may become increasingly dependent economically.

But if basic food self-sufficiency is enforced, serious consequences may be expected. Here the case of Guizhou province is again instructive. The province currently imports between 0.5 and 1.0 million ton of rice annually. Were this, or its inferior nutritional equivalent potatoes to be produced locally it could only be done, if at all, by increasing the current crop area to more than 3 million hectares from the current 1.9 million hectares, of which only 0.8 million are in wet rice. But the crop index is already an astonishing 187 (i.e., 87 percent of the land, much of it unirrigated and unirrigable at present, is cropped twice annually [Hill 1993a]).

Thus an expansion onto marginal land would be needed, similar to that which took place during the "Great Leap Forward" but larger because the population has nearly doubled. But that "Leap" proved to be unsustainable then and another would be unsustainable now.

HOUSEHOLD RESPONSIBILITY SYSTEM

Following Chairman Mao's death in 1976 and the realization that about two-fifths of China's urban population depended on imported grain, the Third Plenary Session of the Eleventh Central Committee of the Party in 1978 recommended major rural policy changes—which initially were opposed. However, despite the official position that the production team was to remain the basic unit of production, income distribution, and accounting, peasants in flood and drought-prone Anhui began to contract land and output quotas to households. Shortly thereafter, such households significantly increased production, and the new system was approved by the central government. By 1983, 93 percent of production teams had adopted household responsibility, most of them the *bao gan dao hu* system of "contracting all actions to the household" (Prosterman and Hanstad 1990, 114–15).

In practice the household responsibility system has shown a number of serious deficiencies. First, the standard fifteen-year period of use-rights is too short for many perennial tree crops, though satisfactory for most annual crops (except where private investments in irrigation are contemplated). For example, in Chinese conditions, *Hevea* rubber is not tappable until the fifth year. Litchi *(Nephelium litchi)* does not begin to yield well until seven to ten years after planting. The economic life of most perennials, except pepper *(Piper nigrum)* and a few others, extends well beyond fifteen years and yet there is no guarantee of renewal.

Second, the contracts for use allow "the state" to resume control over all or part of the household's land. In practice "the state" seems to mean "the cadre" from whom compensation for loss of use and for improvements may or may not be forthcoming. Prosterman and Hanstad (1990, 119) have reported that such resumptions of control do occur, at least often enough for virtually every farmer to have heard of such cases, and several of those they interviewed had either experienced it directly or had it hanging over their heads. Their field research demonstrated that very little in the way of long-term improvements had been made, seemingly because "farmers do not feel adequately assured that they will remain on their present land long enough to recover their investment and reap a profit" (Prosterman and Hanstad 1990, 122).

However, it seems clear, to judge from word-of-mouth reports, that in some upland areas informal long-term use-rights have evolved, though it is difficult to effectively document this process. Thus several Chinese participants in the China Tropical Lands Project (see Parham, Durana, and Hess 1993) noted that in some communities property rights to trees planted by individuals are recognized, though these rights do not extend to actual possession of the land upon which such trees may be planted. This kind of usufruct right has, of course, a long history in the region generally. In such circumstances the issue thus becomes to what extent may such usufruct rights be enforced and the "superior" right of the state be held at bay in the interests of villagers.

But equally it is clear that very large areas remain held in common, land to which all may have access but none exclusively so. Such open access, to some degree informally regulated as it may be with respect to where fuel or fodder may be collected or where animals may be grazed, scarcely permits long-term management or investment for future enhanced yields. The spatial enlargement of local and regional markets has resulted in the "commoditization" of fuelwood, for example, with quantities being fed into local urban markets for use domestically and for industrial purposes such as feeding brick and tile kilns. The demand for these products has increased as a result of increased disposable income derived from the success of the responsibility system.

What, then, is needed to cause the farmer to invest in long-term improvements? Again Prosterman's and Hanstad's fieldwork is instructive. They reported that for their respondents there was ownership. The basic issue was not expected commodity prices nor the difference between a substantial period, say fifteen years or a longer substantial period, but in the credibility of either. They suggest that "so long as the collective [presumably they mean county] still owns the land, the farmers will not make long-term investments, whether the avowed period of their 'rights' is fifteen years or ninety-nine years" (Prosterman and Hanstad 1990, 124–25).

This raises the question of possible kinds of long-term tenure or use-rights. Contrary to general impression, in capitalist countries landholders do not necessarily enjoy absolute rights of possession (freehold). Even freehold does not confer unrestricted rights of use, for these may be controlled by land-use and building regulations. For example, in some countries the state retains forever its absolute right to own land but lets it out on long-term leases. Thus in former British colonial territories, in parts of Malaysia, Singapore, Hong Kong, and parts of Australia both urban and rural lands are let out on long leases—40–99 years, even 999 years. The state retains the right to resume land for public purposes, with compensation for improvements and loss of future earnings. It may also retain the right to determine use. In addition the state retains the right to resume the land for persistent failure to pay land-rent or for failure to cultivate the land at all. Obviously a fairly elaborate and costly system of land survey, registration, and legal process lies behind such institutions but they do avoid the establishment by private individuals of absolute and uncontrolled rights to land and its use.

Alternatively some form of cooperative institution may be appropriate. The record of such in developing country agriculture is not good partly because of weaknesses in administration, sometimes even to the point of criminality, and partly because cooperatives tend to become dominated by a few wealthy, progressive persons who use the organization to improve their status and income at the expense of poorer members. But it should be recalled that cooperatives are a major and effective organizational tool in some developed countries such as New Zealand and Denmark, where, however, they generally operate at the processing, marketing, and farm-input purchasing levels rather than in direct production.

FOREST POLICIES

Since significant proportions of the uplands remain in forest or have been afforested with quick-growing species, mainly softwoods, forest policies form an important component of overall upland policy. With only 12 percent of its land area in forest and a per person forest reserve of only 0.12 hectare (against 1.1 hectares worldwide) of which only a third is accessible to logging, China is seriously underprovided with timber and its derivatives (Ross 1988, 25; Li et al. 1988, 205 ff.). Prior to the Great Leap Forward in the 1950s, farm woodlots were by no means uncommon, serving to supplement public lands as a source of biofuel—the source of four-fifths of China's rural energy needs (Ross 1988, 26). However, during that period most woodlots disappeared as a result of the Maoist policy of "taking grain as the leading factor" and in providing fuel for the notoriously inefficient backyard factories of that day. Thus largely disappeared the integrated production of trees and crops now termed agroforestry.

In line with the macro-economic policy of the time, timber prices were set administratively by location, species, and rotation. In retrospect, prices were clearly too low to reflect true costs of production and, especially, silvicultural control of forests and reforestation. Moreover, artificially low prices encouraged wasteful consumption. This was remedied to some degree at the end of the 1970s and into the early 1980s as administrative control over prices generally began to be relaxed and as timber markets were permitted to develop with consumers and purchasing agents competing with each other for supplies (Li et al. 1988, 232). Finally, in 1985, the compulsory procurement system was "modified" so that while a proportion of output remained subject to compulsory procurement by the state, a second portion was subject to state purchase at above-quota prices and a third portion could be sold on the open market. In theory, all felling, including that of fuelwood trees, was subject to official approval in order that the size of the local harvest did not exceed the annual forest increment (Li et al. 1988, 233).

In practice it is clear that from the end of the 1970s there was increased deforestation despite increases in police and judicial efforts to control cutting and in the face of some well-publicized court cases. Indeed, anecdotal evidence suggests that in Guangdong at least, police and military officers were to some degree involved in illegal cutting, transportation, and sale of timber. The success of the agricultural responsibility system was a stimulus to increased cutting. Not only was there an increased demand for structural timber, especially *Pinus massoniana* and *Cunninghamia lanceolata* for roof beams, for timber for form-work, but also an increased demand for wood-fuel to fire brick and tile kilns. These kilns sprang up in many areas throughout the 1980s to meet the strong demand for those commodities stimulated by the increased house-building stemming in turn from growing wealth and savings in the countryside. Field research in northwestern Guangdong in the mid-1980s revealed that in some villages adjacent to forests great stocks of brush, timber, and even roots were stacked to roof-level for drying prior to sale and shipment. Current reports suggest that some of the wood-using kilns of the 1980s have closed down while others have been forced to convert to coal, the availability of which in some rural areas has clearly improved. Details of the scale of deforestation triggered by the success of the household responsibility system is difficult to assess for lack of data. However, an early 1990s estimate that one-half of all rural houses was no more than ten years old gives some indication of scale.

The household responsibility system has also incorporated a proportion of collective forest farms. As early as 1984 the proportion of workers in that sector had dropped by 40 percent and by the end of the following year some 50 million rural households were responsible for managing 70 million hectares of hills and forest under the responsibility system (Li et al. 1988, 236). As inheritors of the communes, county administrations contract with families or workers to manage forests or to undertake specific silvicultural and related tasks. These contracts are for fifteen to twenty years or for the expected life of the stand and may be inherited. Reports from Shanxi suggest a longer period of use-rights—perhaps fifty or eighty years (Richardson 1990, 174). By 1985 households were said to be responsible for half of the reforestation (Li et al. 1988, 237).

Despite some successes there remain a number of basic problems both in managing existing forests and in reforestation. Given that perhaps four-fifths or more of China's rural domestic fuel needs are met from biofuels, of which at least two-fifths are collected from open-access grass, scrub, and wooded hillsides, it is difficult to see how such lands can now be closed to permit regeneration or reforestation. Indeed field reports from Guangdong suggest that nine-tenths of rural domestic fuel comes from hill slopes where cutting is entirely unregulated. In that province alternative fuels are twice to ten times more costly per unit of energy than such hillside biofuels (Chen 1993). In the same province, hill slopes may also be used for a form of short-cycle supplementary shifting cultivation in the process of which fire is used.

These practical problems are exacerbated by a whole series of structural and managerial difficulties as reviewed by Ross (1988, 34 ff.). He notes (p. 37) that in Hainan, Yunnan, and other frontier areas in the south of the country "deforestation in the name of agricultural and grasslands reclamation is also severe, far exceeding newly afforested land." In particular there are seriously misleading data on areas planted, in some of which long-term survival rates have been notably low. As elsewhere in the region (Thailand, for example), land, especially in the state sector, reported as "forest" is nothing of the kind. For example, Ross (1988, 44) reported that in 1985, of a China-wide total of 33 million hectares under the control of state forest administrations or bureau, only 22 million hectares actually carried trees! He further refers to bureaucratic conflicts in which forestry *(linye)* is administratively part of the agricultural system, whereas forest industry *(senlin gongye)* is administratively part of the heavy industrial sector leading to management problems. Especially, "35 percent of standing timber by volume is left in the forest, hampering regeneration" (Ross 1988, 53).

So far as reforestation is concerned, a number of basic problems has scarcely been addressed. While subsidies are available for planting trees, especially quick-growing species such as *Pinus massoniana, P. yunnanensis, Cunninghamia lanceolata,* and *Eucalyptus,* in many communities the issue of how land under contract for tree-planting will be allocated is unresolved. It would appear that where families cannot mutually agree, social paralysis ensues with little or nothing being done to resolve conflicts and to get on with the job. But a larger issue emerges where reforestation necessitates the withdrawal of hill land from agricultural production whether for grazing or food production. In northwestern Guizhou province, for example, farmers are being paid from central government and loan sources to plant trees in the much-needed interest of controlling erosion in the headwaters of the Chang Jiang. But some of the land is their former source of subsistence and once planting is complete it is a matter of doubt that maintenance payments will suffice for their support. The danger is twofold: First, tree growth will be hampered by the need to continue to graze animals and to produce food. Second, the actual clearance of new plantings will take place to continue agricultural production, thus reducing the effectiveness of the growing forest in soil conservation and potential yields of timber. In China a specialist silvicultural household can generally care adequately for 10–20 hectares, thus giving an average density of 5–10 households, say 20–40 persons per square kilometer. But in some areas designated for reforestation, densities are well above that figure. How, then, is the surplus population to survive, especially where plantings are largely or entirely for conservation rather than commercial purposes?

The question of proper choice of species is still unresolved. Since world softwood prices are continuing to rise, economic imperatives mean that softwood species are the species of choice and that reforestation using local hardwoods is likely to be of limited application. But which softwoods? In terms of rapid yield of timber, several of the Eucalypts are strong performers—*E. globulosa,* for example. They coppice readily and are capable of being used for both pulp and for timber. But common farmer perceptions are that they are profligate users of water, that both quantity and quality of water delivered to streams and irrigation systems are lower than that from slopes in grass, scrub, or secondary forest. The fact that mature *Eucalyptus* tends to suppress the growth of the ground layer and may be susceptible to fire may make this tree a less-than-optimal solution to controlling erosion and maximizing long-term yields, not only of timber but also of fuel for domestic purposes and irrigation water.

CONCLUSION

China's policies and practices in relation to the restoration of degraded lands are embedded within a matrix of past practices and perceptions, as well as of macro-level policies. To conclude, some observations are made concerning important issues. Elsewhere (Hill 1993b) it has been argued that a search by scientists for a single, general formula capable of application to the development of tropical upland areas is both vain and counterproductive. The spectacle of millions of peasants "learning from Dazhai" by cutting terraces whether or not they were economically and environmentally justified in southern China is not an edifying one. Indeed in some research institutions in that region it is clear that the now long-continued "search for the solution" is merely an excuse for avoiding the basic issue of working with farmers and by working with them as equal partners, by applying what is already known, to struggle toward local solutions to local problems.

In Vietnam it is clear that while debate on upland development issues has been comprehensive and open, several basic principles and perceptions have not been challenged. First is the political need to incorporate non-Kinh into the national polity and to ensure a high level of political control over minority peoples, among some of whom disaffection has until recently been expressed by active, if small-scale, irredentism. Whether spoken or not, this imperative has long underlain the long-standing policy of the "sedentarization of the nomads." Whether all those labeled "nomadic" can in any real sense be so regarded is a moot question given that most operate in relatively constricted areas, the majority of which are in grassland, scrub, and secondary forest of no value for timber production. (Although it is difficult to be sure, it seems likely that illegal lumbering is at least as damaging to the remaining mature forests as is shifting cultivation.)

Second is the perception that the lowlands are "overpopulated"—though just what that may be is rarely spelled out—and that the uplands are an appropriate "safety valve" for the "surplus" who need to be moved to enable them to build a better life for themselves. That some have done so is unquestionable. That others have not is equally unquestionable, given the reportedly substantial return migration that apparently exists. The basic question, given Vietnam's steady movement toward market socialism, must be, "What are the costs and what are the benefits?"

A third question is one of demographics. Even if upland colonization schemes are regarded as "successful"—meaning that participants are reasonably well clothed, fed, and housed and produce some economic surplus—how long will such success last? The experience of land colonization in Indonesia and Malaysia is that population growth tends to be so rapid that farm holdings quickly become uneconomic and, in the absence of alternative employment opportunities nearby, poverty and out-migration re-emerge. The irony is that successful pioneering of the land requires large family labor supply—unless cooperative or large-scale fully capitalist forms of organization are employed. Yet the conventional strategy of developing family-sized holdings soon breaks down as holdings are generally too small to support all the young adults of the rising generation.

The "answers" to such questions, if indeed there can be "answers," must lie in the hands of those who make policy and those who advise them. As in any society there will always be those who have a direct, vested interest in maintaining the status quo. But the question remains, "Are there better ways?"

In the Chinese context the papers in *Improving Degraded Lands* (Parham, Durana, and Hess 1993) provide some answers. Unfortunately these are partial at best, for most of the reports discuss interventions carried out on research stations or are simply normative, giving little indication of how desirable objectives may be achieved, still less of economic, as distinct from technical feasibility. (Xu's 1993 paper on trials in Xishuanbanna is a noteworthy exception.) Rather few of those papers contain sufficient economic data to make any judgment as to likely costs and benefits. Yet if farmers, who in the end will be responsible for changes of current practices, cannot see a positive return they are most unlikely to change. In the new, more individualistic situation exhortation will not suffice. With the loss of the commune system, too, the possibility of substituting labor for capital has now disappeared and campaigns simply to "plant more trees," for example, are no adequate substitute.

For Vietnam, there is as yet no comprehensive compilations (at least in English) assessing possible upland development initiatives, though a "look backward" may well provide useful insights toward looking ahead. Here the book by Le Trong Cuc, Gillogly, and Rambo (1990), though confined to a study of the north, provides valuable insights into upland agroecosystems.

Related to this issue is the frequently encountered view that "now" is the time to undertake a "big push," to make a "quantum jump"—a view similar to that there is, or can be, "the answer." China's record in "big pushes," whether "taking grain as the leading factor" or hurling the country into what is now known to have been the abyss of the Great Leap

Forward, is not impressive. So far, informal reports of large forestry projects such as the "Great Green Wall" in Heilongjiang, Liaoning, northern Hebei, Shanxi, and Gansu, or the later "Three Norths" project, suggest, at best, mixed success. There must, in principle, be questions as to the economic desirability of a development strategy that involves a few large "gambler's throw" projects as against a multiplicity of small, local ones. If governments at all levels, county, province, the center, spend money wisely, if they succeed in avoiding the "throw money at it" syndrome that still characterizes some Western development strategy, then progress will be made, not in a quantum leap but in many increments—and these will be on the ground, not just in sequestered research stations where producers are not living on the margin.

But obtaining more funds for upland development is likely to be a matter of considerable difficulty. In the first place, environmental economics is in its infancy globally. In China, for instance, there is no more than a handful of environmental economists in Beijing and reportedly none elsewhere. Consequently decision-makers are unable fully to assess real costs and benefits of proposed development interventions. Second, governments are experiencing serious difficulties in collecting taxes due to them. Consequently they are greatly constrained in investing in anything other than the most remunerative projects. Clearly the highest rates of return are seen to be those involving improved infrastructure mainly in the already relatively wealthy and rapidly growing coastal provinces.

A further question relating to upland development is the pervasive "top-down," "we know" mind-set of scientists. This is but the other side of what may be called the "ignorant farmer" syndrome. It appears several times, for example, in Deng Nan's paper (Deng 1993, 16): "The lack of scientific knowledge among the farmers is another factor [in land degradation]." It is true that farmers may not have the same kind of knowledge as scientists and that their knowledge is not organized in the same way. But few are stupid. Indeed, given the powerful environmental, economic, and institutional constraints within which they must gain their livelihood, it is sometimes extraordinary that they do as well as they do. It is worth being reminded that in technically advanced countries agricultural experimentation is at least partly a joint venture between farmers and scientists.

Since 1986 there has been a decisive shift in China's economy from the countryside to the cities, one that Vietnam is likely to follow. While it is true that those in marginal areas that produce largely for subsistence have not been caught in quite the same cost-price squeeze as the many market-oriented producers in the lowlands—who have seen a recent doubling in the cost of farm inputs whereas prices have increased only by half—subsistence producers are nevertheless affected by rises in the cost of basic consumer goods. Overall, the Ministry of Agriculture has noted, the average rural-urban income gap has widened from 1:1.7 in 1985 to 1:2.4 in 1991. To this may be added an increasing peasant burden of fees and taxes. The *Beijing Economic Daily* (16 December 1992), reporting statistics from twenty-nine provinces for 1990, indicated an average tax burden of 7.9 percent of average per person income, well above the limit of 5 percent set by the State Council. According to a Taiwan source, in which that report appeared, the actual average, including all imports, legal and illegal, averaged 11 percent, more than double the limit

(Inside Mainland China, March 1993, 31). Peasant reaction to such difficulties has been significant and hostile. A recent Hong Kong report notes that "Internal Chinese Government documents . . . have cited more than 200 incidents [of peasant protest] in the last year alone" *(Far Eastern Economic Review,* 15 July 1993). Whether these protests include poverty-stricken upland areas or not is unclear. What is clear is that farmers from such regions, for example adjacent to the burgeoning growth center in the Pearl River Delta, are beginning to take matters into their own hands by becoming "tenants" on the lands of wealthy delta farmers who have moved substantially into urban, industrial employment. A similar path may well emerge in Vietnam.

Lessons

What, then, are the lessons? First, neither Vietnam nor in China has the change in economic structure under way since the 1960s made any significant difference to the employment situation in farming, notwithstanding the significant development of "rural" enterprises in China. Although in both countries the proportion of farmers in the workforce and the proportion of national income derived from the farm sector (especially the latter) have fallen significantly, the absolute number of farmers has nevertheless increased substantially (see Table 15.1). In both countries their rate of increase from 1960 to 1989 has been at a (simple) average of about 2 percent per year. Given the recent and current demographic situation in the uplands where family sizes tend to be rather greater than in the lowlands, and especially in urban areas, it is likely that the number of upland farmers is increasing by about 2.2 to 2.5 percent each year. In China, however, it is clear that work in so-called "rural enterprises"—actually small-town enterprises—as well as in the major cities, has begun to provide employment to temporarily or permanently detached members of upland households. That has led to the emergence of remittances as a means of support in some rural areas and to disintensification of production in others, such as upland Guangdong, especially near Shenzhen. For Vietnam there is anecdotal evidence that a similar process has begun as urban labor markets are beginning to emerge.

The second lesson is that tropical China, though having many similarities with Vietnam in terms of its environment and recent economic history, does not offer a model for

Table 15.1 Basic agricultural statistics: China and Vietnam

	1960				1989			
	China		Vietnam		China		Vietnam	
	No.	(%)	No.	(%)	No.	(%)	No.	(%)
Total population (million)	646.6	(100.0)	30.2	(100.0)	1122.2	(100.0)	65.3	(100.0)
Agricultural population (million)	486.0	(75.2)	24.2	(80.1)	765.2	(68.2)	40.0	(61.3)
Area (1,000 km²)	9597	(100.0)	332	(100.0)	9597	(100.0)	332	(100.0)
Arable and permanent cropland (1,000 km²)	1094	(11.4)	42	(12.7)	961	(10.0)	66	(19.9)
Persons/km² arable and permanent cropland	444		719		1168		989	
Increase of total population, 1960–89 (million)					475.6	(73.6)	35.1	(116.2)
Increase of agricultural population, 1960–89 (million)					279.9	(57.4)	15.8	(65.3)

Sources: Compiled from Production Yearbooks, various years, Rome, FAO.

Vietnam in terms of policy. Indeed, it has been argued that China has no coherent upland development policy, although so far as specific techniques are concerned a body of information exists (Parham, Durana, and Hess 1993) and some are likely to be appropriate in the Vietnamese context. But few of the Chinese upland development interventions have been subject to any kind of cost/benefit analysis, let alone the kinds of analysis now undertaken by modern environmental economics, in which such "externalities" as loss of quantity and quality of irrigation water, soil erosion, even "loss of amenity" may be taken into account. As Vietnam moves toward a macro-economic situation in which the true costs and benefits of the basic factors of production, land, labor, and capital come into play, so too will it become increasingly important to ensure that the true costs and benefits of the potential interventions are established, not just at the project level and for the conventional ten- to twenty-year term. Social costs, including the economic and social costs of inaction or of maintaining the status quo are notoriously difficult to quantify. It is, for example, possible that some population transfers and land colonization schemes may have, by the measures of environmental economics, produced fewer benefits than costs. Even if costs and benefits are difficult to measure, it is usually relatively simple at least to identify them.

Policy is of crucial importance among these parameters for it sets limits within which both farmers and bureaucrats must operate. In the Vietnamese context, several policy areas need careful examination. First is the continuance of new settlement in the uplands by Kinh (ethnic Vietnamese). It seems that on many of the upland colonization schemes undertaken over the last two decades, there has been significant return migration to the lowlands and cities estimated from 20 to 40 percent. With economic liberalization the proportion may well rise. Such loss must involve significant costs. To judge by the experience of China as it has moved to market socialism and as labor markets have emerged, it seems highly likely that people from economically depressed marginal regions will move, legally or illegally, permanently or temporarily. Such movements have characterized most of the major countries of the region, and there is little reason to believe that Vietnam can or will be any different, although rural-urban migration may well be preferential with respect to ethnicity with Kinh rather than minority people moving initially.

Second is the issue of "sedentarization of the nomads" (i.e., shifting cultivators [Hill 1985]). Here, several questions need to be answered. What is the proportion of deforestation initiated by this form of use? In reality some four-fifths appears to be by commercial loggers, both legal and illegal. How much virgin, millable forest is attacked by shifting cultivators? Some two-thirds of the land they clear appears to be scrub and similar forms of young secondary growth, useless for milling at time-spans of less than the century or more it would take for forest to regenerate. That there is a case for the restriction of the attack on millable timber is unquestionable, but need all shifting cultivation be restricted especially among those whose settlements are more or less permanent? Is there not a fair chance, as elsewhere in the region, for example Sarawak, that villagers, of their own initiative or with modest assistance, will gradually sedentarize themselves especially if they can be assured of their food supply via the market mechanism, with the "safety-net" of government intervention if actual famine threatens?

NOTE

1. Much of this dramatic increase, in the early years of reform, was due to release of agricultural products stockpiled against storage to newly open markets. Agricultural production has more recently been stagnant or growing slowly. See William Hinton (1990), *The Great Reversal: The Privatization of China, 1978–1989.*

BIBLIOGRAPHY

Chen Junshi, T. C. Campbell, Li Junyao, and R. Peto. 1990. *Diet, life-style and mortality in China.* Oxford: Oxford University Press.

Chen Rongjun. 1993. Utilization of upland phytomass for fuel. Unpublished Ph.D. dissertation, University of Hong Kong.

Deng Nan. 1993. Sound utilization of land resources and improvement of the eco-environment for promotion of social development. In *Improving degraded lands: Promising experiences from South China,* ed. W. E. Parham, P. J. Durana, and A. L. Hess, 15–18. Bishop Museum Bulletin in Botany 3. Honolulu: Bishop Museum Press.

Far Eastern Economic Review. 15 July 1993. Get off our backs, 68–70.

Hill, R. D. 1985. "Primitives" to "peasants": The "Sedentarization of the nomads" in Vietnam. *Pacific Viewpoint.* 26(2): 448–59.

Hill, R. D. 1993a. Land, people and an equilibrium trap: Guizhou Province, PRC. *Pacific Viewpoint* 34(3): 1–22.

Hill, R. D. 1993b. Quelques considerations sur le developpement des hautes terres en Chine et dans les pays voisins. *Cahiers de geographie du Quebec* 37(100): 161–63.

Hill, R. D. 1994. Improving the use of degraded lands in south China: Contributions to a debate. *Pacific Science Association Bulletin* 45(3/4): 31–34.

Inside Mainland China. March 1993. Dismal agricultural situation, pp. 28–40 (includes report from *Beijing Economic Daily,* 16 December 1992).

Le Trong Cuc, K. Gillogly, and A. T. Rambo. 1990. *Agroecosystems of the midlands of northern Vietnam.* Occasional Paper No. 12. Honolulu: East-West Center.

Li Jinchang, Kong Fanwen, He Naihui, and L. Ross. 1988. Price and policy: The keys to revamping China's forestry resources. In *Public policies and the misuse of forest resources,* ed. R. Repetto and M. Gillis, 205–45. Cambridge University Press.

Mac Duong. 1985. The development of cultural life at the basic units within ethnic minority areas of the Central Highlands. *Tap Chi Cong San* 6:88–94.

Nhan Dan. 4 February 1985. CPV directive on rural mountainous areas (JPRS-SEA-85-057).

Nhan Dan. 7 April 1985. Economic and social study of the Highlands, p. 3 (JPRS-SEA-85-093).

Nhan Dan. 17 April 1985. Party Secretariat directive on mountain region development (JPRS-SEA-85-062).

Nhan Dan. 26 April 1985. [Editorial] Consolidate and improve new production relations in the mountain regions (JPRS-SEA-85-082).

Parham, W. E., P. J. Durana, and A. L. Hess, eds. 1993. *Improving degraded lands: Promising experiences from South China.* Bishop Museum Bulletin in Botany 3. Honolulu: Bishop Museum Press.

Prosterman, R. L., and T. M. Hanstad. 1990. China: A fieldwork-based appraisal of the household responsibility system. In *Agrarian reform and grassroots development: Ten case studies*, ed. R. L. Prosterman, M. N. Temple, and T. M. Hanstad, 103–36. London: Lynne Reinner Publishers.

Prosterman R. L., M. N. Temple, and T. M. Hanstad, eds. 1990. *Agrarian reform and grassroots development: Ten case studies.* London: Lynne Rienner Publishers.

Richardson, S. 1990. *Forests and forestry in China.* Washington, D.C: Island Press.

Ross, L. 1988. *Environmental policy in China.* Bloomington: Indiana University Press.

Socialist Republic of Vietnam. n.d. *Vietnam's integrated rural development programme.* Hanoi.

Truong Dinh Khang. 1985. Our country's uncultivated land; we now have nearly 12 million ha of uncultivated land . . . what patterns should land reclamation operations take? *Nhan Dan,* 17 October (JPRS-SEA-86-015).

Wang Xiaoqiang and Bai Nanfeng. 1991. *The poverty of plenty.* Basingstoke: Macmillan. (Originally published in Chinese in 1986.)

Xu Zaifu. 1993. Agroforestry: A new strategy for development of tropical mountains. In *Improving degraded lands: Promising experiences from South China,* ed. W. E. Parham, P. J. Durana, and A. L. Hess, 129–38. Bishop Museum Bulletin in Botany 3. Honolulu: Bishop Museum Press.

PART SIX

Abstracts

Human Resource Development for the Highlands of Vietnam: Present State and Needs

Nguyen Viet Tung
Hanoi Agricultural University

Human resource development in the highlands of Vietnam has, as its intention, the empowerment of individuals and communities to adapt to changes in technology, society, and the economy. This process is confounded, however, by cultural antagonisms, shortages of extension workers, and low levels of formal education among highland inhabitants, which makes training difficult. Under these conditions, human resource development in the highlands should probably rely on a twofold strategy of broad-based communication of information through the mass media and intense investment in a few key highland centers.

EDUCATIONAL STANDARDS AND CULTURAL BOUNDARIES

As Table A1.1 indicates, upland minority people are less likely to have attended school than the lowland Kinh majority people. The exceptions to this pattern occur among the Muong and Tay, minority groups predominantly located in the midlands, who often live close to Kinh communities. This would suggest that the problem of human resource development in the highlands lies not only in the construction of schools, the enrollment

Table A1.1 Population five years of age and over by ethnic group and school attendance (c. 1982)

Ethnic group	Population	Now attending (%)	Attended in the past (%)	Never attended (%)
Entire Country	54,247,014	23.16	59.56	16.94
Kinh	47,276,666	24.24	62.28	14.96
Tay	976,351	23.21	59.40	17.22
Thai	838,897	15 .49	44.08	40.23
Muong	746,380	19.75	61.26	18.66
Hmong	437,543	2.83	6.90	89.93
Dzao	382,740	7.64	25.79	66.34
Bana	111,190	5.41	13.92	80.59
Xo Dang	76,891	9.55	22.34	68.03
Jarai	197,660	6.77	13.82	79.56
Van Kieu	32,534	6.59	18.14	75.18
Kho Mu	33,916	9.46	22.84	67.34
Stieng	40,988	2.76	10.03	87.17
Han Hi	10,221	5.01	12.43	82.15
Lo Lo	2,559	3.20	9.37	87.14
Co Lao	1,179	1.27	7.03	90.83

of students, and the provision of trained instructors, but in the sociocultural constraints imposed by traditional society.

The primary sociocultural restraint to development in the highlands lies in the inherited beliefs and cultural practices of ethnic minorities. These traditions and practices make it easy for highlanders to resign themselves to an indigent life, as if it were in the course of nature. In such a situation, minority people often have little motivation to change, to improve their living standards, or to invest in formal education.

Overcoming deep-seated cultural constraints is an extremely complicated and delicate task that seems likely to take many generations. As a first step, trade and communications linkages between highland and lowland communities should be encouraged as a means of reducing the isolation of mountainous areas from mainstream society. In a more open context, the highlands will develop new cultural and economic environments that allow local people to break through cultural boundaries and gradually become acquainted to new ways of life.

INVESTMENT PRIORITIES

Given the limited financial resources of the Vietnamese government, it will likely remain impossible to invest in highland development everywhere in the highlands at once. Education, health, and communication investments should therefore be strategically placed in selected communities, established through the resettlement of minority people, which would become centers of diffusion throughout the mountain realm.

Additionally the education and training of minority peoples need to undergo a radical renovation. Quotas are required to guarantee the admission of highlanders in established and more prestigious schools, colleges, and universities throughout the lowlands. Priority should be given to minority peoples and others who currently work or intend to take jobs in the mountains. Within the highlands, special attention must be paid to the effective eradication of illiteracy and the training of grassroots level cadres. School curricula in mountainous areas should be tailored to the special needs of highland communities and coordinated with programs in agricultural extension, economics, and public health. Finally, radio and television programs, in local languages, that support these individual and collective objectives should be both encouraged and given generous financial support.

ABSTRACT NO. 2

Development of Highland Education in Vietnam

Tran Lanh
Highland Education Development Organization, Hanoi

HIGHLAND EDUCATION: AN OVERVIEW

Before the August Revolution of 1945, the few schools available in the mountains of Vietnam, most of which were located in provincial capitals and district towns, remained reserved for the children of mandarins and other colonial collaborators. Since the revolution, many thousands of Vietnamese teachers from the lowlands have been sent to remote highland communes to establish schools, organize cadres, and train local leaderships for future service to the nation. More recent educational initiatives have attracted highland students to boarding schools in provincial and district centers, where they are prepared for entrance to universities, colleges, and vocational institutes (Table A2.1).

Unlike lowland teachers who typically remain in the highlands for only two years, it is hoped that present and future generations of highland students, trained in lowland universities, will return to their native areas for longer periods of service. The challenges they will face are enormous, especially in high mountainous areas. For example, while the illiteracy rate among lowland Vietnamese is currently between 5 and 10 percent, among midland Tay and Nung minorities it ranges between 18 and 24 percent and among high mountain Hmong people it reaches between 90 and 95 percent. In Cao Bang province only 5.7 percent of highland Hmong children between the ages of six and fourteen were enrolled in school in 1992. In Lao Cai, the enrollment rate for Hmong children was 12.6 percent (Ministry of Education and Training 1994). In both provinces, the female enrollment rate was between 1 and 2 percent.

Even when children do attend school, drop-out rates remain extremely high. In Son La province, for example, primary school drop-out rates reached 28 percent in 1972, 25 percent in 1982, and 22 percent in 1992. Among the many reasons for these regional and

Table A2.1 Number of boarding schools for ethnic minorities

Type of school	1989–90 number	School year enrollment	1993–94 number	School year enrollment
Central schools	1	500	5	2,000
Provincial schools	10	1,750	38	10,000
District schools	68	8,172	140	23,000
Total	79	10,422	183	35,000

Source: Ministry of Education and Training (1994).

ethnic disparities are transportation problems, limited demand for non-traditional skills, low levels of school attendance, and early marriages.

THE HIGHLAND EDUCATION DEVELOPMENT ORGANIZATION

The Highland Education Development Organization (HEDO) is a non-governmental organization operating in cooperation with experienced highland teachers. Its purpose is to educate ethnic minority people in ways suitable to their conditions and capacity as a means of ridding themselves of backwardness, poverty, and ignorance.

In recent years HEDO has established formal relationships with fifty-seven non-governmental, governmental, and international organizations throughout the world. Its projects focus mostly on remote and out-of-the-way places such as Bac Ha district of Lao Cai province, Dien Bien district of Lai Chau province, An Khe district of Gia Lai province, and Phong Tho district of Lai Chau province, inhabited by Hmong, Dzao, Bana, and Ede minority groups. During the past four years, HEDO has carried out over thirty projects concerned with the eradication of illiteracy, the improvement of basic and vocational education, and teacher training, as well as providing direct grants to needy pupils. Nevertheless, most of these communities live in difficult straits and are desperately in need of assistance from domestic and international donors. Such funding is necessary to provide equipment for basic and vocational education, guarantee scholarships for minority students to study overseas, and conduct research on problems related to highland education.

ABSTRACT NO. 3

Project Planning and Evaluation for Sustainable Watershed Development in the Uplands of Vietnam

Leslie Lipper
University of California, Berkeley

INTRODUCTION

Vietnam is currently at a critical stage in its development. The Government of the Socialist Republic of Vietnam has set into motion a series of reforms that are transforming the economy from a planned basis to market orientation. The Government of Vietnam, together with international banks and investors, is actively promoting rapid economic development and must consider strategies that will best allow them to achieve their development goals. In Vietnam there are clearly tradeoffs between rapid economic growth, the promotion of equity, and environmental protection.

This abstract examines a methodology that expands the traditional scope of project analysis in the context of the northern mountain region in Vietnam. (The methodology was developed by Professors De Janvry and Sadoulet of the Agricultural and Resource Economics Department at the University of California at Berkeley, and Blas Santos of the Plan Sierra Project in the Dominican Republic.) This methodology incorporates calculations of project financial, social, and environmental impacts upon current and future generations and upon both project participants and non-participants. The consideration of these factors gives rise to the possibility of transfers of project costs and benefits among groups through time and space in order to achieve sustainability while promoting economic development.

For the purposes of this abstract, development will be defined as a process that promotes desirable social objectives such as increase in per capita incomes, improvement in health and nutritional status, educational achievement, and equitable income distribution. Another concept of sustainability, and the one adopted in this abstract, defines sustainability as development that is maintained over generations (i.e., development that results in the maintenance or improvement of capital stock).

This definition of sustainability calls for some difficult calculations. The rate at which man-made capital can be substituted for natural capital is frequently difficult to determine and may vary according to the situation and subjective viewpoint. In this abstract, it is assumed that some system of substitution between man-made and natural capital is estimable, although more detailed studies are required to determine exactly what this rate will be.

In the northern mountain region of Vietnam, economic reforms have resulted in the decollectivization of agricultural production planning and land tenure. Changes in settlement patterns and farming systems have caused changes in cultivation practices resulting in serious environmental degradation. The most serious problem is deforestation leading to erosion, loss of topsoil, watershed degradation, and siltation of irrigation systems. The Government of Vietnam and several international aid agencies have been actively working to design appropriate interventions to improve agricultural productivity while addressing the problems of deforestation and soil erosion.

In this abstract, the issues of conducting an economic analysis with consideration of sustainability are examined for two possible sets of interventions proposed by the Government of Vietnam and aid agencies for a typical uplands area in the northern mountain region. No specific economic values are analyzed, but the key issues that need to be addressed in measuring the sustainability of these measures are outlined and discussed.

In order to conduct an economic analysis of the proposed project interventions, it will be necessary to employ three types of tools: economic and financial analysis (EFA), environmental impact analysis (EIA), and sustainable development analysis (SDA).

The first of these (EFA) is the methodology that is commonly used by development banks when assessing the feasibility of projects. It uses market and non-market values of the benefits and costs the project is expected to generate over time, and discounts them to reflect time preferences. The second (EIA) is widely used in the United States and is becoming more common in the context of development projects. It focuses on externalities generated by the project. An externality is any impact on a third party's welfare that is brought about by the action of an individual and is neither compensated nor appropriated. At present, there is no accepted standard for performing the third type of analysis (SDA), and this abstract suggests one approach that might be taken. SDA focuses on intergenerational equity in the incidence of gains from the project. Sustainable development puts a constraint on the way in which the present generation of decision makers uses natural capital to allow future generations to achieve a level of welfare that is equal to the level achievable by the current generation.

Once the EFA, EIA, and SDA calculations are made, they can be combined in order to derive several criteria by which projects can be judged. These criteria indicate who the beneficiaries and victims of the project interventions are, both in time and in space, and the potential for compensation between them. The criteria are defined as (1) feasibility: net social benefits generated by the project in the current generation are positive, (2) acceptability of the project intervention to the adopting household, and (3) sustainability: impact of the project on future generations.

Feasibility of the project is usually the critical factor that determines whether projects are adopted or not. If a project is unable to generate sufficient financial and social benefits to cover the costs of implementing it, then it probably should never be implemented. However, once projects are determined to be feasible, they should also be assessed according to the acceptability and sustainability criteria. If they do not meet these criteria, then the possibility of taxes and transfers among the affected groups can be considered. Given this framework, project proposals can fall into four basic categories: (1) projects that are not feasible, (2) projects that meet the feasibility, acceptability, and sustainability criteria, (3) feasible projects that require transfers between upstream and downstream users in order to achieve acceptability and sustainability, and (4) feasible projects that require transfers between present and future generations in order to achieve acceptability and sustainability.

Each type of project carries specific institutional arrangements in order to achieve successful implementation. Projects that fall into the first category should not be implemented, as they use more of society's resources than they generate. It is important to note, however, that projects may show economic feasibility but not financial feasibility (i.e., the project may not generate sufficient revenues to cover its costs, but it does result in social benefits that are greater than the costs to society of implementing the project). Examples of projects that fall into this category are education and health improvement programs.

For the second project category, the only barriers to successful project implementation are institutional factors such as land tenure and credit availability. For example, transitioning from annual to perennial crops requires that sufficient long-term credit be available to producers while the perennial crop is in the development stage.

An example of the third type of project includes the introduction of agroforestry on unmanaged forest lands. Agroforestry may not be acceptable to upstream households; therefore, a tax on downstream users who benefit from reduced soil erosion may be transferred to upstream users to achieve acceptability. This may be a tax on electricity or irrigation water provided by downstream water management facilities. The third type of project requires a transfer mechanism between upstream and downstream users.

The fourth project type includes both types: transfers from the current to future generations, as well as transfers from future to current generations. Projects that require transfers from the current generation to the future generation are ones in which the current generation is exploiting the stock of natural capital. In these cases it is necessary for the current generation to compensate the future generation through a sustainability tax. Transfers from future generations to current generations are those that involve generation of natural capital stock in the current period, which will be available for exploitation by future generations. Long-term soft loans of the type extended by the International Fund for Agricultural Development can be seen as fulfilling the function. They permit a forward intergenerational transfer of funds that allows the current generation to engage immediately in sustainable activities. These activities have benefits for the next generation that are larger than the costs of the forward transfers. Most of the cost of these loans (typically forty years with a 10-year grace period and 2 percent interest rate) are effectively paid by the second generation.

Immigration and Health Care in the Vietnamese Highlands: A View from Lam Dong Province

Dominic Montagu
University of California, Berkeley

While the Ministry of Health (1993) may be correct in forecasting improved health conditions for all Vietnamese by the year 2000, health standards in the highlands, the historic home of Vietnam's ethnic minorities, continue to lag behind improvements throughout the rest of the country. As the highlands receive larger numbers of lowland Kinh migrants, regional disparities in health standards, as evidenced in provincial statistics, are likely to decline. Ethnic disparities, however, may continue or, in fact, be exacerbated. This abstract reviews and analyzes the types of health care provided for recent migrants in the uplands, as well as regional disparities in available care and the comparative use of such facilities by immigrants and indigenous minorities in the highlands.

The status of health care in Vietnam allows for a great deal of optimism. Between 1981 and 1993, the immunization rate has risen from 6 percent to 88 percent while child mortality in 1993, at 46 per 1,000, and the maternal mortality rate, at 120 per 100,000, were both well below their respective Southeast Asia regional averages of 57 per 1,000 and 160 per 100,000. Yet there are some indications that the improvements in health care that have occurred in Vietnam in the past decade are not being equitably distributed. Child mortality in the highlands is nearly twice the average of the country as a whole and, according to the director of Vietnam's Ministry of Public Health, the majority of the unvaccinated population are also in these areas.

These lower health standards may be indicative of a fraying of Vietnam's vertical referral network, a system of health delivery that has been largely responsible for health gains in the past. This may be due in part to changes in the economy. As a result of the economic crises of the 1980s, health care, formerly a right written into the constitution, has become partially subject to the market for health-care services. According to the Ministry of Health, fees provided 20 percent of the budget in a typical medical unit in 1990. During that same year, in Lam Dong, a highland province, fees represented less than 10 percent of the cost. Presumably this was related to an inability to pay on the part of local people. Vietnam is now under a great deal of pressure to advance the use of fees to make up an increasingly large portion of the overall medical budget. As this process continues, the highlands face pressure both from low and declining government health-care budgets, and from limited local revenue bases on which to support staff and purchase supplies.

Lower health standards in the highlands may also be due to reductions in medical staff. The Ministry of Health's intention to reduce health staff throughout the country by 20 percent has already begun to affect the highlands. In Lam Dong the number of staff has been reduced by 10 percent between 1991 and 1993. Good management has ensured that the bulk of the cuts in Lam Dong have come from the least skilled tier of personnel. But attracting new and qualified medical personnel from the cities is difficult and the training available in Dalat only goes as far as the "technician" level.

While health standards in the highlands are generally lower than the lowlands, there are also intra-regional ethnic disparities in the delivery of services. Approximately 20 percent of Lam Dong province's population of just over 735,000 people are members of ethnic minorities. Another 20 percent are recent immigrants.

Recent immigrants and ethnic minorities in Lam Dong are segregated by district to such an extent that it is possible to compare districts that are 90 percent minority with districts that are 90 percent northern immigrants. What this segregation means in Lam Dong is that there are large differences in health care offered to the two groups. While ethnic minorities, following national policy, are exempted from most medical fees, their limited population means that they get a smaller allocation from both the national and the provincial budgets. Allocations are based principally on population and the number of hospital beds. As migration continues, those districts with increasing population draw funds away from stable or declining ethnic districts. Under such conditions, it is not surprising to see deterioration in the delivery of health services in some districts while provincial data show improvement.

The World Bank is probably correct in stating that the decline in usage of clinics has also been due to the introduction of fees for many services formerly provided free of charge. In 1988, for example, birth assistance was provided free of charge at clinics in Lam Ha, a Kinh district. In 1990 it cost 1,200 *dong*. By 1994 it cost 15,000 to 20,000 *dong*. While Kinh people in Lam Ha are clearly more wealthy than the minorities of Lac Duong, they still remain among the poorest of Lam Dong province. As Table A4.1 shows, the number of women giving birth in the district hospital of Lam Ha declined by nearly 20 percent between 1990 and 1993.

The challenges for health care in the highlands of Vietnam are how to increase the use of health centers and attack the most endemic illnesses: malaria, acute respiratory infections (ARI), goiters, and chronic diarrhea diseases. There are many ways to address these

Table A4.1 Change in birth site, Lam Ha

	1990	1993	Change	Percent
Hospital deliveries	393	316	–77	–19.6
Home deliveries	946	830	–116	–12.3
Commune/gvt. health worker-assisted deliveries	828	1,234	406	49.0

Source: Provincial and commune statistics.

illnesses, and most of them are already being addressed by the Ministry of Health and the provincial health offices. What is less obvious is how to increase actual usage. In Lam Dong province at least, the differences that exist in health service utilization between immigrants and minorities are fairly clear. That is to say, they are not related specifically to who is minority or immigrant. Rather, the reasons for differences, and the issues that need to be addressed in order to increase use of available health care are (1) costs—both in terms of fees and opportunity costs, (2) materials—what equipment and medicine do the communes have with which to work, (3) accessibility—how to manage a referral system if there are no roads, and (4) education—the awareness of need must be increased. These issues must be addressed and viewed as integral to the health programs of Vietnam. The next step is to evaluate the relative importance of the issues listed above and to begin systematically addressing each of them in the near future. The problems of the highlands are not that people are receiving poor care but that many simply are not receiving any care.

APPENDIX

Contributors and Participants

Seminar on "Defining Highland Development Challenges in Vietnam"
Hawaii Imin International Conference Center at Jefferson Hall
East-West Center, Honolulu, HI 96848 USA
20–22 July 1994

Dr. Bui Cach Tuyen
Deputy Director
Environmental Protection Research Center
University of Agriculture and Forestry
Ho Chi Minh City, Vietnam
Phone: 84-8-966946
84-8-996780
Fax: 84-8-960713

Dr. Chu Huu Quy
Chairman
Vietnam's Integrated Rural Development Program
40A, Ngo Quyen Street
Hanoi, Vietnam
Phone: 84-4-266546
Fax: 84-4-252873

Dr. Eric Crystal
Coordinator
Center for Southeast Asia Studies
University of California, Berkeley
2223 Fulton Street, Room 617
Berkeley, CA 94720-2318 USA
Phone: 510-642-3609
Fax: 510-643-7062

Mr. Michael DiGregorio
Graduate School of Architecture and Urban Planning
University of California, LA
405 Hilgard Avenue
Los Angeles, CA 90025 USA
Phone: 310-825-4491
Fax: 310-206-5566

Mr. Keith Fahrney
Project Assistant
Program on Environment
East-West Center
1777 East-West Road
Honolulu, HI 96848 USA
Phone: 808-944-7244
Fax: 808-944-7298

Dr. Ronald Hill
Reader in Geography
Department of Geography and Geology
The University of Hong Kong
Pokfulam Road
Hong Kong
Phone: 852-859-2838
Fax: 852-559-8994

Mr. Hoang Xuan Ty
Director
Research Center for Forest Ecology and Environment
Forest Science Institute of Vietnam
Chem, Tu Liem
Hanoi, Vietnam
Phone: 014-347434
Fax: 84-4-345722

Dr. Carol Ireson
Professor of Sociology
Willamette University
900 State Street
Salem, OR 97301 USA
Phone: 503-370-6195
Fax: 503-370-6148
E-mail: cireson@willamette.edu

Dr. Neil Jamieson
Program Officer
Winrock International
68 Bui Thi Xuan Street
Hanoi, Vietnam
Phone: 84-4-266618
Fax: 84-4-266618

Dr. Charles Johnson
Senior Fellow
Program on Resources: Energy & Minerals
East-West Center
1777 East-West Road
Honolulu, HI 96848 USA
Phone: 808-944-7550
Fax: 808-944-7559

Mr. Le Duy Hung
Director of Fixed Cultivation and Settlement
Committee for Ethnic Minorities and Mountainous Areas
80 Phan Dinh Phung Street
Hanoi, Vietnam
Phone: 84-4-231569

Dr. Le Trong Cuc
Deputy Director
Center for Natural Resources and Environmental Studies
Hanoi University
Hanoi, Vietnam
Phone: 84-4-266618
Fax: 84-4-266618

Ms. Leslie Lipper
Graduate Student
Department of Agricultural Economics
University of California, Berkeley
Giannini Hall
2223 Fulton Street
Berkeley, CA 94709 USA
Phone: 415-981-3545
Fax: 415-981-6321
E-mail: lipper@ake.berkeley.edu

Mr. Dominic Montagu
International and Area Studies
University of California, Berkeley
2223 Fulton Street
Berkeley, CA 94720 USA
Phone: 510-642-5284
Fax: 510-642-9466

Dr. Nguyen Khanh Quac
President
The Agricultural University No. 3
Thai Nguyen City
Bac Thai Province, Vietnam
Phone: 01-28-55564
Fax: 84-4-264084

Dr. Nguyen Tran Cau
Vice Director
Institute of Geography
Vietnam National Centre for Natural Science and Technology
Nghia Do, Tu Liem
Hanoi, Vietnam
Phone: 84-4-358333, ext. 1234
Fax: 84-4-352483
84-4-361192
E-mail: cau@igg.ac.vn

Mr. Nguyen Van Thang
Ethnologist
Institute of Ethnology
National Center for Social Sciences and Humanities
27 Tran Xuan Soan Street
Hanoi, Vietnam
Phone: 84-4-258867
Fax: 84-4-259071

Dr. Nguyen Viet Tung
Vice Rector
Hanoi Agricultural University
Truong Dai Hoc Nong Nghiep I, Gialam
Hanoi, Vietnam
Phone: 84-4-271654
Fax: 84-4-253844

Dr. Pei Shengji
Division Head
Mountain Environmental Management Division
International Center for Integrated Mountain Development
GPO Box 3226
Kathmandu, Nepal
Phone: 977-525313
Fax: 977-1-524509

Dr. A. Terry Rambo
Director
Program on Environment
East-West Center
1777 East-West Road
Honolulu, HI 96848 USA
Phone: 808-944-7265
Fax: 808-944-7298
E-mail: rambot@ewc.bitnet

Dr. Robert Reed
Chair
Center for Southeast Asia Studies
University of California, Berkeley
2223 Fulton Street, Room 617
Berkeley, CA 94720 USA
Phone: 510-642-3900
Fax: 510-643-7062
E-mail: cseas@uclink.berkeley

Dr. Jeff Romm
Department of Forestry and Resource Management
University of California, Berkeley
2223 Fulton Street
Berkeley, CA 94720 USA
Phone: 510-642-6499
Fax: 510-643-5438

Mr. Michael Rucker
Research Intern
Program on Environment
East-West Center
1777 East-West Road
Honolulu, HI 96848 USA
Phone: 808-944-7250
Fax: 808-944-7298

Mr. Puongpun Sananikone
President
PAC-MAR
115 Anahola Street
Honolulu, HI 96826 USA
Phone: 808-732-8713
Fax: 808-734-2315

Mrs. Thanlo Sananikone
President
TAF International
115 Anahola Street
Honolulu, HI 96826 USA
Phone: 808-732-8713
Fax: 808-734-2315

Mr. Thomas Sikor
145 Wilson Street #67
Albany, CA 94710 USA
Phone: 415-493-3427
Fax: 415-493-3427
E-mail: sikort@garnet.berkeley.edu

Ms. Vy Ton
Project Specialist
Program on Environment
East-West Center
1777 East-West Road
Honolulu, HI 96848 USA
Phone: 808-944-7229
Fax: 808-944-7298

Mr. Tran Lanh
Director's Assistant
Highland Education Development Organization
49 Dai Co Viet
Hanoi, Vietnam
Phone: 84-4-691223
Fax: 84-4-692502

Ms. Catherine Veninga
Asia and Pacific Program
World Resources Institute
1709 New York Avenue, NW, Suite 700
Washington, DC 20006 USA
Phone: 202-662-3094
Fax: 202-638-0036

Dr. Eva Wollenberg
Senior Scientist
Policy Development Program
Center for International Forestry Research
Jalan Gunung Batu 5
Bogor 160001, Indonesia
Phone: 62-251-34-3652
Fax: 62-251-32-6433
E-mail: cifor@cgnet.com